London's Dead

ED GLINERT

London's Dead

ED GLINERT

Collins

Collins, a division of HarperCollins*Publishers*
77–85 Fulham Palace Road, London w6 8jB

www.collins.co.uk

First published in Great Britain in 2008 by HarperCollins*Publishers*
1

Text copyright © Ed Glinert 2008
Photography © Marc Atkins

Ed Glinert asserts the moral right to be identified as the author of this work

A catalogue record for this book is available from the British Library
isbn–13 978 0 00 7254972

Designed by Richard Marston
Printed and bound in Great Britain by Clays Ltd, St Ives plc

Contents

Acknowledgements

I am indebted to Ian Metcalfe of HarperCollins for inviting me to write London's Dead, developing the project, and always being on hand with suggestions and ideas. My agent, Faith Evans, as always, provided much support and help. Also, many thanks to Richard Aron, Clive Bettington, Celia Boggis, Jane Fallowfield, Peter Golds, Martin Morris, Anne Orsi, Vernon Philpot, Tim Richard, Ruth Roff, Adele Rose, Juliet Rose, Martin Rose, Simon Rose, David Stone and Esther Wyatt.

Particular thanks to Marc Atkins for the photos, Bela Cunha, Gill King, John Nicholson, for his extensive library, and of course Katy Walsh Glinert for so enthusiastically following me around necropolitan London.

Introduction

The people featured in this book all, well nearly all, have one thing in common. They are dead. But how they arrived at this probably terminal state is, I hope, what makes this book interesting. Some have died violently, some peacefully; some in mysterious circumstances, some from being in the wrong place at the wrong time. Some were murdered, some executed. A number committed suicide. Most were mourned, but some were booed. The cortège of the early 19th-century peer Lord Castlereagh was jeered in the street. Some, in dying, were thought not to be so. When Tommy Cooper began to fluff his lines at Her Majesty's Theatre in 1984, the audience assumed it was part of the act. Ten minutes later he died in the ambulance taking him to hospital. Many having died, have not been allowed to rest in peace. Thousands who may have thought they had found a final corporeal resting place in St Pancras Old Cemetery have had their graves uprooted and transferred twice – on both occasions so that the railway authorities could fiddle about with the track and nearby station. Some should have died but didn't, well not then. When Carlos the Jackal shot Joseph Sieff in the mouth in December 1973, the Marks and Spencer executive should have expired but … well, you'll have to read on.

How to use *London's Dead*

This is not a guide to London graveyards but a guide to London's dead. It is a series of tales concerned with death and dying in London, written in the form of a guidebook. I have divided the capital into regions and areas based on the traditional postcodes, as these can be seen on almost every road, and can guide the local and visitor alike. Consequently the book opens with the chapter on the City of London, the ancient centre. Chapter 2 is Central London (Bloomsbury, Clerkenwell, Covent Garden,

Holborn), Chapter 3 The West End (Fitzrovia, Marylebone, Mayfair and Soho) and Chapter 4 Westminster. Subsequent chapters are based on the suburbs, such as East London, South-West London, etc. Each chapter is then divided into streets set out in alphabetical order, in which the individual events, sites or buildings are listed. Text displayed in an antique style font denotes that the building or street no longer exists. The book finishes with the London Underground, for under ground is where we are all destined to end up.

CHAPTER 1

The City of London

ALDERSGATE, EC1
Charterhouse Street
Cloth Fair
Cock Lane
Giltspur Street
Greyfriars Passage
Holborn Viaduct
Little Britain
Newgate Street
Snow Hill
West Smithfield

MOORGATE, EC2
Bishopsgate
Cheapside
Gresham Street
Moorfields
Old Jewry
Threadneedle Street
Wood Street

FENCHURCH, EC3
Bevis Marks
Byward Street
Duke's Place
Houndsditch
Lombard Street
Lower Thames Street
Mitre Square
Pudding Lane
St Mary Axe
Seething Lane

LUDGATE, EC4
Bow Lane
College Street
Farringdon Street
Fleet Street
Garlick Hill
Gough Square
Holborn
Holborn Viaduct
Inner Temple Lane
Old Bailey
Queen Victoria Street
St Bride's Avenue
St Paul's Churchyard
Walbrook
Wine Office Court

'Such strange churchyards hide
in the City of London'
The Uncommercial Traveller, Charles Dickens (1861)

The world's leading financial centre occupies one square mile of land
on the north bank of the Thames between the Temple and Tower Hill
and is the oldest settlement in the capital, founded by the Romans in
AD 43. Until the late 19th century, when it was the capital's residential
centre, its many churchyards were the only burial places available.

The Fire of London, which started in a bakery on Pudding Lane just
north of London Bridge on 2 September 1666, destroyed seven-eighths
of the area though it killed only nine people. After the fire the City's
wealthy inhabitants moved west, colonising undeveloped areas in what
are now Mayfair and Marylebone, while the poor stayed put or moved
into the less desirable East End.

In the 19th century the City's Newgate Prison was where the capital's
worst felons were executed, often in public. Twentieth century demo-
graphic changes saw the City lose nearly all its population while
retaining its commercial prestige.

EC1

ALDERSGATE, EC1

Aldersgate was one of the traditional City gates, the one through
which James VI of Scotland arrived in London in 1603 following
the death of Elizabeth I to take the combined English–Scottish
throne as James I. This part of the City is dominated by
Smithfield meat market, St Bartholomew's Hospital (Bart's),
and the winding medieval alleyways around the two sites.

Charterhouse Street

A V2 rocket struck the market building that stood at the corner of
Charterhouse Street and Farringdon Road on 8 March 1945, and burst
through to the railway tunnels below, resulting in the building collapsing into the hole with an explosion that was heard all over London.

More than 100 market workers died on the spot when the rocket fell at 11.30 a.m. as the market was busy with porters, retailers and members of the public queuing for produce. Two weeks later the V2 strikes ceased.

A Plague On All Houses

'Now the grave doth open its mouth without measure,' noted Dr Thomas Vincent, a London clergyman who stayed in the capital throughout the 1665–6 outbreak of bubonic plague which claimed the lives of around 100,000 people living in or near the City. The City churchyards were unable to cope with the tens of thousands of local deaths, and scores of pits were dug to take the bodies, although the dead were rarely covered with enough earth and decomposing corpses were often left exposed.

Aldgate, at the eastern edge of the City, suffered considerably, as Daniel Defoe explained in *A Journal of the Plague Year* (1722): 'There was no parish in or about London where [the plague] raged with such violence as in … Aldgate.' A number of victims, wrapped in blankets and rugs, threw themselves into a hole by St Botolph's church without even waiting to die. 'A terrible pit it was,' Defoe wrote,

> and I could not resist my curiosity to go and see it. As near as I may judge, it was about forty feet in length, and about fifteen or sixteen feet broad, and at the time I first looked at it, about nine feet deep; but it was said they dug it near twenty feet deep afterwards in one part of it, till they could go no deeper for the water.

Those who stayed at home to die were sealed up inside their houses, a red cross painted on the door to ward off visitors, and a guard placed outside to make sure they didn't escape. Some broke free and fled, infecting all those they encountered, but most victims were happy to stay put, for fleeing would be an attempt to escape God's will, they believed, and God would surely hunt down the fugitive.

Household pets were thought to carry the disease, and there was a bounty of two pence on every dog or cat killed, which led to the slaughter of 40,000 dogs and 200,000 cats in a few days. But there was no slaughter of rats which were more to blame for they carried the fleas that spread the disease.

Cloth Fair

Named in honour of the annual medieval festival of Bartholomew Fair, where cloth was paraded and sold, the street was home to the 17th century publisher John Twyn, who was convicted of publishing seditious material and was sentenced to be 'hanged by the neck, cut down before he was dead, shamefully mutilated, his entrails taken out' and have his head cut off and disposed of 'at the pleasure of the king's majesty'. Parts of Twyn's body were later displayed at various city gates 'as an example to all men who advocate death or disobedience to such a monarch'.

Cock Lane

The only place in medieval London where licensed prostitutes could solicit for trade was also where John Bunyan, author of *The Pilgrim's Progress* (1678), died in 1688 from a fever caught during a heavy bout of rain.

In 1762 there were reports that a girl who lived at No. 33, Elizabeth Parsons, had seen an apparition of a dead relative who had been a victim of smallpox. Hundreds of people came to Cock Lane looking for proof of the phenomenon, which became known as the Cock Lane Ghost – without much success. The girl was taken to the rectory of St John's, Clerkenwell, where she was visited by, among others, Dr Johnson, who decried her claims in 'An Account of the Detection of the Imposture in Cock Lane'.

EC1

Giltspur Street

William Walworth, Lord Mayor of London, stabbed to death Wat Tyler, leader of the Peasants' Revolt, outside the church of St Bartholomew the Less on 15 June 1381 after hearing Tyler remonstrate with the king, Richard II. The fatal argument began when Tyler approached the king with a dagger in his hand and shook him saying: 'Brother, be joyful, for you shall have in a fortnight, 40,000 more than you have at present.' The two men bickered for a few moments about the peasants' demands:

> that no lord shall have lordship in future, but that land should be divided among all men ... that the goods of the Holy Church should not remain in the hands of the parsons and vicars and other churchmen ... that their

goods should be divided among the people of the parish ... that there should be no more serfs in England and that all men should be free.'

Richard told Wat Tyler he could have 'all that he could fairly grant' and ordered him to go home without delay, but the peasants' leader asked for a jug of water and rinsed out his mouth before the king in a rude manner, which led to a valet accusing Tyler of being 'the greatest thief and robber in Kent'. Tyler lost his temper and ordered one of his followers to behead the valet, who in turn warned that whoever struck him would be struck in return. When Walworth, the mayor, tried to arrest Tyler, the latter stabbed Walworth but was unable to penetrate the mayor's armour. Walworth struck back at Tyler, cutting him in the neck and dealing him a blow on the head. A member of the king's company then drew his sword and finished off the rebel chieftain.

Tyler was taken to nearby St Bartholomew's but Walworth had him brought out to the middle of Smithfield so that he could be beheaded, after which the mayor placed Tyler's head on a pole and took it to where the king was camped at St John's Fields.

ƒortune of War, *north junction with Cock Lane, west side*

In the 18th century surgeons from St Bartholomew's Hospital used a room at the now demolished ƒortune of War tavern to examine bodies snatched from graves that could be useful for their experiments.

St Bartholomew's Hospital, *east side*

London's oldest hospital, popularly known as Bart's, was founded as a priory in 1123 by Rahere, jester to Henry I, as a thanksgiving after he survived a bout of malaria caught on a pilgrimage to Rome. Rahere became the first prior of St Bartholomew the Great and was buried here in 1144.

Sixteen-year-old Mary Clifford died in the hospital in 1767 after being severely mistreated by her mistress, Elizabeth Brownrigg, a midwife, who forced Clifford to sleep in a coal hole, fed the girl only on bread and water, and chained her to a door when she found the girl had broken into a food cupboard.

Around that time the hospital was at the centre of London's gruesome resurrection industry, in which surgeons and physicians would hire villains to rob graves for fresh cadavers, four guineas a body, as Charles Dickens noted in *A Tale of Two Cities*:

> 'Father,' said young Jerry, 'what's a Resurrection-Man?'
>
> Mr Cruncher came to a stop on the pavement before he answered, 'How should I know?'
>
> 'I thought you knowed everything, father,' said the artless boy.
>
> 'Hem! Well,' returned Mr Cruncher...'he's a tradesman...'
>
> 'What's his goods, father?' asked the lively boy.
>
> 'His goods...is a branch of Scientific goods.'
>
> 'Person's bodies, ain't it, father?'
>
> 'I believe it is something of that sort,' said Mr Cruncher.'

EC1

Dickens had in mind the gang run by Ben Crouch, which had the monopoly on the supply of corpses to Bart's early in the 19th century. If a doctor found an alternative supplier, Crouch and his men would break into the hospital and mutilate any corpses they found, rendering them unusable. The system flourished because the law stated that surgeons could use only the bodies of executed criminals. This changed in 1832 and from then on the corpses of paupers whose relatives could not afford a burial could be sent to the anatomy schools.

Greyfriars Passage

Queen Isabella, wife of Edward II, was buried at the now ruined Franciscan Christ Church, Newgate, in 1358, the heart of her husband placed on her breast. The king himself had been murdered in Berkeley Castle, Gloucestershire, in 1327 by an unknown assailant who ran a red-hot spit through his bowels.

Holborn Viaduct

The Church of the Holy Sepulchre-without-Newgate, *north side*
After London's main hangings began to take place on the Tyburn Tree near Marble Arch in 1388, the condemned prisoners, who were incarcerated in Newgate Prison, would make their way along a tunnel from the prison to this church for a pre-execution ceremony during which a bell would toll and they would be given a nosegay of flowers.

Following a bequest in 1605, a bellman would make his way through the tunnel the night before an execution reciting:

> *All you that in the condemned hold do lie*
> *Prepare you, for tomorrow you shall die;*
> *Watch all and pray, the hour is drawing near*
> *That you before the Almighty must appear;*
> *Examine well yourselves, in time repent,*
> *That you may not to eternal flames be sent:*
> *And when St Sepulchre's bell tomorrow tolls,*
> *The Lord above have mercy on your souls.*
> *Past twelve o'clock!*

Captain John Smith, early 17th-century founder of the US state of Virginia, who was rescued from death by the Princess Pocahontas, is buried in the south-west corner of the church and commemorated in one of the windows.

Little Britain

St Bartholomew-the-Great Gatehouse, *east side*
Mary Tudor, England's last overtly Catholic monarch, who ruled in the 1550s, watched Protestant martyrs burn at the stake in Smithfield from the gatehouse while feasting on chicken and red wine.

Newgate Street

The first recorded undertaker in London was William Boyce, who opened a shop near Newgate Prison in 1675. A rival, William Russell, quick to capitalise on the idea, soon struck up an agreement with the College of Arms, the government office in charge of state funerals and coronations, and would pay its members to attend funerals he organised. This, understandably, conferred gravitas on the proceedings, and meant that customers soon began to prefer Russell's services.

Newgate Prison, Newgate Street at Old Bailey, *south side*

The City's main prison for nearly 500 years was where condemned prisoners were kept in a mass dungeon with only one window before being hanged at Tyburn. The night before their execution they would be woken at midnight by twenty rings of a handbell and given a lecture on sin.

Newgate inmates over the years included Sir Thomas Malory, author of 'Morte D'Arthur' (1485); the notorious thief and escaper Jack Sheppard; and Lord George Gordon, architect of the disastrous Gordon Riots of 1780. Malory wrote 'Morte D'Arthur' while in jail for murder, and is believed to have died in the prison. Sheppard escaped from Newgate in August 1724 dressed as a woman to avoid execution, was recaptured on Finchley Common and sent back to the prison. He escaped from there again on 15 October and was eventually found drunk in a gin shop on Drury Lane. He was again sent back to Newgate, where he was held down by 300 lbs of iron. When Sheppard was finally sent to Tyburn, thousands lined the route to cheer him on.

The prison had a room known as 'Jack Ketch's Kitchen', named after the notoriously incompetent hangman, where body parts of those hanged, drawn and quartered were kept while their relatives sought a normal burial for the deceased. The heads were usually kept in a different part of the jail awaiting a place on a spike for public display.

In 1783 hangings moved to Newgate from Tyburn in the West End following pressure from Mayfair residents. Locals would charge spectators for a vantage point overlooking the place of execution, and once the victim was declared dead a black flag would be hoisted and the crowd would give three cheers. In 1807 twenty-eight people died in a crush when the scaffolding fell as they watched the spectacle.

After 1868 there were no more public hangings and Newgate

executions were held behind closed doors. By then the crimes punishable with the death penalty had been reduced to four: murder, treason, arson in a royal dockyard and piracy. In 1902 the prison was demolished and replaced by an enlarged Central Criminal Court (the Old Bailey).

HANGED AT NEWGATE

‖ **Catherine Murphy** (d. 1789) was the last woman to be executed in England by burning – her crime, coining. Murphy was made to stand on a foot-high platform, secured to the stake with ropes and an iron ring, and surrounded by faggots of straw which the executioner lit. The punishment was abolished the following year when Sir Benjamin Hammett, who had been the Sheriff of London at the time of Murphy's burning, revealed that he had compassionately allowed her to be hanged first, thus technically breaking the law.

‖ **Arthur Thistlewood**, leader of the Cato Street conspirators who planned to assassinate the British Cabinet, went to the gallows in 1820 defiantly, sucking on an orange. Before he died Thistlewood exclaimed: 'Albion is still in the chains of slavery. I quit it without regret.' He was hanged on 1 May as the authorities wanted to mock his socialist beliefs. For being a traitor as well as a murderer, Thistlewood was not just hanged but decapitated – the last British felon to have his head removed by the state.

‖ **Henry Fauntleroy** (1824), a corrupt banker who embezzled a quarter of a million pounds, is rumoured to have escaped death at Newgate by inserting a silver tube in his throat, and being bundled away quickly by friends before heading off to the continent.

‖ The last public execution at Newgate took place on 26 May 1868 when **Michael Barrett**, who had taken part in the Fenian bombing of the Clerkenwell House of Correction (☞ p. 38), went to the gallows.

‖ **Dr Neill Cream**, the Canadian medic who poisoned a number of London prostitutes with strychnine at the end of the 19th century, was hanged at Newgate in 1892 behind closed doors as a screaming mob, 5,000 strong, waited outside, angry that public hangings had been abolished.

Snow Hill

A gunsmith's on Snow Hill was robbed during an aborted attempt to seize London and instigate a revolution in December 1816, and one of the thieves was later hanged in front of the shop – the last time in London history a criminal was executed at the scene of the crime.

EC1

West Smithfield

William Wallace, the Scottish nationalist who was found guilty of treason at Westminster Hall in 1305, was dragged alive through the streets to West Smithfield and hanged here on the gallows. After a few moments Wallace was cut down so that he could recuperate but then his intestines were ripped from his body in front of the crowd. Parts of his corpse were later sent to different locations across the country: his head was stuck on a pole on London Bridge; his right arm was displayed on Newcastle Bridge, the left one exhibited in Berwick; the right leg was displayed in Perth, and the left put on show in Aberdeen.

The last man to be boiled alive in Britain suffered this painful death in West Smithfield. He was Richard Rouse, a cook, who in 1531 was convicted of poisoning John Fisher, the Bishop of Rochester. The bishop failed to eat the infected 'pottage', but 14 guests who did died. Edward VI banned the practice in 1547.

In 1538 John Forest, a preacher who opposed Henry VIII's divorce from Catherine of Aragon, was burnt at the stake in Smithfield.

A wooden holy relic was added to the pyre over which Forest was suspended, and slowly roasted on a bed made of chains.

Forest was one of hundreds of martyrs who met a fiery end at Smithfield during the 16th-century reign of Mary Tudor and the early years of Charles II's rule a century later. The first was a Bible translator, John Rogers, in 1555. When it came to taking Rogers from Newgate Prison to Smithfield, one of the sheriffs, Woodroofe, asked him if he would revoke his 'evil opinion of the Sacrament of the altar'. Rogers replied: 'That which I have preached I will seal with my blood,' to which Woodroofe responded: 'Thou art an heretic.' 'That shall be known,' retorted Rogers, 'at the Day of Judgement.'

Others who lost their lives in the Smithfield burnings included a man called Collins (d. 1538) for mocking the Mass in church by lifting a dog above his head, and Richard Byfield (d. 1664), accused of heresy, whose pre-burning punishment included being tied up by the arms, whipped, and chained by the neck to the wall at Lambeth Palace.

MOORGATE, EC2

The area that covers much of the City's financial centre, including the Bank of England and Stock Exchange, was built near Moorgate, the Roman gate leading to the moor north of the City, which was rebuilt several times and finally demolished in 1762. A hundred years previously, during the bubonic plague, a pit was dug by Bethlem Hospital, near where the modern-day Moorgate station stands, to take the thousands of corpses that the local churchyards couldn't cope with.

Bishopsgate

Named after the Roman gate, demolished in 1760, that led to Ermine Street, the road to Lincoln and York, it was where a sailor, William Brown, mugged a shopkeeper for a shilling during the 1780 Gordon Riots and was punished by being hanged here. When the condemned man saw a cheesemonger, Carter Daking, looking out of the window he held out his hat and exclaimed: 'Damn your eyes and limbs, put a shilling into my hat, or by God I have a party that can destroy your house presently.'

Dirty Dick's, Nos. 202–204, *east side*

'Dirty Dick' was the nickname of Nathaniel Bentley, a local 19th-century ironmonger whose fiancée died on the eve of their marriage, leaving him so distraught he preserved their unused wedding breakfast and spent the rest of his life in squalor, never washing or changing his clothes – not even after disposing of his cats when they died. When Bentley died, the landlord of the inn which stood on this site bought the contents of his shop and house, which were displayed here until the 1980s. Charles Dickens adapted the story for the post-nuptial fate of Miss Havisham in *Great Expectations* (1861).

Cheapside

Cheapside was London's main medieval market and the birthplace of Thomas A Becket, the priest and chancellor to Henry II murdered by the latter's knights in Canterbury Cathedral in 1170. Edward I built Cheapside Cross at the corner of Cheapside and Wood Street in 1290 to commemorate the City resting-place of the coffin containing the body of his queen, Eleanor. He erected other crosses on the long route the cortège took from Lincoln Cathedral to Westminster, including at what became known as Waltham Cross and Charing Cross. The Cheapside Cross, which was decorated with statues of the Pope, the Madonna and Child, and the Apostles, was subjected to violent attacks by the Puritans and demolished in 1643.

Gresham Street

St Lawrence Jewry

An exquisite Wren church situated in the heart of London's medieval Jewish community features a painting in the vestibule which shows its patron saint, Lawrence, being slowly burnt on a gridiron. Lawrence was a third-century deacon and treasurer of the Church in Rome who was ordered by Emperor Valerian to hand over the Church's riches. He gathered the poor and sick, and said to Valerian: 'Here are the treasures of Christ's Church,' which promptly led to his execution. During his ordeal, he allegedly asked: 'This side is now roasted enough; O tyrant, do you think roasted meat or raw the best?'

Moorfields

Bedlam (1675–1815)

London's best-known medieval asylum was the setting for hundreds of pathetic deaths. Typical was that of an early 19th-century inmate, one Norris, who was chained by a strong iron ring riveted round his neck, his arms pinioned by an iron bar, allowing him to move only 12 inches from the wall. After he died a parliamentary inquiry in 1815 led to a more liberal regime being introduced, and that year Bedlam moved to Lambeth (➤ p. 212).

In the last plate of William Hogarth's *A Rake's Progress* (1735) the hero, Tom Rakewell, dies in Bedlam in penury after a life of missed opportunities.

Old Jewry

The street's name recalls the presence of London's medieval Jewish community which grew after William the Conqueror invited the Jews of Rouen in northern France to London to take charge of lending money at interest, Christians being barred from doing so. The Jews were subjected to various privations over the next 200 years. For instance, in 1224 they were accused of ritual murder after it was alleged that gashes found on the body of a dead child were in the form of Hebrew characters and therefore carved by a member of the community. In the mid-13th century the area was beset by violence when hundreds of Jews were murdered after a Jew supposedly charged a gentile too much interest. In 1290 Edward I expelled the Jews from England. No trace of medieval Old Jewry, or its Jewish history, remains above ground.

Threadneedle Street

Thomas Hariot, the early 17th-century scientist, was buried in the remains of St Christopher's church, destroyed in the Fire of London, the site now covered by the entrance hall to the Bank of England. Friends were surprised that Hariot was allowed a church burial given his hostile views on the Creation and his perhaps heretical claim '*ex nihilo nihil fit*' – nothing comes of nothing.

Bank of England

Kenneth Grahame, author of the perennial children's classic *The Wind in the Willows* (1908), who was also the Bank's Secretary, was lucky to survive a shooting in his office in 1903. A customer asked to see Grahame to hand him some documents, some of which were bound in a black ribbon. When Grahame took the documents, the customer pulled out a revolver and fired at him, but some of the bullets were blanks and Grahame survived. The man later claimed he only fired because Grahame had chosen only documents bound with a black ribbon – a sign that he was doomed.

Wood Street

Cripplegate, *north end*

One of eight medieval gates at the edge of the City, Cripplegate was where the body of King Edmund the Martyr was brought into London in 1010. Some historians later claimed that the gate had miraculous powers, including the healing of the lame. Cripplegate was demolished in 1760.

St Giles Cripplegate, *north-west end*

The first church on the site was built by Alfune *c.* 1090 alongside the Jews' Garden, the only place in England where Jews could be buried in those days.

Martin Frobisher, the intrepid explorer who vainly tried to find the North-West Passage and died of wounds sustained while fighting the Spanish, was buried here in 1594 without his heart and entrails which are in St Andrew's church, Plymouth.

The poet John Milton, who worshipped at St Giles and wrote much of his epic biblical poem *Paradise Lost* (1667) locally, was buried here in 1674. A hundred years later workmen exhumed his body during repairs and knocked out some teeth, which they kept as souvenirs. The verger put the poet on display, charging sixpence for a look, and visitors helped themselves to bits of Milton's remains, taking some teeth, hair and even one rib. The 18th-century poet William Cowper was dismayed by the story and thundered:

> Ill fare the hands that heaved the stones
> where Milton's ashes lay!
> That trembled not to grasp his bones
> and steal his dust away!

FENCHURCH, EC3

The heavily commercialised and less glamorous eastern end of
the City was built on the marshy or fenny ground by the banks of
the long-vanished Langbourn stream.

Bevis Marks

The name is a corruption of 'Buries Marks', the burial limits of land
once owned by the abbots of Bury St Edmunds, not that of a local resident, as many believe. The road of the same name, sandwiched between
Camomile Street and Duke's Place, is best known for its long-standing
Spanish and Portuguese Synagogue, the oldest in Britain.

Byward Street

All Hallows Barking

The church, founded by Eorconweald, Bishop of London, in 675 on land
then owned by Barking Abbey, is believed to be the burial place of the
heart – just the heart – of Richard I (Richard the Lionheart). During the
many years when executions took place on nearby Tower Hill the bodies
of the victims were often brought into the church, including those of
Thomas More (d. 1535) and Charles I's Archbishop of Canterbury,
William Laud (d. 1644). Next to Laud's entry in the church's book of burials the word 'traitor' can be seen smeared out.

In January 1650 27 barrels of gunpowder stored on the premises accidentally exploded, blowing up around 50 houses and killing scores of
people.

Duke's Place

The street is named after Thomas Howard, Duke of Norfolk, who was
beheaded in 1572 for participating in a plot to restore Catholicism to
England, and was built on the site of the long demolished medieval
Augustinian Priory of Holy Trinity, Aldgate.

The Houndsditch murders

Three policemen were shot dead by Latvian anarchists during a botched robbery of a jeweller's at 119 Ḩoundsditch on the weekend of 17–18 December 1910. The ten-strong gang, who were looking to raise money for political purposes, included Peter Piatkow, a handyman who went by the nickname 'Peter the Painter'; Jacob Peters, a short, snub-nosed Holloway-based tailor with bristling brown hair; Fritz Svaars, who was on the run after a bank robbery in America; and their leader, Poolka Mourrewitz, who used to walk in the middle of the road to avoid arrest by policemen or what he called 'Tsarist agents lurking in doorways'.

The gang chose the shop at No.119 Houndsditch after being told it contained jewels belonging to the hated Tsar of Russia, the sale of which would raise funds all the sweeter to use for their political escapades. To get closer to the premises they rented a nearby room in €xcḩange Buildings, Cutler Street, and began to dig a tunnel to connect the two over the weekend. But neighbours who heard their hammering alerted the police. A constable knocked on the door, which was opened by Mourrewitz, and when the officer asked him: 'Is anyone working out the back? May we have a look?', Peters fired a pistol at him and his

EC3

Houndsditch

A major road leading from Liverpool Street to Aldgate, named after the ditch in which people left their dead dogs in medieval times, is best known as the setting for the Houndsditch Murders (see above).

Lombard Street

St Edmund the King, *north side at George Yard*
Originally St 'Edmund Grasschurch', named after the nearby herb market, the church is dedicated to the East Anglian king shot by Danes for refusing to renounce Christianity. It was redesigned by Christopher Wren after the Fire of London and was one of the few City churches to be damaged during the First World War.

colleagues. A shot went through the rim of one policeman's helmet and through the shutter behind. Another bullet hit one of the officers in the neck, killing him instantly. When a Constable Choat caught hold of Mourrewitz and tried to wrest the gun from him he was shot eight times by the other anarchists. Choat did, however, manage to partly shield himself with Mourrewitz, who was fatally wounded by a bullet meant for the policeman.

The gang escaped – with the dying Mourrewitz – to a safe house in Mile End, where a doctor, asked to come and heal a man 'accidentally shot by a friend', called the police. They found Mourrewitz dead and a woman frantically throwing papers into the fire. When police realised that they might have stumbled on the Houndsditch gang, they mounted a huge search to find the rest of the villains, putting up posters in English and Yiddish across the East End asking for information. Eventually they caught up with them at 100 Sidney Street, Stepney, which led to the Sidney Street Siege (☛ p. 131).

Peters later rose to a prominent position in the Soviet Union, second in command in Stalin's secret police, the Cheka, but was eventually 'eliminated' on the dictator's orders.

EC3

Lower Thames Street

St Magnus the Martyr, *south side opposite Pudding Lane*
St Magnus was a Norwegian earl murdered by his cousin in 1110, and the church named after him has stood on the site for over 1,000 years. Christopher Wren rebuilt it in 1671–6 after the Fire of London. Until modern times and the resiting of London Bridge the church stood at the bridge's northern approach and was known as St Magnus ad Pontem.

Mitre Square

One of the City's lesser-known squares is built on the site of the cloisters of the Priory of Holy Trinity, Aldgate, founded in 1108 by Mathilda of Scotland.

Location of the fourth Jack the Ripper murder, *south-east corner*

Catharine Eddowes, a Whitechapel prostitute, Jack the Ripper's fourth victim when she was murdered in Mitre Square just before 2 a.m. on 30 September 1888. This was only an hour after the Ripper had murdered another prostitute, Elizabeth Stride, at a different location a mile east (➤ p. 128). At the time of Stride's murder, Eddowes was being arrested on Aldgate High Street for being drunk and running along the road imitating a fire engine. After her release she went looking for a client. At 1.30 a.m. a witness saw her talking to a man, but twenty minutes later Eddowes was dead. Witnesses who were called to the inquest gave a description of a man who might have attacked her, and who was wearing a tweed jacket, deer-stalker cap and red neckerchief.

After these two murders a note, written on a postcard, was sent to the Central News Agency:

> I was not codding [joking], dear old Boss, when I gave you the tip. You'll hear about Saucy Jack's work tomorrow. Double event this time. Number one squealed a bit. Couldnt finish straight off. Had not time to get ears for police. Thanks for keeping last letter back till I got to work again.
>
> JACK THE RIPPER

This was the second such letter sent by someone describing themselves as Jack the Ripper, but experts are divided over whether it was a genuine note from the murderer or a hoax. There would just about have been enough time for someone close to the events other than the perpetrator – such as a journalist – to have written it so that it reached the agency before the details of the murder became widely available.

A couple of weeks later, on 16 October, events took on a gruesome turn in Whitechapel (➤ p. 144).

‖ By a bizarre coincidence a monk from the medieval Holy Trinity Priory, which stood on this site, murdered a woman praying at the altar, in 1530. Ripperologists familiar with the more arcane aspects of the story believe that Eddowes was murdered at a different location and her body then deposited at exactly the spot of the earlier murder for reasons unknown.

Pudding Lane

Despite the devastation it caused to the capital, only nine people died in the Great Fire of London, which started in Farryner's baker's shop on this small turning near London Bridge on 2 September 1666. The Fire raged for five days and destroyed seven-eighths of the City including nearly 15,000 homes and 87 churches, as well as severely damaging major buildings such as St Paul's, the Guildhall, Custom House and the Royal Exchange. Among the dead were Farryner's wife and child. A French Huguenot, Robert Hubert, who falsely confessed to starting the blaze, was hanged at Tyburn (☛p. 67).

St Mary Axe

The street is named after the now demolished church of St Mary Axe, properly known as St Mary the Virgin and St Ursula and the Eleven Thousand Virgins. It took its name from the legend of the royal English princess who journeyed to Germany with 11,000 handmaidens but met a bloody end at the hands of Attila the Hun, who killed them with three axes, one of which was later stored in the church.

An IRA bomb that exploded in the street on 10 April 1992 killed three people and injured 91. Many buildings were heavily damaged, including the Baltic Exchange which was replaced by Norman Foster's unforgettable Swiss Re tower, popularly known as the 'Erotic Gherkin'.

EC3

St Andrew Undershaft, *east side*

The church had a tall maypole erected alongside which in medieval times was used during the annual spring festivities. On 1 May 1517 the celebrations were marred by a riot against immigrants and foreign goods, which resulted in 14 locals being hanged for inciting the destruction of foreigners' homes.

John Stow, the pioneering London historian, was buried inside the church in 1605 and is commemorated with a marble monument. The hand of the statue contains a quill pen, which is replaced every year by the Lord Mayor who then hands the old pen to the child who has written the best essay on the capital.

Seething Lane

St Olave's, *at Hart Street*

Charles Dickens called St Olave his 'best beloved churchyard, the churchyard of ghastly grim, its ferocious strong spiked iron gate like a jail ornamented with skulls and cross bones' in 'Uncommercial Traveller: City of the Absent' (1861).

The church is named after King Olaf of Norway who fought with Ethelred the Unready in the Battle of London Bridge in 1014 and was canonised soon after his death. The diarist Samuel Pepys (d. 1703) and his wife, who lived locally, are buried here. Pepys wanted fellow diarist John Evelyn to be a pallbearer for him but Evelyn refused. A bust of Pepys's wife in the nave was sited so that the diarist could see it from his pew.

LUDGATE, EC4

The oldest section of the square mile includes the City's most important building, St Paul's Cathedral, and its most famous street, Fleet Street, former home of the British newspaper industry.

The land between the Temple and Blackfriars, answerable in medieval times to no local government, became the most lawless in London in the 1550s after Edward VI abandoned Bridewell, the palace his father, Henry VIII, built here. It acquired the nickname 'Alsatia' in mock honour of Alsace, the disputed land between France and Germany and wasn't cleaned up until the early 19th century.

Bow Lane

St Mary-le-Bow

The most famous of the City's 39 churches, for only those born within the sound of its bells are true cockneys, was where William Fitzosbert, a radical orator known as Longbeard, took sanctuary in 1196 after speaking out against new taxes and the greed of the wealthy. When Archbishop Hubert instructed that the church be set on fire, Longbeard fled. He was soon captured, stabbed to death, taken to the gallows at Tyburn and hanged on a gibbet as a warning to others thinking of publicly criticising the king. His was the first recorded Tyburn execution.

St Mary-le-Bow has twice partly collapsed, killing people in the street below. The first occasion was when the roof blew off in 1090, the second in 1271 when the tower fell down.

College Street

Previously known as Elbow Lane, on account of the sharp turn which the River Walbrook took here en route to the Thames.

St Michael Paternoster Royal

A church has stood on the site since the 13th century, but has no royal connection, its name being a corruption of La Reole, a town in France from where local vintners imported wine. Dick Whittington, who had been Lord Mayor of London, paid for the church to be rebuilt with an attached college in 1409, and was buried here in 1423. His remains were disturbed in the mid-16th century when the rector, Thomas Mountain, broke open the monument in the hope of discovering treasure, and on finding nothing tore the leaden sheet off the corpse. Mountain was removed from office when Mary Tudor succeeded to the throne, and Whittington's body was once again covered with lead.

The church was destroyed in the 1666 Fire of London, rebuilt by Christopher Wren, and redesigned by William Butterfield in 1866. In 1944 it was hit by a flying bomb, but was later restored.

EC4

Farringdon Street

Built in 1737, when the River Fleet was arched over, the street was named after William de Farringdone, a 13th-century goldsmith, and is today part of the main route between King's Cross and Blackfriars Bridge. The Fleet formed the Romans' western London boundary. In the City it was long a sewer, running red with the blood of animals slaughtered at Smithfield Market, or as the *Tatler* noted in 1710, full of 'Sweepings from Butchers' Stalls, Dung, Guts and Blood,/Drown'd Puppies, stinking Sprats, all drench'd in Mud,/Dead Cats and Turnip-Tops [which came] tumbling down the Flood'. It now flows underground from Hampstead and Highgate into the Thames at Blackfriars.

Fleet Street

From the mid-19th century to the end of the 20th many of Britain's best-known newspapers had their headquarters on or near Fleet Street. Among those who have stayed alive long enough to read their own obituaries was Lord Alfred Douglas, Oscar Wilde's lover, who opened a 1906 edition of the *Daily News* to find himself dead and described as a 'degenerate'. When *The Times* updated its obituary file for the sports commentator Rex Alston in 1985 it accidentally published it as a genuine obituary. Alston remarried the following year at the age of 85 and therefore enjoyed the unusual distinction of having his marriage announced in the papers after his obituary. That for Dave Swarbrick, the leading folk violinist, was published in the *Daily Telegraph* in April 1999 after the musician was admitted to hospital with a chest infection, prompting him to quip: 'It's not the first time I have died in Coventry.'

Temple Bar

At the western end of Fleet Street until modern times stood Temple Bar, the City's western gateway, where the heads of those executed were displayed, and spyglasses were hired out to morbid onlookers at halfpenny a look. In 1745 Temple Bar exhibited the heads of members of the Manchester Regiment, executed for supporting the claims to the throne of Charles Edward Stuart, the Young Pretender, during the unsuccessful Jacobite Rebellion. When it was announced that the head of Captain Towneley was still dripping with blood, the crowd began placing bets on which head was Towneley's as the hangman and his assistants ascended the ladders to place the heads on spikes. The hangman was so disgusted that he refused to say. Two of the skulls stayed on the pole for thirty years before finally falling down.

Wren's Temple Bar was removed in 1878 and taken to Theobalds Park, Hertfordshire. It was recently returned to the City but placed inappropriately at St Paul's, not here.

Sweeney Todd's barber shop, No. 186

Sweeney Todd, the so-called 'demon barber of Fleet Street' may have murdered more than 150 customers in his Fleet Street shop at the end of the 18th century, thereby making him the biggest serial killer in British history – if he existed. Few historians have been able to agree on even the most basic details surrounding Todd's existence. In a 1993 biography Peter Haining explained that Todd vowed to avenge himself on mankind when he was imprisoned in Newgate for theft. After his release in 1785 he established himself as a barber at 186 Fleet Street under the sign 'Easy shaving for a penny – as good as you will find any'. There he terrorised customers with a cut-throat razor while they sat in a revolving chair poised over a trap door to the cellars. The shop was supposedly connected by tunnel with a building on nearby Bell Yard where Todd's lover, Margery Lovett, cooked the flesh of the victims in meat pies.

EC4

The Sweeney Todd legend may have arisen from an article in the *Daily Courant* (Fleet Street's first newspaper) of 14 April 1785 about a 'horrid murder committed in Fleet Street on the person of a young gentleman from the country while on a visit to relatives in London who fell into conversation with a man in the clothing of a barber'. After an argument the barber 'took from his clothing a razor and slit the throat of the young man'.

Garlick Hill

St James Garlickhythe

In 1855 workmen clearing out a vault found a corpse they dubbed Jimmy Garlick. For nearly 100 years it was kept in a glass case inside the church alongside the legend:

> *Stop Stranger Stop As You Pass By*
> *As You Are Now So Once Was I*
> *As I Am Now So Shall You Be*
> *So Pray Prepare To Follow Me*

On Sundays the choirboys would take Garlick out and place him on a pew with a ruff collar around his neck. Since the Second World War he has led a less dramatic afterlife, housed in an upper room of the church tower. It is now believed that Jimmy Garlick was a 16-year-old fever victim, Seagrave Chamberlain.

Gough Square

Only Dr Johnson's house remains out of the original buildings on Gough Square, the statue outside being that of the Dictionary compiler's much-loved cat, Hodge. Those houses which have been demolished include No. 3, home in Johnson's day of a surgeon who once brought home the body of a man hanged at Tyburn, sold to him for medical purposes. When a maid, unable to resist a peek, approached the corpse, it came to life. The surgeon cleaned up the man, who seemed to be none the worse for his ordeal, and arranged for him to be sent to America, where he made a fortune, which he bequeathed to his saviour.

Holborn

Langdale's Brewery, *opposite Leather Lane*

The brewery obtained its water not from the nearby filthy Fleet River
but from the Clerk's Well on Farringdon Lane. It was set ablaze during
the 1780 Gordon Riots when a mob rolled out the casks and smashed
them open. The raw spirit caught fire, sending pillars of flame up to the
sky and hot gin running down the road. Locals who gorged themselves
on the spoils were soon screaming from internal burns and keeling
over, dead drunk or just dead. When firefighters attached their hoses to
taps in the cellars the blaze burned fiercer: the taps were connected to a
supply of gin, not water.

Holborn Viaduct

St Andrew

Originally it was a wooden Saxon church, first mentioned in 951, and
those buried here include the Jacobean playwright John Webster, who
once wrote 'O, that it were possible, we might hold some two days' conference with the dead!'

It was at St Andrew that the mid-17th-century cleric John Hackett, an
opponent of Oliver Cromwell, came close to losing his life in 1624 when
the latter's troops invaded the church, looking to punish him for using
the then outlawed Book of Common Prayer. Finding Hackett with the
banned book, a soldier pointed a gun to his head. The cleric replied: 'I'm
doing my duty. Now do yours.' They backed down. Hackett later became
Bishop of Lichfield.

In 1827 William Marsden, a surgeon, came upon a young woman
dying in the churchyard. When he couldn't find a bed for her he decided
to set up a free surgery in Holborn, and later founded the Royal Free
Hospital in Gray's Inn Road, which is now in Hampstead.

The church crypt was cleared of dead bodies as recently as 2002, sixty
years after the task was first planned following wartime bombing.
Thousand of corpses were found, some dating back to the 14th century,
including hundreds of plague victims. Before going below to watch the
exhumations the author Stephen Smith had to be inoculated against
smallpox and examined on site by a government medic due to the risk
of disease from the flesh remaining on some of the corpses.

EC4

Inner Temple Lane

The Inner Temple and Middle Temple, two of London's four Inns of
Court, where lawyers live and work, are named after the Knights
Templar, a body of medieval French warrior monks who protected pilgrims travelling to the Holy Land, and who owned the land here in the
12th century.

Temple Church

The first Gothic church to be built in London, erected between 1160 and
1185, escaped the Great Fire and was refurbished in the late 17th century
by Christopher Wren.

A recess in the south wall contains a Purbeck marble effigy of Bishop
Sylvester, 13th-century Bishop of Carlisle, who was killed in 1255 when he
fell off his horse in London, and was buried here. Others buried in the
church include the 16th century lawyer Edmund Plowden, who never
left the Temple's precincts in the three years he was studying for the Bar,
and the 18th century writer Oliver Goldsmith who was supposed to be
buried in Westminster Abbey but was so in debt that the funeral had to
be cancelled.

A door in the north-west corner of the choir leads to the Penitential
Cell, where knights who had disobeyed the master or broken Temple
rules were imprisoned and in some cases starved to death.

Old Bailey

The street gave its name to the Central Criminal Court, which is based
by the junction of Old Bailey and Newgate Street by the site of the
medieval Newgate Prison.

Magpie and Stump, No. 18

The closest public house to Newgate Prison was originally known as the
Magpie, the 'Stump' suffix being added in mock honour of the headless
victims executed at the prison in the 19th century. Before 1869, when the
Newgate executions were held in public, spectators would pay £10 to
gain a good view of events from the first floor of the house.

Central Criminal Court

Britain's most famous law court, which opened in 1907 to replace those that joined Newgate Prison, has been the setting for many of the most famous murder trials of the last 100 years.

TRIED AT THE OLD BAILEY

‖ The first major murder trial held at the Old Bailey was that of **Horace Rayner**, who was charged in 1907 with murdering his estranged father, the wealthy grocer William Whiteley, at his Westbourne Grove shop, and was acquitted amid a wave of public sympathy (☛p. 263).

‖ **The Kray twins**, Reggie and Ronnie, were tried here for the gangland murders of George Cornell (☛p. 141) and Jack 'The Hat' McVitie (☛p. 184). They were sentenced to life in March 1969 with the recommendation that they serve 'not less than 30 years'.

A year earlier the Krays had planned the daring murder of a witness who was due to appear in court. The would-be assassin was an associate who wanted to prove his worth to the Krays' organisation. He was meant to take into court an attaché case containing a hypodermic needle and a syringe filled with cyanide attached to a small brass ring which, when pulled, would push the needle out, jabbing the witness as he walked by. The victim would die of poisoning five minutes later, by which time his assailant would have escaped. The plan failed when the witness did not walk through the designated spot on the relevant day.

The Krays were unaware at that time that they had been set up by a man working for Scotland Yard's undercover team.

‖ In 1983 civil servant **Dennis Nilsen** was found guilty on six counts of murder and two of attempted murder after probably killing twice that number, mostly homosexuals he'd picked up, in Cricklewood and Muswell Hill in the late 1970s and early 1980s (☛p. 197 and p. 182).

‖ In July 2000 **David Copeland**, a loner whose house was decorated with Nazi posters and who bore a grudge against immigrants and homosexuals, was jailed for life for planting a bomb that killed three people in the Admiral Duncan pub in Soho. Two other Copeland bombs, one in Brixton market, one on Brick Lane, caused mayhem but no deaths. Copeland pleaded not guilty, declaring he was a righteous messenger from God, but was convicted nonetheless.

EC4

Queen Victoria Street

St Nicholas Cole Abbey, *east of Distaff Lane*

The church name is misleading given that it never was an abbey, nor
was there a relevant Nicholas Cole; it is in fact a corruption of the word
'coldharbour', a type of shelter. The church was destroyed on Sunday
11 May 1941 in a Second World War raid in which more than 3,000 were
killed, and was later restored to Christopher Wren's designs.

St Bride's Avenue

St Bride

Still known as the journalists' church, despite the exodus of newspaper
offices to east London, St Bride stands on a pagan site of worship
dedicated to Brigit or Brighde, the Celtic goddess of healing, childbirth
and fire.

The diarist Samuel Pepys, who was baptised in the (surviving) font in
1633, was obliged to bribe the gravedigger to 'jostle together' bodies so
that he could make room for his late brother, Tom, 31, later. As Pepys
wrote in his diary for Friday 18 March 1663 or 1664:

> But to see how a man's tombes are at the mercy of such a fellow, that for
> sixpence he would, (as his owne words were,) 'I will justle them together
> but I will make room for him;' speaking of the fulness of the middle isle,
> where he was to lie; and that he would, for my father's sake, do my brother
> that is dead all the civility he can; which was to disturb other corps that
> are not quite rotten, to make room for him; and methought his manner
> of speaking it was very remarkable; as of a thing that now was in his
> power to do a man a courtesy or not.

Those buried at St Bride include Wynkyn de Worde (d. 1535), William
Caxton's assistant, who brought the first printing press with movable
type to Fleet Street in 1500.

Following Second World War damage an American academic visited
the church to try to save some of the artefacts, and found coffins and
corpses stacked one on top of the other awaiting reburial. He also managed to touch the body of the long deceased 18th-century novelist
Samuel Richardson on the nose.

St Paul's Churchyard

Paul's Cross

Paul's Cross, a wooden pulpit, stood in front of St Paul's Cathedral from 1299 until 1643 when the Puritans pulled it down. Its purpose was to inspire passers-by to pray for the souls of the dead, and it eventually became a medieval 'speakers' corner' as well as a place where royal proclamations were made.

A preacher by the name of Beal stirred up the crowd at Paul's Cross so passionately on May Day 1517 that riots broke out across London on what later came to be called Evil May Day. Troops eventually restored order and took 400 rioters as prisoners. The leaders of the riots were hanged, drawn and quartered.

In 1540 the vicar of St Dunstan and All Saints, William Jerome, was burnt alive for preaching an Anabaptist sermon (rejecting infant baptism) at Paul's Cross.

St Paul's Cathedral

Britain's major cathedral was founded in 604 by Ethelbert, King of Kent, and Mellitus, Bishop of the East Saxons. It burned down in the 1666 Fire of London but was reworked by Christopher Wren. During rebuilding work layers of burials from earlier ages were uncovered. At the top were recent graves from the previous few centuries. Below them were Saxon era burial places lined with chalk stones, followed by Roman urns, and deeper still ancient Briton burial sites surrounded by ivory and wooden pins.

One corpse found by Wren's men was that of John Colet, Dean of St Paul's, who had died in 1519. A hole was made in the coffin and it was found to contain a preserving liquid. This was sampled by a Mr Wyld and Ralph Greatorex, who said it had a kind of 'insipid tast, something of an Ironish tast…perhaps it was a Pickle, as for Beefe whose Saltness in so many years the Lead might sweeten and render insipid'.

When it came to laying the foundation stone of the rebuilt cathedral, Wren asked a workman to bring him the first lump of stone he could find. It was a gravestone, appropriately inscribed *Resurgam* – I will rise again. Wren's own grave contains the brilliant epitaph *si monumentum requiris circumspice* – if you seek his monument, look around.

BURIED AT ST PAUL'S

‖ The lead coffin of the great Elizabethan poet **Sir Philip Sidney** (d. 1586) was exposed by the Fire of London that burned down St Paul's.

‖ The memorial to the metaphysical poet and one-time St Paul's rector **John Donne** (d. 1631), was the only one to survive the Fire.

‖ **Christopher Wren**, who rebuilt the cathedral after the Fire, was buried here in 1723.

‖ A number of well-known artists are buried at St Paul's rather than at Westminster Abbey, including **Joshua Reynolds** (d. 1792), **J. M. W. Turner** (d. 1851), **Lord Leighton** (d. 1896), **John Everett Millais** (d. 1896) and **William Holman Hunt** (d. 1910).

‖ The body of **Lord Nelson** (d. 1805) lies in a coffin made from the mast of the French ship *L'Orient*. During the great warrior's funeral at the cathedral the sailors bearing his coffin tore to shreds the flag that covered it for souvenirs.

‖ In St Paul's crypt, the largest in Europe, is the 11-ton funeral coach used for the **Duke of Wellington**'s cortège on 18 November 1852 in what was the most elaborate state funeral of the era – grander even than Queen Victoria's or Prince Albert's. The coach was made from the metal of the guns used during the Battle of Waterloo, and was pulled by 12 horses with black ostrich plumes on their heads. Their journey from the duke's Apsley House home by Hyde Park Corner to the cathedral took four and a half hours.

ǁ When **Prince Albert**, Victoria's beloved consort, died in 1861 the bells of St Paul's rang what *The Times* called 'the solemn tones of the great bell of St Paul's – a bell of evil omen – [which] told all citizens how irreparable has been the loss of their beloved Queen'. At the same time churches outside London, unaware of the news, were still praying for the prince's recovery.

ǁ Although **Arthur Sullivan**, the composer of the Gilbert and Sullivan operettas, had insisted that he wanted to be buried with his parents at Brompton Cemetery, the Dean of St Paul's offered the crypt of the cathedral when the prolific composer died on 22 November 1900. After the coffin was lowered, Sullivan's hymn 'Brother, Thou Art Gone Before Us' was sung.

Walbrook

St Stephen Walbrook

Long missing is the gravestone of the playwright-architect Sir John Vanbrugh (d. 1726), inscribed with an epitaph supposedly written by fellow architect Nicholas Hawksmoor which read:

> *Lie heavy on him, Earth! For he*
> *Laid many heavy loads on thee.*

EC4

Wine Office Court

Licences for the sale of wine were formerly issued from this court off Fleet Street.

Ye Olde Cheshire Cheese, *at Fleet Street*

One of London's oldest taverns, for a century or so the most popular with newspapermen from the nearby offices, was home early in the 20th century to a parrot whose language shocked even the journalists and whose death in 1926, at the reputed age of 40, was marked by obituaries in many publications.

CHAPTER 2

Central London

CLERKENWELL, EC1
Bleeding Heart Yard
Brooke Street
Charterhouse Square
Clerkenwell Close
Clerkenwell Road
Coldbath Square
Corporation Row
Great Bath Street

FINSBURY, EC2
Bunhill Row
Charlotte Road
Rosebery Avenue

BLOOMSBURY, WC1
Bloomsbury Square
Bloomsbury Way
Calthorpe Street
Gower Street
Great Russell Street
High Holborn
Red Lion Square
Red Lion Street
Tavistock Square

COVENT GARDEN, WC2
Bedford Street
Garrick Street
Long Acre
St Giles High Street
St Martin's Place
Southampton Stret

HOLBORN, WC2
Aldwych
Bell Yard
Chancery Lane
Drury Lane
Lincoln's Inn Fields
Little Queen Street
St Clement's Lane

STRAND, WC2
Fountain Court
Savoy Court
Strand
Trafalgar Square
York Place (formerly Of Alley)

CLERKENWELL EC1

Clerkenwell was London's first suburb, dominated in medieval times by religious institutions such as St John Priory and Charterhouse, which was founded in 1371 as a chapel to help ease the suffering of the souls of those buried locally during the Black Death. After the mid-16th-century dissolution of the monasteries the area was colonised by Huguenots (French Protestants fleeing persecution), who set up workshops for watch-making and leather work.

In recent decades Clerkenwell has attained a fashionable cachet owing to its unfussy Victorian architecture, and its proximity to both the City and the West End.

Bleeding Heart Yard

The unusual name of this dingy, well-concealed courtyard, mentioned by Charles Dickens in *Little Dorrit* (1857), dates back to a myth that grew up around the fate of Lady Elizabeth Hatton, who in 1626 supposedly danced here with the devil and was found the next morning dead, her heart still pumping blood.

Brooke Street

The street, which leads north from Holborn, is named after the long-demolished Brooke House, inhabited in the late 16th century by Fulke Greville (Lord Brooke), Elizabeth I's Chancellor of the Exchequer. He was murdered in the house by his manservant when the latter discovered he had been left out of Greville's will.

Thomas Chatterton's death place (1770), No. 39

Chatterton, the romantic poet described by John Keats as 'the purest writer in the English language', died at 39 Brook Street at the age of 17 from arsenic poisoning. He had taken a fatal dose in a fit of depression. Some say this was induced by a publisher's rejection of his poems, although others believe it was due to the venereal disease he was suffering from and was trying to cure.

After Chatterton's death, poems which he had claimed were written by Thomas Rowley, a 15th-century monk, were found among his papers.

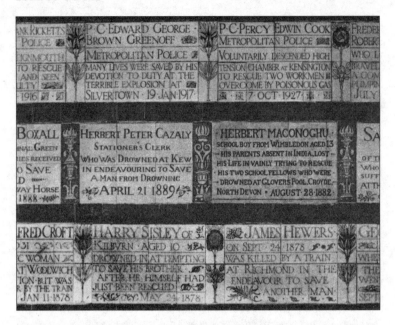

They were published in 1777 and hailed as masterpieces. A few years later however, a scholar proved that the poems could not have been written by the monk, as they used grammatical constructions unknown at that time, and so must have been the work of Chatterton himself, who was then hailed as a poetic genius.

In 1856 Henry Wallis painted *The Death of Chatterton* in the room in which the poet had died, with the novelist and poet George Meredith posing as the doomed romantic poet.

A branch of Barclays Bank now stands on the site.

Charterhouse Square

A Black Death burial site containing 50,000 bodies later became home to Charterhouse School, which was based here until the mid-19th century. Pupils used to tease newcomers by taking them into the square and pressing their ears to the ground to test whether they could hear the anguished cries of those Black Death victims who had been buried alive underneath.

Charterhouse

The arm of John Houghton, prior of the medieval Carthusian monastery that stood on this site, was nailed to the gate after he was hanged, drawn and quartered at Tyburn in 1534 for high treason during the dissolution of the monasteries. Over the next few years 16 more Carthusian monks met the same fate at Tyburn.

During Second World War bombing of 1941 parts of the original monastery were uncovered. When the coffin containing the body of the founder, Walter de Mauny, was unsealed the corpse immediately disintegrated. Some of the ancient buildings remain and are now used by St Bartholomew's Hospital as a medical college.

Clerkenwell Close

In his 1889 novel *The Nether World*, George Gissing describes the funeral of the Peckovers, residents of Clerkenwell Close:

> Each guest having taken a quaff of ale or spirits was led down into the back-kitchen to view the coffin and the corpse. Could Mrs. Peckover have buried the old woman in an orange-crate, she would gladly have done so for the saving of expense; but with relatives and neighbours to consider, she drew a great deal of virtue out of necessity, and dealt so very handsomely with the undertaker, that this burial would be the talk of the Close for some weeks.
>
> The coffin was inspected inside and out, was admired and appraised. At the same time every most revolting detail of the dead woman's last illness was related and discussed and mused over and exclaimed upon. 'A lovely corpse, considerin' her years,' was the general opinion.

Clerkenwell Road

Turnmill's, No. 63b

Frankie Fraser, the infamous late 20th-century gangland enforcer, should have died when he was shot outside Turnmill's nightclub on 23 August 1991, but somehow survived. As Fraser himself explained: 'The bullet was a .22, it came in by my right eye, went all round my face under my nose and lodged by my left eye. But it was good fun, good action, it makes a good night's drink after all.'

Coldbath Square

Coldbath Prison

The prison built here in 1794 had a fearsome reputation, as the poet
Coleridge noted in 'The Devil's Walk', in which he wrote:

> As he went through Coldbath Fields. He saw a solitary cell
> And the devil was pleased for it gave him a hint
> For improving his prisons in hell.

John Williams, the seaman accused of committing the 1811 Ratcliffe
Highway Murders (☛p. 125 and p. 133), was found hanged in his cell at
the end of December that year before he could be brought to trial.
Evidently, many believed, he was the murderer, and had decided to take
his own life rather than face the court and the mob. He was buried in a
ghoulish ceremony (☛p. 121), but a few weeks later it emerged that it
would have been physically impossible for Williams to have hanged
himself in the cell, and therefore he must have been murdered, which
only added to the mystery.

In May 1816 Mary Lewson died at the age of 116, having lived in the
square for 90 years. During that time she rarely left her house or saw
visitors, and never washed, believing that water brought on colds.

Coldbath Prison closed in 1877 and the square was then mostly
demolished.

Corporation Row

The first terrorist bomb ever set off on mainland Britain exploded on
Corporation Row on Friday 13 December 1867, killing six people and
injuring 120 others. The bomb was planted by the Fenians, Irish nationalists, as part of an unsuccessful attempt to release two of their leaders,
Burke and Casey, from what was then the Clerkenwell House of Detention
that stood here.

Although the Dublin authorities had warned the Metropolitan
Police that there would be an attempt to spring the Fenians from
Clerkenwell, few precautions were taken and a constable who saw a
group of men drag a barrel to the prison wall, light a fuse, and drag it
away as it smouldered and fizzled out failed to report the incident to
his superiors.

Two days later, on 13 December, three men and a woman hauled a

30-gallon cask containing more than 500 lbs of gunpowder to Corporation Row, and asked a girl playing in the street to fetch a match. There was a massive blast which caused deaths and injuries, particularly to those crushed in their homes. Michael Barrett, who lit the fuse, was hanged at Newgate (☛ p. 9) a year later in what was London's last public execution. The prison closed in the 1890s and the buildings were converted into a school.

Great Bath Street

Emanuel Swedenborg, the Swedish scientist and mystic, died at 26 Great Bath Street, off Farringdon Road (the street has long been demolished). One of his predictions was that in heaven there would be a special part set aside for the English.

FINSBURY, EC2

Bunhill Row

Bunhill Fields

Daniel Defoe's 'great pit in Finsbury Fields', the first cemetery in London, was established in 1657 by Dissenters – Protestants who rejected the Church of England at a time when burial in old-style small churchyards was associated with popery. Indeed the early 19th-century poet laureate Robert Southey described Bunhill as the 'Campo Santo of Noncomformity', such was its status from when it opened to 1854 when burials ceased.

The site had been known as Bone Hill Fields since the authorities moved a quantity of bones here from St Paul's Churchyard in 1549. Just over 100 years later 'many [plague victims] who were infected and near their end, came here to die in their desperation,' according to Daniel Defoe in *A Journal of the Plague Year* (1722). 'Delirious also [they] ran wrapped in blankets or rags and threw themselves in and expired there.'

Dr Thomas Emes, a self-styled prophet, who died in December 1707, was buried in Bunhill Fields. Many believed he would be resurrected five months later, and huge crowds turned up at the cemetery the following May. When there was no sign of Emes, his supporters explained

EC1 | EC2

EC2

that the miracle had been cancelled for fear that the sizeable crowd would endanger the safety of the risen prophet.

The inscription for Dame Mary Page, the wife of an East India Company merchant, who died in 1728, reads: 'In 67 months she was tap'd 66 times, had taken away 240 gallons of water, without ever repining at her case, or ever fearing the operation.'

BURIED AT BUNHILL FIELDS

‖ **John Bunyan** (d. 1688), author of *The Pilgrim's Progress* (1684), which includes much death imagery, caught a cold on his way to London and died at a friend's house in Snow Hill. He was buried in the vault of his friend, Strudwick, a Holborn grocer.

‖ The writer **Daniel Defoe** (d. 1731) had been hiding from creditors and other enemies when he died and so his simple tombstone was marked 'Mr Dubow'. More suitable would have been: 'The best of men cannot suspend their fate. The good die early, and the bad die late' – one of his best quotes. Nearly 150 years later an obelisk was erected by his grave after an appeal in The *Christian World* newspaper. It later disappeared but was discovered in the 1930s in Southampton and moved to Stoke Newington Library.

‖ **Susanna**, mother of the founder of Methodism **John Wesley**, was interred in 1742 at a service conducted by Wesley himself in front of a large crowd.

‖ The exact location of the grave of **William Blake** (d. 1827) who died peacefully at home in his apartment off the Strand, is unknown. Bunches of fresh flowers are regularly laid at his stone.

‖ The **Thomas Hardy** (d. 1832) buried here is not the romantic Victorian novelist but the early 19th-century radical who in 1794 was accused of high treason and committed to the Tower of London. A mob attacked Hardy's house, frightening his pregnant wife into fleeing, and she later died in childbirth, which led to public sympathy for Hardy. The campaigner was acquitted and died nearly 40 years later.

‖ In **J. B. Priestley**'s 1930 novel *Angel Pavement*, Mr Smeeth goes to Bunhill Fields and 'stared through the iron railings of the old graves' until he is stopped by a passer-by and told that Defoe, Bunyan and Blake 'lie in the sooty earth while their dreams and ecstasies still light the world'.

EC2

Charlotte Road

Factual Nonsense (1990s), *No. 44a*

The avant-garde artist Joshua Compston died in his bed at No. 44a in March 1996 after taking a mixture of alcohol and ether. At the beginning of the decade Compston had opened the premises as a gallery that became central to the new Young British Artists movement. The opening featured a street party at which the stalls were manned by up-and-coming artists such as Tracey Emin, who did palm readings, and Damien Hirst, dressed as a clown, who hired out spin-painting equipment to anyone who wanted to try their hand at producing a work in his style at 50p a go.

Rosebery Avenue

Spa Fields

The large expanse of open land between Sadler's Wells and Charterhouse was covered by Spa Fields before the mid-19th century. Part of the site was occupied by Spa Fields burial ground, where gravediggers burned coffins and corpses. Those brave enough to go there despite the tales about victims of 'putrid fever' would often see gravediggers carrying human remains to the furnace.

BLOOMSBURY, WC1

The intellectual and academic heart of the capital – thanks to the various colleges attached to London University, the presence of the British Museum and the many barely damaged Georgian terraces – is also where one of the July 2005 London transport bombers blew himself up on a bus, and where 30 years previously the Israeli secret service carried out the assassination of a target in the street.

Bloomsbury Square

The long-demolished No. 29 was home in the late 19th century to Lord Mansfield, the Lord Chief Justice, who had accumulated here what was said to be the world's greatest law library. During the 1780 Gordon Riots a mob besieged the property and burned it down to show their distaste for the government's plans to give more rights to Catholics. Some of those responsible were later hanged in the square, forced to face the burnt-out house as the noose tightened.

Bloomsbury Way

St George, *north side between museum street and bury place*

A Nicholas Hawksmoor church built on a constrained site, its burial ground was unpopular until Robert Nelson, the religious pamphleteer, was interred here, leading the historian John Timbs to remark: 'People like to be buried in company, and in good company.'

The funeral of the suffragette Emily Davison, who threw herself under the king's horse at the 1913 Derby, was held at St George.

Calthorpe Street

Robert Cullery, the first policeman to be killed in London, was stabbed to death in Calthorpe Street in 1833 when a demonstration at nearby Coldbath Fields in support of working-class suffrage ended in violence. Men fought for several hours in the neighbouring streets, culminating in the stabbing of Cullery, who staggered into the yard of the Calthorpe Arms public house at the corner of Gray's Inn Road and Calthorpe Street and died there. The jury, surprisingly, returned a verdict of justifiable homicide, on the grounds that the police had charged the crowd without first reading the Riot Act.

Gower Street

University College Hospital, *west side*

The *Animal Farm* and *1984* author George Orwell died on 21 January 1950 in the hospital at the age of 46 when his lung burst while he was being treated for tuberculosis. A few weeks before, on his hospital bed, Orwell married Sonia Brownell, a long time target, whom he had depicted as the scheming Julia in *1984*. Because the author was so ill they needed special dispensation from the Archbishop of Canterbury to marry, there being a law designed to protect the dying rich from gold-diggers. And yet it was Sonia who inherited Orwell's estate – the vast royalties accruing from *Animal Farm* and *1984* – to the consternation of those who had known Orwell's popular first wife, Eileen, who had died during a routine operation a few years previously.

Controversy surrounds Sonia's actions around the time the author died. Some accused her of cavorting in a nightclub off Tottenham Court Road on the night of Orwell's death. She claimed she was discussing with the painter Lucian Freud plans to transfer the writer to a sanatorium in the countryside.

In 2006 a high profile death at the hospital in more sinister circumstances was that of the former KGB agent Alexander Litvinenko. Litvinenko, who had been living in exile in London, died from what turned out to be radiation poisoning from polonium-210 administered by a political opponent during a meeting at a West End hotel (☞ p. 76). Before losing consciousness in hospital, Litvinenko told a friend: 'I want to survive, just to show them. The bastards got me, but they won't get everybody.'

University College, *south of Gower Place*

The embalmed corpse of Jeremy Bentham, the 18th-century philosopher who bequeathed a large of sum of money to the University (founded in 1826), resides in a prominent public position in the south cloister of the college. Bentham made the bequest on condition that his own skeleton be preserved and displayed every year at the annual general meeting. 'I direct that the body thus prepared shall be transferred to my executor. He will cause the skeleton to be clad in one of the suits of black occasionally worn by me.'

Consequently every year the mummified Bentham is taken along to the AGM enclosed in a mahogany case with folding glass doors, seated in an armchair, holding his favourite walking stick. The late philosopher is also taken to the board of governors' meeting once a week, where he is registered as present but not voting. Over the years the university authorities have made some cosmetic alterations to the skeleton, and changed Bentham's underwear as recently as 1935, because a visiting academic insisted on it before giving a lecture. The head is a wax model, the original being stored in the college safe.

Bernard Spilsbury, the Home Office pathologist, poisoned himself in his UCL laboratory in 1947. Spilsbury gave evidence at many of the major murder trials of the mid-20th century, nearly all of which resulted in the conviction of the accused. It was said that he only had to turn up at the mortuary for an accused man to be condemned. He carefully planned his demise after suffering several strokes, realising that, with his mental faculties impaired, his professional usefulness was at an end. After dining at his club, Spilsbury returned to his laboratory and gassed himself by placing his head in an oven.

Great Russell Street

British Museum

The country's foremost museum was founded in 1753 to preserve the artefacts bequeathed by the physician Sir Hans Sloane, and contains one of the world's greatest collections of antiquities, including a number of Egyptian mummies. Rooms 62 and 63 have the bulk of the museum's Egyptian collection, including the (female) mummy of the 18th Dynasty Katebet, wrapped with a gilded mask, wig and pierced earrings. Room 64 is the home of 'Ginger', often featured in books about Egyptian mummies. Nearby is a 1st Dynasty basket coffin, an unwise choice of material given that it would have trapped moisture, which must have quickly rotted the body.

In a corner of the museum is Lindow Man, the well-preserved remains of a body found near Manchester in 1984.

For over 200 years until 1997 the museum was home to the British Library, now situated next to St Pancras station. Many of Britain's greatest writers – Charles Dickens, George Bernard Shaw, Virginia Woolf – enjoyed associations with the library, as did the probably fictitious late 19th-century poet Enoch Soames. He was so upset at lack of recognition by the public that he supposedly sold his soul to the devil in return for the chance to be projected 100 years into the future. According to a story written by Max Beerbohm, Soames arrives in the library a century later, looks himself up in the catalogue, but finds only the briefest mention and no entry in the *Dictionary of National Biography*. In despair he turns to an assistant, who shows him a 1990s newspaper article about an imaginary poet called Enoch Soames who sells his soul to the devil in exchange for the chance to be projected into the future to discover what posterity thinks about him.

High Holborn

The Israeli secret service, Mossad, assassinated one of the Munich Olympics terrorists, who had murdered 11 Israeli athletes during the 1972 games, by running him over in their car on High Holborn. MI5 and Whitehall were annoyed – publicly – that a foreign power had taken the law into its own hands on the streets of London.

Less successful was the stay of the two Mossad agents in the Europa Hotel in London in 1974. One evening after dinner a glamorous blonde struck up conversation in the hotel bar with the pseudonymous agent 'Avner'. As Avner left to go to his room – alone – his colleague passed him going the other way, to the bar. Avner later returned to the bar to socialise with his friend but found him and the girl gone. On his way back to his room, he smelt the woman's perfume in the corridor outside his fellow agent's room. When his friend failed to come down to breakfast the following day, Avner summoned help. They found the Mossad agent dead on his bed, naked, with a bullet wound to the chest, and the girl gone.

The George and Blue Boar, Nos. 268–270

The George and Blue Boar was a medieval inn where those being taken from Newgate Prison to be hanged at Tyburn could stop for a glass of ale. Jonathan Swift described this in his 1727 poem 'Tom Clinch':

> As clever Tom Clinch, while the rabble was bawling
> Rode stately through Holborn to die in his calling
> He stopt at The George for a bottle of sack
> And promised to pay for it when he came back.

WC1

The inn lost much trade when the railways were built and was replaced by a hotel.

Red Lion Square

Originally Red Lion Fields, the square was developed in 1684 by Dr Nicholas Barbon, a surgeon and speculative builder. A demonstration organised by the National Front in Red Lion Square on 15 June 1974 ended in violence when Front members clashed with members of the International Marxist Group. Warwick University student Kevin Gately was killed in the fighting.

Red Lion Street

Dolphin, No. 44

Three people were killed when a Zeppelin bomb fell on the pub on 9 September 1915. The clock in the bar is frozen at the time of the explosion – 10.40 p.m.

Old Red Lion, *Nos. 68–70*

The bodies of those responsible for executing Charles II in 1649 – Oliver Cromwell, who replaced the king; Cromwell's son-in-law and right-hand man Henry Ireton; and John Bradshawe, who gave the order for execution – were dug up from Westminster Abbey where they had been buried, after Charles II returned to the throne on 4 December 1660 and were displayed overnight at the Red Lion. As Bradshawe's corpse had not been properly embalmed and was badly decayed, a nauseous stench filled the tavern during the exhibition. The next day the trio were taken to the Tyburn gallows and publicly 'executed' in a grotesque final humiliation (p. 67).

Within a few years rumours circulated London that prior to his death Cromwell had transposed the royal tombs in the Abbey so that the body exhumed in 1661 might not have been his, and might even have been that of Charles I whom he sent for execution. The story was not completely discounted until the 19th century when the remains of Charles I were discovered undisturbed at Windsor.

Tavistock Square

WC1

Hasib Hussain blew himself up and 12 other people on a No. 30 bus as it travelled through Tavistock Square on the morning of 7 July 2005. It is not known whether he planned to detonate the device at that moment or whether it exploded accidentally. Hussain was thwarted in his original mission – to blow himself up on a packed tube train – when the Underground system was evacuated following the explosions caused by his fellow bombers at three other points on the network. He was one of thousands evacuated from King's Cross station and went into a nearby McDonald's to phone his colleagues. Receiving no reply – they were already dead – Hussain left a panicky message for Mohammad Sidique Khan: 'I can't get on a train. What should I do?' He left the same message for the other two bombers, Shehzad Tanweer and Germaine Lindsay. Walking west, he boarded the No. 30 bus near St Pancras church, and when it turned left towards the West End set off the bomb. Survivors claimed Hussain seemed 'flustered' as he rummaged inside the large black rucksack on his lap.

His demise was similar to that of Martial Bourdin, a French anarchist, who was carrying a bomb to the Royal Observatory in Greenwich in 1895. It blew up prematurely in the park, but killed only him.

COVENT GARDEN, WC2

Now mostly a centre of shopping and tourism, thanks to the revamped Covent Garden Market, WC2 is built on what was the Saxons' Thames port of Lundenwic. Westminster Abbey bought the land at the beginning of the 13th century to found a *convent garden*, which grew into London's major flower and vegetable market, giving its name to the area in a corrupted form. The market is now located in Battersea.

Alfred Hitchcock's 1972 movie, *Frenzy*, which is set among the stalls of Covent Garden and was filmed just before the market moved to Nine Elms, tells the story of a fruit seller who is also a serial sex killer.

Bedford Street

St Paul

London's first classical revival building, the work of Inigo Jones in the 1630s, is also known as the actors' church as it is where Ellen Terry (d. 1928), Margaret Rutherford (d. 1972), Dame Edith Evans (d. 1976) and Hatti Jacques (d. 1980) are buried. The church also contains memorials to the actress Vivien Leigh and the music-hall star Marie Lloyd.

The 17th-century writer Samuel Butler was buried here rather than Westminster Abbey when the executors of his estate realised they could not afford the abbey's burial fees.

Garrick Street

Garrick Club, No. 15

Shortly after the death of the Savoy Opera composer Arthur Sullivan a club member, unaware of the news, spotted Sullivan's long-time collaborator, W. S. Gilbert, in the club and asked him what Sullivan was doing. 'He is doing nothing,' Gilbert replied. 'Surely he is composing?' the man persisted. 'On the contrary,' Gilbert quipped. 'He is decomposing.'

Long Acre

St Martin's Hall/Odham's, No. 94

Thirty-eight people died when a bomb fell on the printing works owned by the publishers, Odham's, at 94 Long Acre on 29 January 1918. Odham's produced magazines such as *Racing Pigeon*, *Vanity Fair* and *John Bull*. The company was owned by Julius Elias, an eccentric who continued to run his papers from the grave after his death in 1946 according to his successor, A. C. Duncan, a keen spiritualist, who claimed he held regular 'consultations' with his deceased predecessor.

WC2

St Giles High Street

A Roman road, despite its curved shape, St Giles High Street was a major stop on the route the condemned took from Newgate Prison to the Tyburn Tree Gallows. It was where they would take a last drink from what became known as 'the St Giles bowl' at one of the street's many inns. The road's status declined following the construction of New Oxford Street in the 1840s and is now a backwater.

St Giles

Sir John Oldcastle, leader of the Lollards, who preached an early form of Protestantism in the early 15th century and who provided Shakespeare with the model for Falstaff, was hanged near the church gate in 1417. Once he had expired his corpse was burnt even though it was still bound in chains.

Richard Penderell (d. 1671), who smuggled Charles II out of England after the execution of his father, is commemorated with a fulsome epitaph:

Unparalell'd Pendrell, thro' the universe
Like when the Eastern Star from Heaven gave light
To three lost kings; so he, in such dark night,
To Britain's Monarch, toss'd by adverse War,
On Earth appear'd, a second Eastern Star,
A Pope, a Stern, in her rebellious Main,
A Pilot to her Royal Sovereign.
Now to triumph in Heav'n's eternal sphere,
Whilst Albion's Chronicles, with matching fame,
Embalm the story of great Pendrell's Name.

Twelve Catholics denounced by Titus Oates as part of the so-called Popish Plot, which alleged that Catholics were about to seize the throne, were executed here from 1678–81 and buried in the churchyard.

In his 1792 *Account of London* Thomas Pennant railed against St Giles churchyard

with many rows of coffins piled one upon the other, all exposed to sight and smell; some of the piles incomplete, expecting the mortality of the night. I turned away disgusted at the view, and scandalized at the want of police, which so little regards the health of the living, as to permit so many putrid corpses, tacked between some slight boards, dispersing their dangerous effluvia over the capital, to remain unburied.

The *Weekly Dispatch* of September 1838 described the churchyard as a 'horrid place, full of coffins, up to the surface. Coffins are broken up before they are decayed, and bodies are removed to the bone house [where] you may see bones with flesh still adhering to them.'

St Martin's Place

St Martin-in-the-Fields

The well-known church, located by Trafalgar Square, was the burial place of Nell Gwynn (d. 1687), Charles II's mistress. Her welfare must have been the king's paramount concern: on his deathbed, two years earlier, he had whispered: 'Let not poor Nell starve.'

In 1724 Jack Sheppard, thief and escaper, was buried here after his execution at Tyburn in front of a crowd of 200,000, some of whom stopped bodysnatchers making off with the corpse.

Findings made in 2006 during the rebuilding of the church included a Roman style grave in a limestone coffin. Carbon-dating has determined that the remains are from the early fifth century, making it the earliest body from London's Roman period ever discovered. St Martin's clergy are hoping to find proof that the Roman burial was conducted in the Christian manner, as there are few Christian remains from Roman Britain and no identifiable churches from Roman London.

Southampton Street

There was an outcry when Arthur Conan Doyle killed off Sherlock Holmes in the short story 'The Final Problem' (1893). Thousands cancelled their subscriptions to *Strand* magazine, which premiered the Holmes stories, and some readers descended on its Southampton Street offices to protest.

HOLBORN, WC2

In his 1752 engraving *Gin Lane*, set in Holborn, William Hogarth illustrates the powerful hold gin had over 18th-century London society in a tableau heavy with spectacular funereal imagery. In Hogarth's picture the skeletal figure who sells gin and ballad sheets is based on a real local character whose cry was: 'Buy my ballads and I'll give you a glass of gin for nothing.' Over the doorway of the gin cellar is the legend:

> *Drunk for a penny*
> *Dead drunk for two pence*
> *Clean straw for nothing.*

In the middle distance the parish beadle watches as a dead woman is dropped into a coffin, and a suicide is hanging from the rafters, presumably unable to face life without gin.

Gin became popular after William III introduced an Act in 1690 to 'encourage the distilling of brandy and spirits' that would boost the grain market and benefit farmers. This led to a half-century of excessive gin consumption, but was particularly troublesome for the poor who were used to drinking pints of beer, were ill prepared for gin and now had a greater chance of dying of alcoholic poisoning. One such victim was a labourer by the name of George Wade who went to a public house in Westminster, 'drank a Pint of Gin off at a Draught, and expired in a few Minutes'.

After the prime minister Robert Walpole brought in an Act in 1736 restricting the sale of the drink, Londoners took to the streets in mock funeral processions for Queen Gin and hung black drapes over gin shops. The Gin Act rewarded informers who squealed on illegal vendors, many of whom were severely beaten and some even killed.

Aldwych

Nearly 200 people lost their lives when a German V1 rocket fell on Aldwych at lunchtime on 30 June 1944. The rocket exploded just outside the Air Ministry building opposite Bush House. Many died from injuries caused by flying rubble, while some workers at the ministry were sucked out of office windows by the blast and perished. Initially the authorities claimed that only 48 people were killed, but it later emerged that the number of casualties was higher, a fact the authorities deliberately concealed because many of those killed were government officials or military personnel.

Edward O'Brien, an Irish terrorist, blew himself up when a bomb he was carrying on a No.171 bus travelling along Aldwych exploded prematurely on 18 February 1996. Eight others were injured.

Bell Yard

Margery Lovett, lover of Sweeney Todd, the so-called 'demon barber of Fleet Street', ran a shop on Bell Yard in the 1780s where she cooked meat pies supposedly containing the flesh of his many victims. The bodies were brought to the shop along a tunnel which linked her premises with Todd's barber shop at 186 Fleet Street (p. 25), 100 yards to the east.

Charles Dickens obliquely referred to Lovett's vile practice in *Martin Chuzzlewit* (1844) in which Tom Pinch is afraid that his friend will think he has strayed 'into one of those streets where the countrymen are

murdered, and ... made [into] meat pies'. The site of the shop is now
occupied by Butterworth's publishers.

Chancery Lane

In Charles Dickens's *Bleak House* (1853), mostly set in this locale, Tom
Jarndyce 'in despair blew his brains out at a coffee-house in Chancery
Lane', thus setting in motion the relentless Jarndyce *v* Jarndyce legal
case which powers the novel.

Drury Lane

The 1665 outbreak of bubonic plague started in this area of London
when a parcel containing clothes imported from Holland was opened
and unleashed fleas carrying the disease. The diarist Samuel Pepys
came here a year later and noted a number of houses on Drury Lane
marked with a red cross and the words 'Lord have mercy upon us' written on the door in regulation one-foot-high letters. This meant that the
occupants had fallen victim to the plague and had been sealed in to die
so as not to infect others. Around 100,000 Londoners died of the disease in 1665 and 1666.

In 1750, four years after his farcical execution of Lord Kilmarnock at
Tower Hill (☛p. 136), the incompetent executioner John Thrift was
attacked by a gang near his Drury Lane home. During the mêlée a man
was killed, and Thrift was charged with murder and sentenced to death.
The punishment was later commuted to transportation to the
American colonies, although this move was shelved on the grounds that
an executioner was too valuable to lose. He was pardoned on condition
that he agreed to continue his trade.

Charles Dickens modelled the graveyard featured in his 1853 novel
Bleak House on a Drury Lane burial ground that had been opened in
1850 and was described by the local Board of Health as being 'quite
greasy to the touch'. Seven years previously, when a family would not
accept a burial in a shallow hole in the Drury Lane graveyard, the dig-
gers pickaxed open a coffin, 'exposing the mortal remains of its pale
tenant', tipped out the corpse, 'smashing and mixing it up with the
clay', and then dug up two more coffins to make room.

WC2

Lincoln's Inn Fields

Lincoln's Inn Fields is London's largest square and was used in medieval times for sports and jousting. It was here in September 1586 that the 14 Babington Plotters who had planned to murder Elizabeth I and install Mary Queen of Scots on the throne were hanged, drawn and quartered. In 1683 the square was again the setting for a political execution when Lord Russell was implicated in a Whig plot to assassinate Charles II. A century later those found to have been holding illegal mass at the nearby Ship Inn were executed for heresy here.

Sir John Soane Museum, Nos. 12–14

The crypt of this remarkable museum, once the home of the late 18th-century architect John Soane, replete with classical artefacts and architectural oddities, contains the sarcophagus of Pharaoh Seti I (1279 bc). The tomb was carved out of a single piece of Egyptian alabaster and was discovered in the Valley of the Kings in 1817 by Giovanni Belzoni. Soane arranged for it to be shipped to London seven years later, but when it arrived in Lincoln's Inn Fields he realised the sarcophagus was too big to get into the house. Most of the back wall had to be demolished to allow the block through. Soane celebrated its arrival with a three-day party attended by around 1,000 people, including the painter J. M. W. Turner and the poet Samuel Taylor Coleridge. At the time the hieroglyphics had not been deciphered, but we now know they to refer to the passage of the soul through the underworld. The sarcophagus has since turned yellow in the London air.

Royal College of Surgeons, Nos. 35–43

In January 1803 the body of the murderer George Forster was pulled down from the gallows at Newgate Prison and taken to the college. Before a large audience, a doctor, Giovanni Aldini, began trying to return the corpse to life. He connected conducting rods, wired to a battery, to Forster's face and soon, according to witnesses, 'the jaw began to quiver, the adjoining muscles were horribly contorted, and the left eye actually opened'. The climax came when Forster's clenched fist punched the air, his legs kicked and his back arched violently. There was no spark of life in the late murderer, however. Aldini had simply sent an electric current through the body.

Little Queen Street

Mary Lamb, the writer who collaborated with her brother, Charles, on *Tales from Shakespeare* (1807), killed their mother on 22 September 1796 with a kitchen knife at No. 7 (close to the junction of Kingsway and Parker Street). The stabbing was a mistake. Mary had intended to injure an annoying apprentice who was assisting her mother with her needle-work, but the latter intervened. The coroner pronounced a verdict of murder while temporarily insane, and Mary was sent to an asylum in Islington.

St Clement's Lane

Enon Chapel

Opened in 1823 to alleviate overcrowding in the City churchyards and built over an open sewer, the Enon Chapel took an extraordinary number of 'burials' – some 12,000 – over the following 20 years. The vicar would soak the bodies with quicklime and sell the coffins a few weeks after death to make space for more of the dead. Sometimes he and his colleagues poured human remains into the nearest sewer, so that they could float away in the Thames, and if the need to find space became particularly acute he would arrange for the bodies to be carted off and dumped directly in the river.

A letter sent to *The Times* on 25 June 1839 noted how the 'effluvia' from the Enon burial ground was:

> so offensive that persons living in the back of Clement's Lane are com-pelled to keep their windows closed; the walls even of the ground which adjoins the yards of those houses, are frequently seen reeking with fluid, which diffuses a most offensive smell. Who can wonder, then, that fever is here so prevalent and so triumphant?

In *London by Day and Night*, his 1852 guidebook, David W. Bartlett noted how graves had been dug for typhus victims on St Clement's Lane but left open only yards from where people lived. The gravedigger at the nearby St Clement Danes church told Bartlett that the ground was so full he could not make a new grave without coming into other graves:

> We have cut parts away with choppers and pickaxes. We have opened the lids of coffins, and the bodies have been so perfect that we could

WC2

distinguish males from females and all those have been chopped and cut up. During the time I was at this work, the flesh has been cut up in pieces and thrown up behind the boards which are placed to keep the ground up where the mourners are standing – and when the mourners are gone this flesh has been thrown in and jammed down, and the coffins taken away and burnt.

His story, however, was not as upsetting as that of one of his colleagues who, chopping off a head in the graveyard, realised in horror that it was his own father's.

The Enon graveyard closed at the end of the century when the area was redeveloped. Excavations in 1967 prior to the building of a block for the London School of Economics uncovered large quantities of human bones.

STRAND, WC2

Fountain Court

William Blake death place (1827), *No. 3*

The revered poet-painter lived in what the diarist Henry Crabb Robinson described as a 'squalid place of but two chairs and a bed' off the Strand with his wife, Catherine, for the last seven years of his long life. Mostly unknown outside a small group of associates at that time, Blake spent his last days in poverty, but he consoled himself with the thought that 'God had a beautiful mansion for me elsewhere.'

By February 1827 Blake said he was feeling 'feeble and tottering', and by April was talking of how 'we must all soon follow, every one to his own eternal house'. On the day he died – 12 August 1827 – he stopped work and turned to his wife saying: 'Stay Kate, keep just as you are – I will draw your portrait for you have ever been an angel to me.' He began singing hymns and verses and at six in the evening died.

Savoy Court

The name Savoy dominates the tiny lanes and blind alleyways to the west of Waterloo Bridge: Savoy Buildings, Savoy Court, Savoy Hill, Savoy Place, Savoy Row, Savoy Steps, Savoy Street and Savoy Way as well as the

Savoy Hotel, the Savoy Theatre and Savoy Chapel. The name is in honour of the medieval Savoy Palace, built in 1245 and sacked during the Peasants' Revolt of 1381, when some of the rebels found the wine cellars and during their drunken revelry threw barrels into the flames only to discover too late that the casks held gunpowder. Following the explosions they were unable to make their way out and were trapped in the cellars where they drank themselves to death while the blaze raged.

Savoy Hotel

Stanley Gibbons, who founded the famous philately business that bears his name, died in strange circumstances, probably in the arms of a lover, overexcited by her charms, at the Savoy Hotel in 1913. No authoritative account of his death has been established, and one story claims that his corpse was immediately bundled up in a carpet and removed from the hotel to a nephew's apartment in Piccadilly. There are even rumours that Gibbons was a serial wife-killer who poisoned all four of his brides.

Five years later, in November 1918, the starlet Billie Carleton was found at the Savoy dead from a drugs overdose – the first 'celebrity' drug casualty in London history. The previous evening she had starred in a Great War victory ball at the Albert Hall. The inquest found Carleton had died of cocaine poisoning, and police established that she had obtained the drugs from the opium dens of Chinatown, then in Limehouse. The sensationalist writer Sax Rohmer quickly capitalised on the tragedy, weaving the story into a novel, *Dope: a Story of Chinatown*.

In 1956 the prime minister, Anthony Eden, was overheard in the hotel shouting down a telephone: 'I want Nasser [the president of Egypt] assassinated.' Britain and Egypt were then at loggerheads over the ownership of the Suez Canal, and MI6 devised a plot to poison Gamal Nasser with nerve gas dispersed through the ventilation system of one of the presidential buildings. The scheme was dropped when the foreign secretary, Selwyn Lloyd, panicked. Eden resigned the premiership after his attempt to invade Egypt backfired.

Strand

Adelphi Theatre, No. 414

Built as the Sans Pareil in 1806 by John Scott, a tradesman who wanted to launch his daughter, Jane, as an actress, it became the Adelphi in 1819 and was rebuilt in 1858 by T. H. Wyatt to resemble the Opéra Comique in Paris. The actor William Terris was stabbed to death by a jealous colleague outside the theatre on 16 December 1897.

Somerset House, *south side*

Following James I's death in 1625, his body lay at Somerset House, traditionally the Queen of England's palace, for five weeks, surrounded by half a dozen silver candlesticks the new king, Charles I, had bought in Spain.

Some 30 years afterwards the late Lord Protector, Oliver Cromwell – Charles's nemesis – lay in state at Somerset House after his death. The diarist John Evelyn, a contemporary of Samuel Pepys, wrote that he saw 'the superb funeral of the Protector. He was carried from Somerset House in a velvet bed drawn by six horses … [he was] lying in effigy in royal robes and crowned with a crown, sceptre and globe like a king.'

However, the ceremony was a farce. Cromwell had already been buried in Westminster Abbey three weeks previously, because the embalming went wrong, or as his physician George Bate revealed 'his Body filled with Spices, wrapped in a fourfold Cerecloath, put first into a Coffin of Lead, and then into a Wooden one, yet it purged and wrought through all, so that there was a necessity of interring it before the Solemnity of his Funerals'. Consequently the coffin paraded through the streets was empty. Cromwell's corpse later had to endure the ignominy of exhumation from Westminster Abbey and a hanging at Tyburn (☛ p. 67).

Charing Cross station

The memorial outside Charing Cross station is not Charing Cross, but Eleanor's Cross, in memory of Edward I's queen, Eleanor of Castile. It is a Victorian replica, for the original, which stood 100 yards to the west from 1290, was pulled down in 1647 by the Puritans. When Charing Cross station was being built in the 1860s, the authorities thought it would be a good idea to celebrate the old cross so they commissioned Edward Middelton Barry to create a copy of the original.

On 10 May 1927 station staff noticed an unpleasant smell coming from the left luggage department. There they found a trunk containing the dismembered body of a woman, the legs hacked off at the hips and the arms removed from the shoulders. The limbs had been wrapped in brown paper and tied with string.

Fortunately there was a label on the woman's clothes and she was soon identified as Minnie Bonati, a former cook who had been working as a prostitute. A police appeal for information was answered by a taxi driver who reported that he had picked up a man and helped him move a heavy trunk. The man was indentified as John Robinson, estate agent. When confronted by officers, he confessed to Bonati's murder. He was hanged at Pentonville on 12 August 1927.

Trafalgar Square

Two people were killed in the square on 'Bloody Sunday', 13 November 1887, when violence marred a demonstration against the jailing of the radical Irish MP William O'Brien. The protest was led by the Socialist League, whose numbers included the great Victorian polymath William Morris, Annie Besant (leader of the match girls' strike) and the playwright George Bernard Shaw. They were at the head of a crowd that had set off from Clerkenwell Green and on reaching Trafalgar Square were rushed by the police.

WC2

York Place (formerly Of Alley)

In his will George Villiers, 2nd Duke of Buckingham, power broker of
Charles I, stipulated that the streets around his York House mansion,
which was situated close to modern-day Charing Cross station, be
renamed after him using all parts of his name, thereby leading to the
creation of George Court, Villiers Street, Duke Street, Buckingham
Street and the absurd Of Alley.

CHAPTER 3

The West End

THE WEST END, W1
Oxford Street
Regent Steet

FITZROVIA, W1
Charlotte Street
Newman Passage

MARYLEBONE, W1
Cato Street
Cavendish Street
Duke Street
Harley Street
Manchester Street
Upper Berkeley Street
Welbeck Street
Wimpole Street

MAYFAIR, W1
Berkeley Square
Curzon Place
Curzon Street
Grosvenor Square
Hill Street
Mount Street
Park Lane
Piccadilly
St George Street
Savile Row
Stratton Street

SOHO, W1
Broadwick Street
Coventry Street
Frith Street
Gerrard Street
Goslett Yard
Great Windmill Street
Old Compton Street
Romilly Street
St Anne's Court
Wardour Street

THE WEST END, w1

The West End, the retail and nightlife centre of London, radiates in four quarters – Fitzrovia, Marylebone, Mayfair and Soho – around Oxford Circus with Oxford Street running east–west and Regent Street north–south through its centre.

Oxford Street

In pre-Victorian times the condemned were taken along Oxford Street for public hanging at the Tyburn Tree.

Tyburn, *junction with Edgware Road*

The most famous London gallows, located by the Tyburn stream a few yards from the modern-day Marble Arch, was where more than 50,000 people were hanged from 1196 to 1783.

Originally Tyburn was a basic gallows bounded by a row of elms, the trees the Normans equated with justice. In 1511 it was expanded into the Tyburn Tree, an enormous construction of three posts, 18 feet high, capable of hanging 24 prisoners at the same time, eight on each horizontal beam, and known popularly as the 'Never-Green Tree'.

Hangings took place seven or eight times a year and the occasions were treated as public festivals and attended by tens of thousands. (The 'official' record gate was 80,000 for the forger Henry Fauntleroy in 1824.) The most expensive seats were by the tree, and space could be rented in the rooms of the upper-storeys of nearby houses and pubs. But most spectators had to make do with a free, if obstructed, view from the crowd where there was always the added thrill of maybe having one's pockets picked by someone who might end up at Tyburn a few months later.

In charge of the seating arrangements were the so-called Tyburn pew-openers such as Mammy Douglas. She raised her prices from 2/- to 2/6 in 1758 for the demise of a Dr Florence Henesy (a man, despite the name) and was publicly decried for profiteering. The public paid up, grudgingly, but at the last minute when doctor was reprieved, which understandably led to a riot as the mob tried to replace the fortunate doctor with Mammy Douglas.

The day was run according to a well-arranged timetable. Victims would rise at seven o'clock at Newgate Prison, where they were held prior to execution, and led in chains into Newgate Yard where the Yeoman of the Halter would tie their wrists in front of them so that the hands would be in praying position when they reached Tyburn. He would then place a rope round their necks, the free end left to coil about their bodies, and lead them to the start of their journey.

The first stop was St Sepulchre's church on Newgate Street, where the condemned were given a nosegay of flowers. The Newgate church bell would sound and the clerk would chant: 'You that are condemned to die, repent with lamentable tears; ask mercy of the Lord for the salvation of your souls.' The procession would then move through the City – along Snow Hill, across the River Fleet and up the hill to High Holborn.

In the narrow streets of St Giles the party would head for a tavern by St Giles's Hospital where prisoners took their last drink – the Cup of Charity – without having to pay, although some jokingly promised to buy a round on the way back. Then it was back on to the wagon once more – never to drink again (hence the phrase 'on the wagon') and along Tyburn Road (Oxford Street) where they were placed behind their coffin on a hurdle and dragged along for the rest of the trip for several hours.

As the condemned went to the gallows they would be approached by authors seeking approval to publish material already written as 'last confessions'. The condemned would advertise the forthcoming works to the crowds before they were executed, and the families would be rewarded.

Finally there was the execution itself. The blindfolded, hooded victim, hands tied, would stand on a wagon with a rope around the neck and wait while the horse was whipped into running off. When the wagon moved away the prisoner would be left to dangle and would die a slow death from asphyxiation. This could often take as long as an hour. The crowd knew that death had overcome life when they saw urine dribble down the leg. (Those singled out for really severe punishment would be disembowelled while half-hanged.) The public enjoyed such spectacles and would cheer if the prisoner put up a fight, especially if they struggled to the end.

The hangman was allowed to keep the clothes of the dead, and so many prisoners wore rags. However, some of the condemned put on quality threads hoping that a grateful executioner would ease their suffering by pulling on their legs and beating on their chests so that they died quicker. The hangman could also make a little cash charging the public for the right to stroke the dead, which was believed to have health benefits. Finally, at the end of the day's events he could sell the rope. The more notorious the victim the higher the price.

Sometimes a pardon would arrive just in time. In 1447 five men who had been placed on the gallows were lucky enough to win a reprieve while still alive. The hangman cut them down but stripped them and insisted on keeping their garments, despite the pleas of the men who would now be obliged to walk home naked.

Some who were hanged lived to tell the tale. One man pushed open the lid of his coffin and asked for a drink. A kindly spectator offered him a jug of wine which he drank, only to drop down dead on the spot, this time for good. A John Smith, who was hanged at Tyburn on Christmas Eve 1705, was left to dangle for 15 minutes until the crowd shouted 'reprieve'. He was cut down and taken to a nearby house where he soon recovered. Asked what it was like to be hanged Smith replied:

> When I was turned off I was, for some time, sensible of very great pain occasioned by the weight of my body and felt my spirits in strange commotion, violently pressing upwards. After I was cut down, I began to come to myself and the blood and spirits forcing themselves into their former channels put me by a prickling or shooting into such intolerable pain that I could have wished those hanged who had cut me down.

He was known for ever more as 'Half-hanged Smith'. Sixteen year old William Duell, who was hanged in 1740 for rape and murder, recovered at the Surgeons Hall on Newgate just as he was about to be dissected. He had his sentenced commuted to transportation.

In 1759 the authorities introduced a trapdoor. Now victims no longer asphyxiated slowly but died very quickly, falling through the opening. By then, however, roughly half of those condemned to death were being spared the gallows for a worse punishment – banishment to Australia.

It was around this time that the residents of growing Mayfair and Marylebone put pressure on the authorities to stop the Tyburn hangings, not out of human compassion or revulsion at the process but out of distaste for the rabble coming through their increasingly affluent neighbourhood. From 1783 hangings took place within the prison walls at Newgate in the City.

Events at Tyburn were captured by Samuel Pepys in his diary, where he noted on 21 January 1664 that he 'got for a shilling to stand upon the wheel of a cart, in great pain, above an hour before the execution was done'. They were also recorded by William Hogarth, whose 1747 painting *Industry and Idleness: The Idle 'Prentice Executed at Tyburn*, depicts a huge crowd gathered to enjoy the executions, indulging in feasting, drinking and making merry while a group of boys overturn a fruit cart and pick the pocket of a cake salesman.

Hanged, Drawn and Quartered

The sentence for those found guilty of high treason was the severest of all punishments in medieval times – hanging, drawing and quartering. Miscreants would be half-hanged so that the rest of the sentence could be carried out while they were still aware of it, and began with lingering death by slow strangulation. During this male victims would be castrated so that they would be unable to 'spread their seed', a mostly symbolic act given that they would soon have no seed to spread.

Next came the 'drawing' of the bowels and other organs, which were removed with a knife and thrown on the fire. Then the condemned was decapitated, and the body quartered – chopped into four pieces – and boiled in a salty solution laced with cumin seed to discourage birds from pecking the flesh. Finally the body parts were exhibited.

The sentence was first used against William Maurice for piracy in 1241, and deployed excessively a few decades later by Edward I while subjugating the Scots and Welsh. One of the most famous victims was William Wallace, the Scottish patriot 'Braveheart', in 1305. Typical was the way the punishment was handed out to John Rouse and others at Newgate in 1683. The official court record notes:

Then Sentence was passed, as followeth, viz. That they should return to the place from whence they came, from thence be drawn to the Common place of Execution upon Hurdles, and there to be Hanged by the Necks, then cut down alive, their Privy-Members cut off, and Bowels taken out to be burnt before their Faces, their Heads to be severed from their Bodies, and their Bodies divided into four parts, to be disposed of as the King should think fit.

The ordeal ended because of the concerns of the medical profession. Doctors wanted the corpses intact. So did relatives, not to help the dissectors, but because it was commonly believed that only having an intact body could lead to life after death.

HANGED AT TYBURN

Most Tyburn victims were commonplace felons. Some were murderers, more were bread thieves, others had simply tampered with haystacks, and many more had fallen foul of the bewildering number of 'crimes' that could result in hanging in those days.

- The first recorded Tyburn execution was that of **William Fitzosbert** in 1196, hanged for urging the public to oppose new taxes.
- **Elizabeth Barton** (d. 1534), dubbed by some 'the English Joan of Arc', was a religious visionary who became a Benedictine nun in Canterbury. She protested against Henry VIII's divorce from Catherine of Aragon, wrote to the Pope, and was hanged for her views.
- The Jesuit, **Robert Southwell** (d. 1595), convicted of treason, survived 13 torture sessions in various prisons and a botched hanging at the Tyburn Tree in 1595 when the noose was placed improperly around his neck. Fortunately the hangman took mercy on Southwell and pulled his feet to end his agony. To make sure there were no more mistakes Southwell was also beheaded, quartered and disembowelled.

ǁ Those held to be responsible for executing Charles I – **Oliver Cromwell**, his son-in-law **Henry Ireton** and **John Bradshawe** – were exhumed from their tombs at Westminster Abbey in December 1660, after the country had reverted to a monarchy, drawn to the gallows, and hanged and buried under it.

ǁ **Robert Hubert**, a French silversmith, took the blame for the 1666 Fire of London, freely admitting that he had started the blaze at Farryner's bakery on Pudding Lane in the City (☛ p. 21) on the order of the Pope's, even though it was easily shown that his confession was riddled with inconsistencies and impossibilities.

No one knows why Hubert was so keen to be the scapegoat. Alongside him at Tyburn an effigy of the Pope, its head filled with live cats, was set alight. As the flames rose the cats, who could not be seen, screamed in torment and it looked as if the 'Pope', rather than the animals, was being burned alive – to the delight of the large crowd.

ǁ When **Jack Sheppard**, the burglar and recidivist escaper, was executed in 1724 he was quickly removed in a hearse hired by the writer Daniel Defoe so that he could be revived. The crowd attacked the vehicle, assuming it contained bodysnatchers making off with prize booty.

ǁ **Jonathan Wild**, London's arch early 18th-century thief-taker, was hanged in 1725 after his career collapsed and he unsuccessfully tried to commit suicide. Wild was one of the most powerful figures London had ever known, self-styled Thief-Taker General of Great Britain and Ireland, who sent more than 120 men to the gallows, but he also organized his own groups of highwaymen and thieves.

Wild's forte was the double cross. When he had gathered enough evidence to convict a man he would put an 'X' against his name. If he decided he was going to betray him he would put an extra 'X'. On his journey to Tyburn, Wild was booed and pelted with missiles, including human stools, and in a drugged state faced one of the largest crowds ever seen at the tree. He did not give the customary last speech and his body was cut down before resurrectionists could seize it.

ǁ Dr Johnson's biographer, James Boswell, saw the highwayman **Paul Lewis** hanged in May 1763 and noted: 'I was most terribly shocked, and thrown into a very deep melancholy.'

ǁ **Dr Dodd**, a clergyman who forged a £4,200 bond in the name of the Earl of Chesterfield, was hanged in 1777 but soon cut down by friends, who took the body to a Goodge Street undertaker's. There John

Hunter, the eminent surgeon, tried unsuccessfully to bring Dodd
back to life, even going as far as giving him a hot bath, in vain.

‖ In 1780 scores of Londoners were hanged for their involvement in
the anti-Catholic **Gordon Riots**. Some were executed just for watching as the mob burned down the homes of Catholics. Samuel Rogers,
a witness, recollected seeing 'a whole cartload of young girls, in
dresses of various colours, on the way to be executed at Tyburn'.

Regent Street

One of London's foremost Victorian mourning shops was Jay's London
General Mourning Warehouse, which opened on Regent Street in 1841
and provided a full range of funereal wear, specialising in black silks,
crapes, paramattas, cashmeres, grenadines and tulles. As Richard Davey
noted in *A History of Mourning* in 1889:

> Private mourning in modern times, like everything else, has been greatly
> altered and modified, to suit an age of rapid transit and travel. Men no
> longer make a point of wearing full black for a fixed number of months
> after the decease of a near relation, and even content themselves with a
> black hat-band and dark-coloured garments. Funeral ceremonies, too, are
> less elaborate, although during the past few years a growing tendency to
> send flowers to the grave has increased in every class of the community.

FITZROVIA, W1

The area to the north-east of Oxford Circus was jokingly so
named early in the 20th century by regulars at the Fitzroy Tavern,
a haunt of writers and artists in the 1920s. Near the well-known
pub are Fitzroy Street and Fitzroy Square, themselves named
after Henry Fitzroy, illegitimate son of Charles II.

Charlotte Street

Richard Dadd, the Victorian artist responsible for the intricately fantastic *Fairy-Feller's Master Stroke* (1855–64), shared digs on Charlotte Street
with fellow painters W. P. Frith and Augustus Egg, an associate of
Dickens, until Dadd was sent to an asylum for stabbing his father to

death. The tragedy took place while the two were walking in the Surrey woods, and was caused by an 'imbalance in Dadd's mind', experts claimed, brought about by sunstroke he had suffered in Egypt.

A few days after the killing a passenger travelling in a coach in France awoke to find Dadd's hands round his throat. The artist was arrested, tried, found to be insane, and sent to Bedlam (☞p. 14). During a search of his Charlotte Street studio a painting on the wall behind a screen came to light. It contained portraits of Egg and Frith – both with their throats cut.

A passing motorcyclist, Alex de Antiquis, was shot when he tried to prevent a robbery at Jay's store, 73–75 Charlotte Street, in April 1947, and was found lying wounded in the street by two men. The two passers-by just happened to be Superintendent Robert Fabian (the policeman who inspired TV's 'Fabian of the Yard') and Britain's most famous hangman, Albert Pierrepoint, who were on their way to the Fitzroy Tavern. De Antiquis died soon after in Middlesex Hospital, but police eventually caught up with the robbers, two of whom were hanged... by Pierrepoint.

The head and hands of a missing French woman, Emilienne Gerard, whose husband was away fighting in the French Army, were found at 101 Charlotte Street towards the end of 1917 after a dramatic search across London. It all began on the morning of 2 November when a road sweeper found a bundle in Regent Square, Bloomsbury. He opened it, and came upon the trunk and arms of a woman. He contacted the police who began looking for the rest of the body. A search of Regent Square yielded the legs in a sack stencilled with the words *Argentina La Plata Cold Storage*, a laundry mark and a scrap of brown paper enscribed *Blodie Belgiam*.

The police traced the laundry mark to 50 Munster Square, Somers Town, which had been occupied by Mme Gerard – until she had gone missing a few weeks previously during a German Zeppelin raid. There were bloodstains on the premises and an IOU signed by one Louis Voisin, who turned out to be a French butcher working in London. Voisin, who lived at 101 Charlotte Street, was taken in for questioning and asked to write the phrase 'Bloody Belgian' five times. Each time he spelt it *Blodie Belgiam* – just like it was spelt on the paper used to wrap Gerard's body. Voisin had in his possession a key to a coal cellar beneath his address. It was searched and the rest of Mme Gerard was uncovered. He was hanged at Pentonville.

Newman Passage

An obscurely sited dog-leg alley just west of Charlotte Street was where the film director Michael Powell shot the murder of the prostitute at the beginning of his 1959 film *Peeping Tom*. The scene is witnessed through the viewfinder of the murderer's camera, who chillingly films himself committing the crime.

MARYLEBONE, w1

The church of St Mary-by-the-Tyburn or St Mary-a-le-Bourne, built *c.* 1400, originally stood at what is now the northern end of Marylebone High Street and has since been rebuilt nearby. The surrounding land was used as a hunting ground by Henry VIII, and was developed from 1719 by the architect James Gibbs. Its rigidly straight streets of smart, if austere, architecture are mostly home to wealthy companies, which makes it the quietest section of the West End.

Cato Street

A band of anarchists who set up their headquarters at a still-surviving mews cottage on Cato Street, just off Edgware Road, in February 1820 planned to assassinate the entire British Cabinet, including the prime minister, the Duke of Wellington. The anarchists were led by a farmer, Arthur Thistlewood, and counted among their number George Edwards, who supplied them with blunderbusses and cutlasses; shoemaker Richard Tidd; James Ings, a butcher; and William Davidson, son of the attorney general of Kingston, Jamaica, who suffered from what he himself described as 'psychotic tendencies'.

From Cato Street it was only a mile or so to their targeted location, No. 39 (now 44) Grosvenor Square, home of Lord Harrowby, where, they had found out the entire Cabinet would be dining on 22 February. Thistlewood and Co. planned to rush the door, overcome the servants, storm the dining room and attack the party. 'We are going to kill His Majesty's ministers and will have blood and wine for supper,' Thistlewood boasted. 'We will cut off every head in the room and bring away the heads of Lord Castlereagh and Lord Sidmouth in a bag.'

Things didn't go according to plan. George Edwards was an *agent provocateur*, a government stooge. The dinner was a ploy; the participants were ready and waiting for their attackers. However, the would-be assassins never arrived. The police caught up with them at Cato Street, which they raided, finding 20 or so men armed with guns, swords and other weapons standing next to the two sacks in which they intended toZcarry off the heads of the ministers. At the start of the raid one constable, PC George Ruthven, shouted: 'We are officers! Seize their arms!', but Thistlewood picked up his sword and thrust it into the body of another officer, Richard Smythers, who cried out: 'Oh my God, I am done.' As the *Morning Chronicle* recounted the following day: 'Smythers was carried away quite dead.'

In the mêlée four of the conspirators, including Thistlewood and John Brunt, escaped out of a window. They were soon arrested, but Thistlewood broke free, only to be recaptured the following night near Moorgate. After being imprisoned in the Tower, he was hanged outside Newgate Prison on, ironically, 1 May. For being a traitor as well as a murderer Thistlewood was decapitated after being hanged – the last condemned person to be treated this way in Britain. Brunt's demise was equally dramatic. He refused a blindfold, calmly took a pinch of snuff, and announced to the crowd: 'It is better to die free than to live like slaves.'

Cavendish Square

On the west side of Cavendish Square stood Harcourt House, an 18th-century mansion designed by Thomas Archer for Lord Bingley. A hundred years later it was at the centre of one of the strangest legal tussles London has ever witnessed. A Mrs Druce, the daughter-in-law of a local shopkeeper, the late Thomas Druce, petitioned the home secretary for permission to open her father-in-law's coffin on the grounds that Druce and the Duke of Portland, who had also passed away, were one and the same; and that the duke had created the shopkeeper persona as an elaborate hoax. The coffin would be empty, she explained, and she would be entitled to a share of the millions that the childless Duke of Portland had left in his will.

A legal battle of Jarndycean proportions ensued, but Mrs Druce remained unsuccessful in her attempts to prove that her father-in-law's coffin was empty. It remained unopened, and after seven years Mrs

Druce was consigned to a mental hospital, the case unsolved. Meanwhile, the Druce family formed a public company to pursue the matter, and speculators, sensing a killing, took up their cause. At last, in 1907, the coffin was opened. Inside, to no one's surprise, was the body of Druce. The case collapsed.

Duke Street

10 Duke Street, near Selfridge's, now a restaurant, was where French Resistance leader Charles de Gaulle set up his Free French government-in-exile – *Le Bureau Centrale de Renseignements et d'Action* – during the Second World War. Here the French Resistance arranged for agents to go to France to engage in espionage and sabotage against the collaborating Vichy government, as well as the Nazis. When a suspected German agent was found hanged in the basement at No. 10 in 1943 it took much persuasion by the various security services before the police agreed to drop the matter. De Gaulle then moved the office to Algeria.

Harley Street

In 1828 John St John Long, the so-called 'King of the Quacks', opened a clinic for wealthy female clients at No. 84. He treated them by asking them to inhale from a long length of pink tubing filled with a potent gas. Long's star waned after the death of two of his patients, and he was convicted of manslaughter, for which he received a mere £250 fine.

Manchester Street

Joanna Southcott, the early 19th-century millennial prophetess who identified herself with the biblical 'woman clothed with the sun', died at No. 38 in 1814 shortly after announcing that she was pregnant, at the age of 64, despite being a virgin.

Southcott would give birth to 'Shiloh', the biblical man-child of *Revelation* 12, and she was examined by around 20 doctors, who confirmed her pregnancy. Gifts were sent, and a cradle was decorated with a gold crown and the name Shiloh embroidered in Hebrew letters at the head. Southcott acquired a husband prior to the birth, so that the child would not be declared illegitimate, but by November 1814 the signs of pregnancy had disappeared.

She grew increasingly weak and died on 27 December. Supporters placed hot water bottles around her body to keep it warm, in expectation of either a resurrection or the appearance of Shiloh. When four days had passed and neither had happened, Southcott's remains were taken to St John's Wood Cemetery, where she was buried (☛p. 205)

Upper Berkeley Street

Mason's Arms, No. 51
The inn's cellar was a dungeon used in the 18th century to hold some of those who were to be executed at the nearby Tyburn gallows.

Welbeck Street

Lord Gordon, the architect of the 1780 anti-Catholic Gordon Riots, the most violent disturbances London has ever witnessed, was targeted for assassination a couple of years later by the Vatican, which sent two Jesuits to his Welbeck Street address, No. 64, to poison him. The Jesuits brought with them a vial of liquid and a note supposedly written by the local chemist urging the peer to drink the mixture for his health. Suspicious of the strangers, and their unusual request and package, Gordon had the contents examined and found out that they contained poison.

The Victorian novelist Anthony Trollope died in a nursing home at No. 33 in 1882 following a stroke.

Wimpole Street

This is the setting for Alfred Lord Tennyson's 1850 poem 'In Memoriam', in which he stands in the 'long unlovely street' contemplating the demise of his friend, Arthur Hallam, who had lived here.

MAYFAIR

Named after the annual spring festival held in what is now
Shepherd Market until 1735, Mayfair became one of the most
luxurious quarters of the capital, with its greatest concentration
of the rich and powerful, once the fair moved away. At the
outbreak of the Second World War most of its residents left, but
the area has retained its exclusivity by attracting wealthy
companies to move into its elegant buildings.

Berkeley Square

One of Mayfair's three main squares, Berkeley has long fascinated ghost
lovers. The narrow alley alongside Lansdowne House was the setting for

The Curse of Tutankhamun

The capital was gripped throughout the 1920s by the supposed curse of
Tutankhamun, the Egyptian boy-king of antiquity, whose tomb in the
Egyptian sands was uncovered in February 1923 by the British archaeol-
ogist, Howard Carter. The site was looted, and over the next few years
more than 20 of those involved in the exhumation or in handling the
contents of the tomb perished in strange circumstances – indeed only
one lived into old age – prompting the myth of the so-called 'curse of
Tutankhamun'.

Nowhere in the world – particularly the West End – appeared to be
safe for those who had provoked the ire of the Egyptian death gods.
At Kate Meyrick's exclusive 43 Club near Leicester Square the brother
of King Fuad of Egypt told the hostess: 'It is ill work. The dead must
not be disturbed. Only evil can come of it.' A few weeks later Lord
Carnarvon, who had sponsored the expedition, was fatally bitten on
the cheek by a mosquito. At the exact moment of his death there was a
power failure in Cairo.

Seven years after the tomb was opened Howard Carter's personal
secretary, Richard Bethell, was found slumped over in a chair at the
Bath Club on Mayfair's Brook Street. The cause of death was never
scientifically determined. A few months later Bethell's father, Lord

Michael Arlen's 1920s ghost story 'The Loquacious Lady of Lansdowne Passage', while No. 7 is supposedly haunted by two generals who died when they fell through a trap door arguing about how the Duke of Marlborough should have waged the Battle of Blenheim.

Curzon Place

Two well-known rock stars, Mama Cass, the Mamas and Papas singer, and the Who's drummer, Keith Moon, died in the 1970s, four years apart, in Flat 12, 9 Curzon Place, a property then owned by the singer Harry Nilsson. Press reports claimed that the cause of Cass's death in July 1974 was inhalation of vomit after choking on a sandwich, but the pathologist found no traces of food blocking her trachea and concluded that she had died of natural causes, even though she was only 32. Four years later, on 7 September 1978, Moon overdosed on pills

Westbury, leapt from a window of his seventh-storey apartment near Piccadilly. Although Westbury had never even seen the tomb, he possessed a small collection of Egyptian antiquities, and had frequently been heard to mutter 'the curse of the pharaohs'. He left a note which read: 'I really cannot stand any more horrors and hardly see what good I am going to do here, so I am making my exit.'

As the hearse made its way down the street a week later an eight-year-old girl was accidentally killed. Some time afterwards the curse also claimed a radiologist, Sir Archibald Douglas Reid, who died of an unknown illness after signing an agreement with the Cairo authorities to x-ray Tutankhamun's body.

By 1929, eleven of the people connected with the discovery of the tomb had died. The credulous pointed to the legend written in hieroglyphics near the entry of the tomb: 'Death will slay with his wings whoever disturbs the peace of the pharaoh.' Proof, surely, of the curse of Tutankhamun. Medical experts suggested a more prosaic explanation after examining the health records of museum workers: many had been exposed to a fever-inducing fungus, *Aspergillus niger*, which may have survived in the tombs for thousands of years.

W1

prescribed to fight his alcoholism. Thirty-two Heminevrin tablets were found in his stomach, 26 of them undissolved.

Curzon Street

The formidable Victorian prime minister Benjamin Disraeli died in 1881 at No. 19, a house he bought with the proceeds of his novel *Endymion*. On his deathbed Disraeli rejected Queen Victoria's offer of a visit on the grounds that 'She will only ask me to take a message to the Albert [the late Prince Consort].' As Disraeli lay dying, straw was spread on the road outside so that the statesman would not be disturbed by passing carriages. The politician left instructions that he was not to be given a state funeral, and was buried in a church despite being born Jewish.

Grosvenor Square

A group of anarchists plotted to kill the entire British Cabinet, including the prime minister, the Duke of Wellington, while they were dining at No. 39, on the south side of the square, in February 1820, but were arrested at their Cato Street headquarters (☛p. 70) in time.

Millennium Hotel, No. 44
It was here on 1 November 2006 that Russian dissident Alexander Litvinenko is believed to have been poisoned with polonium-210 by agents avenging the honour of the Russian secret service (FSB) which they considered Litvinenko had betrayed. After Litvinenko died in University College Hospital (☛p. 44) on 23 November, police inspected many London sites which had also been similarly contaminated, as had the aeroplanes the Russian agents had travelled on.

Hill Street

Admiral Byng who lived at No. 6 in the 1750s was executed by his own employers, the British Navy, for 'failing to do his utmost' during the Battle of Minorca in 1757. He has endured an infamous afterlife thanks to Voltaire's memorable quote that Byng was shot *pour encourager les autres*.

Mount Street

Martin van Butchell, an eccentric 18th-century dentist, exhibited his late wife as an attraction at No. 56 Mount Street after her death in January 1775. Doctor colleagues injected the body with preservatives and additives, and it was then placed in a glass-topped coffin. The gruesome show continued until van Butchell's new wife objected. The display was then sent to a museum.

Park Lane

Park Lane in the 19th century was *the* address for any self-respecting magnate. Many of these were diamond merchants – the Randlords, they were called – such as Ernest Cassel, Edward VII's closest confidant, whom the king called to his deathbed for a last message. Another was Barney Barnato, a former East End music hall performer, who acquired a property at Park Lane's junction with Stanhope Gate but died when he fell overboard from the ship taking him from South Africa to London for his housewarming party. Even over 100 years later, at the beginning of the 21st century, his granddaughter was adamant that he had been pushed – by his own nephew, Solly, who knew he would inherit Barnato's fortune.

Arthur Conan Doyle set the empty house of the Sherlock Holmes short story of the same name, where the Honourable Ronald Adair was dishonourably and mysteriously killed, at the fictitious 427 Park Lane. When Adair can't be roused after a high-stakes card game, the door is broken down and he is found with his head 'horribly mutilated by an expanding revolver bullet'. But it is Holmes's appearance in London to solve the crime that is of most interest, given that he is missing, presumed dead, after supposedly falling into the Reichenbach Falls in Switzerland in the previous story.

Piccadilly

Itsu Sushi Bar, *No. 167*
One of a number of London locations where traces of radioactive polonium-210 were found following Alexander Litvinenko's poisoning. (☛Millennium Hotel, p. 76; Highgate Cemetery, p. 169).

St George Street

One of the first modern cremations took place in the churchyard of
St George, Hanover Square, in 1769 when one Honoretta Pratt ordered
that her corpse be burnt after her death as the vapours emanating from
the graves of the London churchyards were, she believed, harmful to the
capital's inhabitants.

Savile Row

One of a number of Savile Row properties occupied by high-quality
gentlemen's outfitters is No. 1 where the corpse of the Africa explorer
David Livingstone lay in state after his death in 1874 before being
interred at Westminster Abbey.

Richard Brinsley Sheridan death place (1816), *No. 14*

'I won't die, Bridget. I don't like death,' joked Sheridan, the early 19th-
century playwright, using a line from one of his plays, as he lay dying
in poverty, having been bedridden for a week, at his Savile Row address.
Dying didn't free Sheridan from the clutches of his creditors, however.
A bailiff posing as a relative came for a 'last look', but when the coffin
was opened promptly arrested the late playwright for non-payment
of bills.

Stratton Street

After his cremation at Golders Green in October 1905 the ashes of the
popular Victorian actor Sir Henry Irving were placed in a coffin in a
flower-filled room at 1 Stratton Street, home of his long-time companion Angela Burdett-Coutts, the leading philanthropist of the age, which
was visited by streams of well-wishers. The next day Irving was taken to
Westminster Abbey. Burdett-Coutts herself died at 1 Stratton Street on
30 December 1906. She too was visited by thousands and buried at the
Abbey.

SOHO

Soho is the London area traditionally most associated with sleaze and violence, albeit a kind of glamorous, film world violence dominated by high-class hookers and pin-striped mobsters. It witnessed a number of high-profile murders during the 20th century as generation after generation of gangland bosses tussled to control local vice and protection. In the 1950s the Soho godfather was Billy Hill. When he took over he issued an edict proclaiming 'No guns' and then promptly set up a criminal sideline called 'Murder Incorporated'. For a price, his team would eliminate an opponent, they boasted. In reality Hill simply pocketed the fee without carrying out the murder. If the client complained, they would be dealt with violently, but nothing worse. In later decades there has been no one controlling figure to rival Hill, nevertheless Soho has remained a popular venue for those intent on murder.

Broadwick Street

At the corner with Lexington Street stands the John Snow pub, named after the mid-19th-century Soho surgeon who single-handedly solved the local cholera problem that killed some 10,000 people. Snow claimed the disease was spread through dirty water, but the authorities rubbished his findings, as did the local water companies who maintained it was caused by a 'miasma in the atmosphere'.

Early in September 1854 Snow interviewed the families of 127 local people who had died of cholera and discovered that all the victims had drunk from a well on Broad Street (now Broadwick Street). He took samples of the water, found that it contained infectious organisms and urged the guardians of the local parish to remove the pump handle.

After they did so the outbreak dwindled away, but still the authorities were not convinced. They cited the death of a Hampstead woman and her niece in Islington, neither of whom had been in Soho, to boost their argument. Snow visited the relatives and discovered that the woman had previously lived in Broad Street. She liked the taste of the water there so much that she sent her servant to Soho to raise water from the well and take it back to her house in Hampstead.

Coventry Street

Café de Paris

When 1930s bandleader Ken 'Snakehips' Johnson announced at the beginning of the Second World War: 'I'm determined to make them like swing at the Café or die in the attempt,' he doubtless didn't consider that he might achieve both. On 8 March 1941 two bombs fell on the venue near Leicester Square, killing the bandleader and 33 others. The explosion was so intense that musicians and dancers were killed instantaneously, frozen in their dance poses.

Frith Street

After Thomas de Veil, London's best-known 18th-century magistrate and a hated figure for his implementation of the Gin Act, died, his body was removed from his house in Frith Street as quickly as possible, before the mob found out and stormed the building. De Veil was Justice of the Peace for Middlesex and Westminster, in charge of what became Bow Street Magistrates' Court, and he also ran a network of informers. In William Hogarth's *Times of the Day: Night* (1738) he is depicted making his way along St Martin's Lane, Covent Garden, as a disgruntled local pours a pitcher of urine out of the window on to him.

Hazlitt's/William Hazlitt's address (1830), *No. 6*

Now a charming hotel, one of few in the area, Hazlitt's was where the early 19th-century essayist William Hazlitt died, in the small back room on the third floor, on 18 September 1830 at the age of 52. The cause was either cholera, stomach cancer or drinking too much tea; the story varies. A few weeks before Hazlitt expired, he dictated a note to the magazine editor Francis Jeffrey which read: 'Dear Sir, I am dying. Can you send me £10 and so consummate your many kindnesses to me.' On his deathbed Hazlitt remarked: 'Well I've had a happy life,' which came as something of a surprise to friends such as the essayist Charles Lamb, who had just witnessed the latest in a series of bouts of the writer's depression. The poet Samuel Taylor Coleridge claimed that Hazlitt's manners were '99 in a 100 singularly repulsive'.

Gerrard Street

One of a number of murders perpetrated probably by the Chinese
Triads since Chinatown moved to Soho in the 1960s was that of Yu Yi
He, an illegal immigrant and money-lender, shot dead in June 2003 in
the crowded BRB bar on Gerrard Street. A week before his murder Yu Yi
He had been ejected from Napoleon's Casino on Leicester Square for
attacking customers. After the BRB bar killing the murderer calmly left,
mingling with the crowds outside. Surprisingly, the weapon was a gun.
Usually the Triads use a meat cleaver or a machete.

Goslett Yard

The boxing champion Freddie Mills was found shot dead in his car in
Goslett Yard, a small dog-leg alley west of Charing Cross Road, on 25
July 1965. Mills had financial difficulties, but it is not known whether his
death was murder or suicide, though the latter was the official verdict.
If it was murder, as many have claimed, he may well have been a victim
of a gangland feud involving the Kray twins, for he owned a nightclub
at 143 Charing Cross Road, which backs on to Goslett Yard, and mixed
with them. Experts who accept the suicide version believe that Mills
was responsible for killing a number of prostitutes in London between
June 1959 and February 1965 – the so-called 'Jack the Stripper' murders
(☞ p. 267).

Great Windmill Street

Red Lion, No. 20, east side
Karl Marx and fellow communists ran a debating club above the Red
Lion pub (now closed) in the 1850s unaware that one of them, Wilhelm
Stieber, who posed as a devotee, was in fact an agent of the Prussian
government. Stieber was watching Marx under instructions from the
Prussian Minister of the Interior, Ferdinand von Westphalen, who just
happened to be Marx's brother-in-law. Von Westphalen revealed to the
British government that the communists were plotting in code to kill
Queen Victoria, but Lord Palmerston, then foreign secretary, sat on the
information. The Prussians complained that Britain was not showing
sufficient concern about the imminent regicide, but the home secretary
wrote back explaining that 'under our laws mere discussion ... does not

constitute sufficient grounds for the arrest of the conspirators'. The
communist cell was wound up in September 1850 and moved to
Cologne, where it was then rounded up by the Prussian police. They
never did kill Queen Victoria.

Old Compton Street

Soho's high street and the centre of the capital's gay scene was the setting for a nail bombing in 1999 (☛p. 83), and was where sixty years
previously Italian anarchists plotted to assassinate Benito Mussolini
(also ☛p. 83).

Play To Win amusement arcade, *No. 38*

Alfredo Zomparelli, a small-time villain, was shot in the back as he
played the Wild Life pinball machine in what was then the Golden
Goose arcade, on 4 September 1974. Mystery has since surrounded the
identity of the gunman or gunmen responsible. Zomparelli had been
involved in the murder of David Knight, brother of Barbara Windsor's
husband, Ronnie, an underworld figure, in a fight at a nearby club, and
the police, assuming that Zomparelli had been killed in revenge, took
Ronnie Knight in for questioning.

Knight admitted that he was pleased to hear of the demise of
Zomparelli, but denied any involvement. He was released without
charge, and the file remained closed until 1980 when George Bradshaw,
who had been a regular visitor to Knight's club in Charing Cross Road,
confessed to the killing and implicated Knight. Again Knight was
arrested and again he was cleared. He later admitted in his autobiogra-
phy *Memoirs and Confessions* (1998) that he had indeed been involved in
Zomparelli's murder.

No. 34

Woislav Maximus Petrovitch, an ex-attaché to the Serbian Legation
in London, gassed himself in his Old Compton Street room on
24 November 1934 after taking a cocktail of whisky and drugs. At the
inquest he was described as a dangerous alien, and accused – probably
unfairly – of being involved in the assassination of the Yugoslav king,
Alexander, in Marseilles a month earlier. Experts cast doubts on the
suicide theory and believe a terror group, the Black Hand of Serbia, was
responsible for Petrovitch's death.

King Bomba (1920–71), No. 37

Italian anarchists meeting at this café in the 1930s plotted to assassinate the Italian fascist dictator Benito Mussolini. They met here because King Bomba, situated in the heart of what was then the West End's large Italian colony, was owned by Ernidio Recchioni, an anarchist who in 1899 had escaped from the prison island of Pantelleria, where he had been interned for his involvement in an assassination attempt on the Italian prime minister, Francesco Crispi.

When the Italian fascist party opened an office at 25 Noel Street, Soho, in 1921, Recchioni began using King Bomba as a centre of opposition to Mussolini's dictatorship. In 1931 he travelled to Brussels to meet Angelo Sbardellotto, another Italian anarchist, who offered to go to Rome and personally kill *Il Duce* if Recchioni could provide money and weapons.

Several failed assassination attempts later, Sbardellotto was arrested in Rome, and found in possession of two bombs and a loaded revolver. He made a full confession, listing the dates when he had met Recchioni in Paris. The Italian authorities requested Recchioni's extradition from London, but the café owner stood his ground, and when the *Daily Telegraph* named him as being involved in the failed assassination plot, he sued for damages to his reputation as a 'virtuous man' and was awarded £1,177.

A home office file released at the end of the 20th century, though originally due to remain sealed until 2035, revealed that the government suppressed evidence of the plot against Mussolini, fearing that details would be made public during the libel hearing. It also showed that Herbert Samuel, home secretary in the 1930s, and the Metropolitan Police Commissioner Lord Trenchard decided that it would be in the public interest to obstruct the course of justice rather than allow sensitive information to come to light.

Admiral Duncan, No. 54

Three people were killed and scores of bystanders injured in the Admiral Duncan, one of London's leading gay pubs, on 30 April 1999 when a bomb went off. The explosion was the work of David Copeland, a Nazi sympathiser waging a one-man war against minority groups. He hid a holdall containing a bomb packed with 500 nails in the bar before nervously asking the barman directions to the nearest bank before leaving the building. Copeland had detonated similar bombs in Brixton and Brick Lane over the previous few weeks, though by chance they had caused much less damage. It later transpired that the police, suspecting that Old Compton Street could be a target, had alerted some organisations but that the warning letter they sent the gay rights group Stonewall had a second-class stamp and failed to arrive until 30 April, the day of the bombing.

Romilly Street

The small street near Old Compton Street is named after the early 19th-century lawyer Samuel Romilly who campaigned successfully to remove the death penalty as punishment for a host of crimes, including shoplifting. In February 1810 Romilly told the House of Commons: 'There is no country on the face of the earth in which there [have] been so many different offences according to law to be punished with death as in England.' Shoplifting was then one of 220 offences that could result in execution.

St Anne's Court

A narrow alleyway between Dean and Wardour streets, it was known as 'the street of the dead' because it was particularly hit during the 1850s cholera epidemic – enduring twice the national death rate.

Wardour Street

West End Bridge and Billiards Club (mid-20th century), No. 37

Wartime fighting between Soho's Jewish and Italian gangsters culminated in the fatal stabbing in 1941 of Harry 'Little Hubby' Distleman, doorman of the West End Bridge and Billiards Club. The knifeman was the Italian Antonio 'Babe' Mancini, and as the blade went in five times Distleman cried out: 'Babe's stabbed me in the heart. I'm dying.' In October 1941 Mancini became the first 'drop' for the man destined to be Britain's most famous 20th-century hangman, Albert Pierrepoint. Indeed he was the only Soho gangster ever hanged for murder.

St Anne

The former church of St Anne contains the grave of Theodore von Neuhoff (d. 1756) who styled himself the 'King of Corsica' and staged a coup to take the island, but died in poverty, his treasure buried somewhere in West Ham. Von Neuhoff would have had a pauper's grave but for a local tradesman, who was amused at the idea of paying for a king's funeral expenses.

In the 1840s the caretaker of the graveyard made a handy profit for himself out of selling lead, handles, nails and screws from the coffins of those buried here. Also buried here are the essayist William Hazlitt (d. 1830), remembered by the Soho hotel of the same name where he died (☞ p. 80), and the author Dorothy L. Sayers (d. 1957) who was a St Anne's churchwarden.

CHAPTER 4

Westminster

The nation's great buildings of state – the Houses of Parliament, Buckingham Palace, Westminster Abbey, 10 Downing Street, the Treasury, the Home Office and the Foreign Office – can all be found in Westminster, centre of British politics and royalty since the 11th century. The Abbey is London's foremost place of burial for royals, politicians and important cultural and civic figures, as well as the home of the much visited Poets' Corner with its myriad memorials to the country's greatest writers.

Birdcage Walk

Guards Chapel, Wellington Barracks

A German V1 rocket fell on the chapel on 8 June 1944 while the building was packed with Guards, their families and friends. A few minutes after 11 a.m. the congregation heard a distant buzzing which gradually grew louder and turned into a roar that drowned out the hymn singing. The engine then cut out and the V1 hit the roof of the chapel, exploding on impact. The roof collapsed on the congregation, killing 121 people and seriously injuring another 141. The only one unhurt was the Bishop of Maidstone, who was conducting the service. News of the tragedy was suppressed on propaganda grounds until after the end of the War.

Broad Sanctuary

Westminster Abbey

One of Britain's most important religious buildings, 'the place of sepulchre for the philosophers, heroes and kings of England', according to the 18th-century writer Oliver Goldsmith, contains the burial site or memorial of nearly all monarchs who have ruled England or the United Kingdom since the 13th century. Poets' Corner, situated within the Abbey's walls, is similarly filled with the tombs or dedications to the country's greatest writers.

ROYALTY AT WESTMINSTER ABBEY

II **Edward the Confessor (d. 1066)** was canonised in 1163 during the 12th-century reign of Henry II after his tomb was opened and the body found to be immaculately preserved. When Westminster Abbey was rebuilt early the next century the king's body was placed in a shrine, but the coffin was removed from it during the dissolution of the monasteries in the 16th century, and buried nearby. By 1685 Edward's body had started to decay. It was last examined in 1916.

‖ **Henry III (d. 1272)** – The first of the Plantagenets to be buried within the Abbey, Henry was also one of the first English kings to die in London, passing away at the Palace of Westminster in November 1272. Henry was briefly laid to rest in the tomb of Edward the Confessor while his own sarcophagus was built. He was given a proper burial in May 1290 and his heart was given to the Abbey of Fontevraud. The heart later passed through several owners until it was acquired by a museum in Orleans. In 1864 Lord Palmerston, the prime minister, refused to have it interred at Westminster.

‖ **Edward I (d. 1307)** – Following Edward's death in Carlisle while on his way to fight Robert the Bruce, the late king was taken to Waltham Abbey where he lay for 16 weeks prior to burial. Edward wanted his corpse to be boiled, so that his bones could be carried on future military expeditions to Scotland and his heart on Crusades, but his wishes were ignored. The body was embalmed and placed in a black Purbeck marble tomb in the Westminster Abbey chapel of Edward the Confessor, marked by a stone slab which bears the simple epitaph: 'Here lies Edward, the Hammer of the Scots'.

‖ **Edward III (d. 1377)** died undramatically at Sheen (Richmond) Palace on 21 June 1377, whereas his father, Edward II, had an eventful death at Berkeley Castle, Gloucestershire, when a red-hot poker was inserted into his entrails with a horn. Edward III was buried in Westminster Abbey, south of the Confessor's shrine. His corpse has been undisturbed since, unlike those of most of his fellow monarchs.

‖ **Richard II (d. 1400)** – Although Richard arranged for a tomb in Westminster Abbey, he was originally buried in King's Langley, Hertfordshire, after being starved to death in a dungeon at Pontefract Castle. Richard had been imprisoned there for being a tyrant, musing on, as Shakespeare claimed, 'graves, worms and epitaphs'. It was not until 1413 that the body was exhumed and transferred to Westminster. In 1871 the Abbey authorities opened the tomb and found chaotic disarray inside the coffin: the skulls of Richard and his wife, Anne of Bohemia, were resting by their feet. The copper crowns they had once worn were missing, but strangely a set of iron shears had been put in the coffin. The royal couple's bones were reordered afterwards.

‖ **Henry IV (d. 1413)** – Although the Lancastrian king is not buried in the Abbey, he died here, from a seizure while praying at St Edward's shrine, after which he was carried to the abbot's house. He had been suffering from either leprosy or syphilis.

‖ **Henry V (d. 1422)** – An intricately wrought set of iron gates leads to the Abbey's monument to the Agincourt king who died of dysentery in 1422, eight years after the battle. Because Henry died in France, an elaborate means of preserving the body was set in motion in preparation for the funeral in England. With the help of butchers, the corpse was disembowelled, cut into pieces and boiled in vinegar mixed with spices. The flesh was sealed up with the bones in a lead case. Although Paris and Rouen made claims to be the eventual burial site, Henry's wish, to go to Westminster, was honoured, two months after he died. There have since been a number of thefts of items connected with the tomb.

‖ **Katherine de Valois (d. 1438)** – When Henry VII demolished the Lady Chapel in 1502 the body of Henry V's wife was taken out of its decaying wooden coffin so that the remains could be re-interred in a new chapel. However Henry himself died soon after and little was done to protect Katherine, as the antiquary John Weever noted in 1631: 'Katherine, Queen of England, lieth here in a chest or coffin with a loose cover, to be seen or handled of any who will much desire it.'

By 1669, Katherine's coffin had still not been repaired, as Samuel Pepys recorded in his diary in an amusing passage for 23 February, after he had visited the Abbey with his wife and daughters:

> I now took them to Westminster Abbey, and there did show them all the tombs very finely, it being Shrove Tuesday; and here we did see, by particular favour, the body of Queen Katherine of Valois; and I had the upper part of her body in my hands, and I did kiss her mouth, reflecting upon it that I did kiss a Queen, and that this was my birth-day, thirty-six years old, that I did first kiss a Queen.'

In later years scholars from Westminster School took great delight in mutilating bits of the body, which was not formally protected until 1877. An examination carried out on them showed that while the torso and head had become skeletal, the left arm was still in perfect condition. The late queen was then put in a new coffin beneath the altar slab in the Henry V chantry chapel.

‖ **Edward V (1483)** – One of the two 'Princes in the Tower' who, with his brother, Richard, Duke of York, was murdered in 1483 either by their uncle, Richard III, or by Henry VII. A chest containing the bones of two children was found under a staircase in the Tower in July 1674 and transferred, ironically, to the Henry VII Chapel in the Abbey. Four years later they were put in an urn. In 1933 the urn was opened and animal bones were found alongside the human bones. These were then wrapped separately in linen and placed back in the urn.

‖ **Henry VII (1509)** – The first Tudor king is buried in the chapel he built here, now known as Lady Chapel, his tomb in the centre, enclosed by railings. Popular legend at the time claimed Henry died of a broken heart after the deaths of his son and heir, Arthur, and his wife, Elizabeth of York.

‖ **Edward VI (d. 1553)** – Aged only 15, Edward VI died at Greenwich Palace, possibly of arsenic poisoning or more likely syphilis. His dying words were 'Oh my Lord God, defend this realm from papistry and maintain Thy true religion.' The king's death was kept secret for several days so that preparations could be made for Lady Jane Grey's accession. Unfortunately for Jane the public were keener on the rightful heir, Mary Tudor, and Lady Jane Grey was executed. Edward was buried in the Henry VII Lady Chapel but rumours spread for decades that he had survived, and in the meantime several impostors were proposed as king, a theme later taken up by Mark Twain in the novel *The Prince and the Pauper*.

‖ **Mary Tudor (d. 1558)** – After her death at St James's Palace, Mary was taken to Westminster where she was placed in the Henry VII Chapel. The vault was opened after the death of Elizabeth I forty-five years later. In 1670 during the funeral of General Monck the coffin was opened and her heart was handled by a schoolboy, William Taswell.

‖ **Elizabeth I (d. 1603)** was buried in the Abbey and succeeded by James – the Scottish descendant of her aunt, Margaret Tudor – against the wishes expressed by her father, Henry VIII, in his will. Had Henry had his way the next monarch after him would have been Lady Anne Stanley.

James I later moved Elizabeth's coffin to another part of the Abbey. More controversially he brought the body of his mother, Mary Queen of Scots, to the Abbey, which meant that the two rival queens, who never met in life, lay only feet away from each other in death.

‖ **James I (d. 1625)** was buried in the Henry VII Chapel. Three years later the body of the assassinated Duke of Buckingham was buried next to him. Some historians believe the two were lovers.

ıı **Charles II (d. 1685)** was buried in a vault in the Henry VII Chapel immediately after his execution, or as John Evelyn wrote in his diary: 'obscurely buried in a vault without any manner of pomp [as the king had died in a] different religion to his people'. This referred to the idea that Charles may have belatedly converted to Catholicism, although it is more likely that Evelyn was simply confused owing to the speed with which Charles was interred. During the installation of heating pipes in 1867 the coffin was found. The corpse was badly decayed. The same vault houses (Queen) Mary Stuart, his niece (d. 1694); her husband, William III (d. 1702); and their successor, Anne (d. 1714).

ıı **George II (d. 1760)** was afforded the new vault created for his wife, Caroline, in the Henry VII Chapel. He was the last British king to be embalmed in the traditional way and the last to be buried in the Abbey.

POETS' CORNER

This famous section of the Abbey owes its existence to Geoffrey Chaucer, author of *The Canterbury Tales* (c. 1400), who moved into a house where the Henry VII Chapel now stands in 1399. When he died the following year he was buried in the Abbey in what is now Poets' Corner. Admissions are granted by the dean, and incumbents of the post rejected Lord Byron (d. 1824) for amorality and George Eliot (d. 1880) as an agnostic.

ıı At the funeral of the poet **Edmund Spenser**, who died from starvation in 1598 at a house near the Abbey, a number of his fellow poets threw their own works into his grave. No one now knows exactly where in Poets' Corner his grave is.

ıı **William Shakespeare** (d. 1616) is commemorated with a memorial designed by William Kent which was erected in 1740 and described by the 20th-century hack writer Hugh Walpole as 'preposterous', probably because it misquotes lines from *The Tempest*.

ıı **Thomas Parr** was a Shropshire farmer who lived during the reigns of ten monarchs and died, allegedly aged 152, in November 1653. It wasn't until he was 80 that Parr got married for the first time. He was married again at the age of 122.

ıı **Ben Jonson** (d. 1637) was buried upright, having told the dean 'Six foot long by two foot wide is too much for me. Two feet by two is all I want.'

‖ **John Milton** (d. 1674) is buried in St Giles Cripplegate (☛p. 16) but was awarded a memorial here 63 years later when his republican views were no longer deemed so controversial.

‖ The Restoration playwright **William Congreve** died in Bath in 1729 after his carriage overturned.

‖ **John Gay** (d. 1732), author of *The Beggar's Opera* 1728, is buried under his own epitaph: 'Life is a jest, and all things show it/I thought so once and now I know it.'

‖ There is a memorial to the major early 19th-century poet **Percy Shelley**, who died in the Gulf of La Spezia in 1822 and was cremated on the beach nearby. Shelley's ashes were taken to the British consulate building in Rome, stored in the wine cellar for a few months, and then buried in the city.

‖ The Dean of the Abbey refused to take **Lord Byron** (d. 1824) because of what he called the poet's 'open profligacy … an obstacle to his commemoration'. Byron was buried in the family vault at Hucknall parish church in Nottinghamshire.

‖ There is a seated statue of **William Wordsworth** (d. 1850) who is buried in the Lake District.

‖ The bust of **William Makepeace Thackeray** (d. 1863) by Marachetti so annoyed the novelist's daughter that she had it removed. Another sculptor then altered the moustache until she felt it was the right length.

‖ **Henry James** (d. 1916), one of the few non-poets honoured in Poets' Corner, was cremated at Golders Green.

‖ **Thomas Hardy** (d. 1928) had satirised the dean who refused to bury Byron in his poem 'A Refusal' four years earlier and specifically requested not to be buried in the Abbey but in Dorset, near his family. However Hardy's agent ignored his client's wishes and organised the Abbey funeral, with the small compromise that the heart be removed and taken to Dorset (in a biscuit tin) and buried in the churchyard of St Michael, Stinsford.

‖ **D. H. Lawrence** (d. 1930) is a surprising inclusion given the Abbey's objections to Byron and George Eliot, which may explain why his memorial didn't appear until 1985.

‖ There was no memorial for the Welsh poet **Dylan Thomas** (d. 1953) until the 1970s when US president Jimmy Carter complained about the lack of one.

‖ After the ashes of the actor **Laurence Olivier** (d. 1989) were buried here the Abbey decided Poets' Corner was full.

POLITICIANS

‖ Two years after being buried in the Abbey the corpse of **Oliver Cromwell** (1658) was sent for 'punishment' at Tyburn (☛ p. 67), preceded by humiliation at the Red Lion, Holborn (☛ p. 47), along with those of fellow regicides **Henry Ireton** and **John Bradshawe**. As Samuel Pepys wrote in his diary for 4 December 1660:

> This day the Parliament voted that the bodies of Oliver, Ireton, Bradshawe, &c., should be taken up out of their graves in the Abbey, and drawn to [Tyburn] gallows, and there hanged and buried under it: which (methinks) do trouble me that a man of so great courage as he was, should have that dishonour, though otherwise he might deserve it enough.

‖ In the North Transept is a monument to **William Pitt the Elder**, Earl of Chatham (d. 1778), around which are memorials to a number of eminent politicians, including his son, **William Pitt the Younger** (d. 1806). Both Pitts served terms as prime minister.

‖ **Lord Castlereagh** (d. 1822) – Following a financial scandal the deeply unpopular Castlereagh, early 19th-century Tory foreign secretary, committed suicide. People booed in the street as his corpse was borne on a gun carriage to Westminster Abbey, among them the Tory politician George Canning. As a suicide, Castlereagh should not have been buried here.

‖ **Viscount Palmerston** (d. 1865) – American author Charles Adams was amazed by the lack of grief on the faces of the crowd as Palmerston's coffin passed. Although the Liberal statesman wanted a quiet burial at his ancestors' church, Romney Abbey, the Cabinet insisted on the full Westminster Abbey treatment, and his widow agreed as long as she could be buried alongside him when her time came.

‖ **Andrew Bonar Law** (d. 1923) – The coffin of the inconsequential Canada-born Conservative prime minister was carried by Herbert Asquith, himself a former Liberal premier, who remarked: 'It is fitting that we should have buried the unknown prime minister by the side of the Unknown Soldier.'

‖ **Beatrice Webb** (d. 1943) – The ashes of the socialist and pioneer of Fabianism were at first placed on a mantelpiece in the Webb household. When visitors called, her husband, Sidney, would point and explain: 'That's Beatrice, you know.' The ashes were later buried in their garden in Suffolk. After Sidney died the ashes of both Webbs were interred in the Abbey.

OTHER DIGNITARIES

‖ **Henry Purcell** (d. 1695) – The composer is buried in the north choir aisle with an epitaph, probably written by the poet John Dryden, which reads:

> *Here Lyes*
> *HENRY PURCELL esq*
> *Who left this life*
> *And is gone to that blessed Place*
> *Where only his Harmony*
> *Can be exceeded.*

‖ Other greats buried here include the pioneering scientist **Isaac Newton** (d. 1727), the composer **George Frederic Handel** (d. 1759), the anti-slavery campaigner **William Wilberforce** (d. 1833), the explorer **David Livingstone** (d. 1873), the iconoclastic biologist **Charles Darwin** (d. 1882), and **Ernest (Lord) Rutherford** (d. 1937) who first split the atom. The ashes of Britain's greatest composer, **Ralph Vaughan Williams** (d. 1958), are buried in the north choir aisle. There is only a memorial to Vaughan Williams's favourite conductor, **Adrian Boult** (d. 1983), as he left his body to medical science.

THE UNKNOWN WARRIOR

‖ During the First World War a British chaplain, the Revd David Railton, devised the idea of burying an unidentified soldier in the Abbey to commemorate those with no other memorial. The idea came to him after seeing a grave in Armentières marked only with a wooden cross which bore the inscription: 'An unknown British Soldier (of the Black Watch)'.

After the war Railton wrote to the Dean of Westminster, who approved the idea. The bodies of four unknown British servicemen were exhumed and covered with a Union Flag, and one was chosen at random and placed in a plain sealed coffin as the Unknown Warrior. His epitaph in Westminster Abbey reads:

> *Beneath this stone rests the body*
> *Of a British Warrior*
> *Unknown by name or rank*

Broadway

A blind match-seller standing outside St James's Park station in the late 1930s was in reality a German intelligence officer who spent his time photographing those entering and leaving MI6's 'secret' headquarters opposite, at 55 Broadway. The ruse was discovered only when several British officers were arrested in Germany during the Second World War and accused of being spies before being executed.

Carlton Gardens

Lord Northcliffe's death place, No. 2

Lord Northcliffe, the powerful early 20th-century press magnate, one-time owner of the *Daily Mirror*, *Daily Mail* and *The Times*, died of general paralysis of the insane in 1922 in a hut on the roof of 2 Carlton Gardens, incarcerated there for his own safety.

For the last few years of his life Northcliffe had been suffering from a mixture of stomach pains and acute paranoia, sleeping alongside a loaded revolver which he once cocked at his own dressing gown believing it to contain a body. He told aides that his stomach problems stemmed from having had his ice cream poisoned during the First World War by a German gang as he visited the Dutch border, a claim which was not as far fetched as it seems, for Northcliffe was the Allies' director of propaganda during the war, and may have been recognised by enemies during his trip to Holland and poisoned.

Carlton House Terrace

An exquisite cream-coloured stucco Georgian terrace, it stands on the site of Carlton House, a Georgian mansion where Frederick, Prince of Wales, died in 1751, aged 44, following a bout of pleurisy. While trying to recover Frederick took part in a game of cards, but went into a fit of coughing and cried out: 'Je sens la mort,' his last words. The *Gentleman's Magazine* put it slightly differently. 'He complained of a sudden pain and an offensive smell and immediately threw himself backwards and expired.'

The post-mortem revealed that Frederick had died 'by the breaking of an imposthume between the pericardium and the diaphragm'. Friends explained that the cause may have been a tennis ball which had

hit him in the stomach and led to an abdominal ulcer and pleurisy.
A ballad was published in the popular press which ran:

> *Here lies Fred*
> *Who was alive and is dead*
> *…Had it been his sister*
> *No one would have missed her*
> *Had it been the whole generation*
> *Still better for the nation*
> *But since it was only Fred*
> *Who was alive and is dead*
> *There's no more to be said.*

Ashraf Marwan, an Egyptian billionaire who was the son-in-law of the
1960s Egyptian president, Gamal Nasser, and a spy for the Israeli secret
service agency Mossad, was found dead outside his Carlton House
Terrace flat on 27 June 2007 after supposedly falling four floors. Marwan
had become a 'walk-in' spy in 1969 when he entered the Israeli embassy
in London and offered his services. He was ejected but told a security
guard: 'Send my name to Tel Aviv. They'll know who I am. I'll be back in
a week's time.'

Extensive checks convinced Mossad that Marwan was not acting as a
double agent. He was exposed as working for the Israelis in a book published in 2004, after which he told friends he feared he would be
assassinated, either by the Arabs for betraying them or by the Israelis for
being found out. Following Marwan's death the only copy of his memoirs – presumably incriminating– disappeared from his apartment.

Caxton Street

Caxton Hall

Udham Singh, an Indian nationalist, shot and killed Sir Michael
O'Dwyer, former lieutenant governor in the Punjab region of India, at
a public meeting at Caxton Hall on 13 March 1940. Singh, who had managed to be taken as O'Dwyer's chauffeur, held him responsible for the
1919 massacre at Amritsar.

Cleveland Row

St James's Palace

London's major royal residence prior to Buckingham Palace – foreign ambassadors are still accredited to the Court of St James. The palace was built by Henry VIII in 1532–6 on the site of a leper hospital.

Following the death of Henry, Prince of Wales, at the palace in 1612 (see below), a young man of about the same age appeared here a few days before the funeral, stark naked, claiming to be the late prince's ghost visiting from heaven with a message for King James. He was given several lashes and imprisoned overnight, still naked.

Charles I stayed in the palace the night before his execution in January 1649 so that he would not be able to hear the hammering of the carpenters building the scaffold for him on Whitehall. Also staying here the night before the momentous event was the executioner, Richard Brandon. The king awoke at six the following morning and called to his servant: 'I will get up. I have a great work to do this day. This is my second marriage day; I would be as trim today as may be for before tonight I hope to be espoused to my beloved Jesus.'

Charles dressed in extra shirts so that the crowd would not see him shivering from the cold and think it cowardice, and was taken across the park to the scaffold outside Banqueting House by a regiment of soldiers including the Yeomen of the Guard, their flags flying and drums beating. After the execution Charles's head was returned to the body, which was put in a wooden coffin, placed in a lead case and taken to St James's Palace, where it was displayed only to the inner royal circle. It was then taken to Windsor, as Parliament had ruled, for fear that a London burial site might be turned into a place of pilgrimage.

George III was lucky not to die when a servant, Margaret Nicholson, tried to kill him at St James's Palace on 2 August 1786. As the king alighted from his coach to attend a function, Nicholson approached him, holding out a piece of paper the king assumed was a petition, and suddenly produced a knife. She tried to stab him and managed to tear his waistcoat, but he was unhurt. Courtiers grabbed the woman, but the king was magnanimous. 'The poor creature is mad,' he said. 'Do not hurt her. She has not hurt me.'

The Duke of Cumberland was similarly fortunate not to be killed on 31 May 1810 when a would-be assassin charged at him with a sabre as he slept at the palace. When the guards arrived on the scene they began a search of the building and found a valet, John Sellis, dead in his room, his throat cut. Whether Sellis killed himself after trying to assassinate the Duke or the Duke killed him after being roused is not known.

In 1997 the coffin of Diana, Princess of Wales, lay at the Chapel Royal before her funeral at Westminster Abbey.

St James's Palace is now headquarters for a number of institutions including the Royal Collection Department, the Marshal of the Diplomatic Corps, the Central Chancery of the Orders of Knighthood and the Chapel Royal.

Constitution Hill

Edward Oxford, an 18-year-old potboy, fired a pistol at Queen Victoria on 10 June 1840 but missed and was overpowered. Oxford avoided capital punishment for high treason on the grounds of insanity, and spent 27 years in an asylum. In 1842 cabinet-maker John Francis also shot at the monarch on Constitution Hill. Not only did he miss, but he happened to be standing next to a plainclothes policeman, who arrested him. It was another nine years before Victoria again became a target for assassination, again on Constitution Hill. This time the gunman was William Hamilton, an Irishman, whose aim was faulty. He was sentenced to seven years' transportation.

Downing Street

No. 10

Only one prime minister, Henry Campbell-Bannerman, has died at No. 10, official home of British prime ministers since the mid-18th century. The Liberal Campbell-Bannerman took over as premier in 1905, when he was 69. His ailing wife was not impressed with the property, which she described as a 'house of doom' when they moved in. After her death in Marienbad, Campbell-Bannerman grieved intensely, and a month later he suffered the first of several heart attacks at No. 10, where he died in April 1908.

Following William Gladstone's resignation in 1894 No. 10 was occupied not by the new prime minister, Lord Salisbury, but by Stafford Northcote, First Lord of the Treasury. A year later Northcote, by now Lord Iddesleigh, and no longer resident, visited No. 10. He collapsed at the top of the stairs and died in the White Drawing Room.

Death the Stuart Way

Prince Henry, James I's sickly eldest son, died of typhoid at St James's Palace on 12 November 1612, aged only 18. The prince's woes had begun 12 days earlier after an epic tennis match with Frederick, the Elector Palatine, when he went to chapel at St James's Palace and heard a depressing sermon on the book of Job that included the infamous line: 'Man that is born of woman is of few days and full of trouble...'

Henry took to his bed after dinner and never left it through nearly a fortnight of anguish, despite being treated with the finest medicines, including 'sharpe tarte cordials and cooling juleps ... a cocke, cloven by the backe [applied] to the soles of his feet.'

As a last resort the royal family sent for Walter Ralegh, who at the time was imprisoned in the Tower. Only his secret remedy (herbs and spices, tinctures of Bezoar stone, hartshorn, musk, pearls dissolved in oil of vitriol) could now work. When it didn't there were accusations that Ralegh had poisoned the sickly prince.

Near the end the prince's parents – King James and Queen Anne – left him, not out of malice but because they had never been that close to their son, who was virtually a stranger to them, and they had no wish to contract whatever disease he was suffering from. Only the Princess Elizabeth was close to Henry. She disguised herself and attempted to bribe the footmen to gain access to her brother. Even that was not enough, and each time she tried to visit him she was turned away. She was even more distraught when she found out that her brother's dying words were: 'Where is my deare sister?'

Great Smith Street

Church House, *east side, north junction with Little Smith Street*
The headquarters of the Church of England was where the box left by the millennial prophetess Joanna Southcott before she died in November 1814 ended up. Southcott insisted it should be unlocked only after her death, in the presence of 24 bishops. It was not until 1927 that it was opened – and even then in the presence of just one bishop – but it was found to contain nothing of spiritual value, just coins, a pistol, a nightcap, a lottery ticket and a cheap novel.

Haymarket

Her Majesty's Theatre

The much-loved comedian Tommy Cooper died in the ambulance taking him to hospital after collapsing on stage at the theatre on 15 April 1984 during a live television broadcast. He was wearing a long cloak from which he was supposed to produce large objects. A ladder was to come through his legs followed by a milk churn and a long pole. When the comic fell backwards, the show's host, Jimmy Tarbuck, thought Cooper was about to engage in a levitation trick from under his cloak. Understandably the audience also assumed the comedian's fall was part of his routine. Ten minutes later Cooper was dead.

Old Palace Yard

Guy Fawkes and some of his fellow Gunpowder Plot conspirators – Thomas Wintour, Robert Keyes and Ambrose Rookwood – were hanged, drawn and quartered in Old Palace Yard outside the Palace of Westminster in 1606 following their failed attempt to blow up Parliament.

After their arrest the Gunpowder Plotters were interrogated in the Tower, tortured on the rack, and drawn on a hurdle to Westminster – to the 'very place which they had planned to demolish in order to hammer home the message of their wickedness', as the authorities put it.

On the ladder to the gallows Robert Keyes, 'not staying the hangman's turn, turned himself off with such a leap that, with a swing he brake the halter. But after his fall, was quickly drawn to the block, and there was quickly divided into four parts'. As he was being dragged to the execution spot, Ambrose Rookwood passed his house in the Strand and asked if he could have one last look at his wife, Elizabeth, to whom he cried: 'Pray for me, pray for me.' She replied: 'I will, and be of good courage. Offer thyself wholly to God. I, for my part, do as freely restore thee to God as He gave thee unto me.' At the scaffold Rookwood confessed and asked God to bless the king and his family, that they might 'live long to reign in peace and happiness over this Kingdom'. He also beseeched God to make the king a Catholic, a plea which went unanswered. The speech was well received and earned him a hanging almost to the point of death, rather than a slower and more painful punishment.

Fawkes, the main conspirator, had his punishment at the end, or as a contemporary wrote:

> Last of all came the great devil of all, Guy Fawkes, who should have put fire to the powder. His body being weak with the torture and sickness he was scarce able to go up the ladder, yet with much ado, by the help of the hangman, went high enough to break his neck by the fall. He made no speech, but with his crosses and idle ceremonies made his end upon the gallows and the block, to the great joy of all the beholders that the land was ended of so wicked a villainy.

Before his execution in Old Palace Yard on 29 October 1618, carried out as a result of barely believable accusations of treason by the Spanish ambassador, Sir Walter Ralegh ate a hearty breakfast and smoked his last pipe. When asked if he liked the wine served, he replied: 'It was a good drink, if one could tarry over it.' As Ralegh was being escorted to the execution site, he noticed in the crowd a friend, Sir Hugh Ceeston, who was struggling to find a good spot. 'I know not whether you will get there,' he shouted to Ceeston, 'but I am sure to have a place.'

In his final speech Ralegh announced: 'So I take my leave of you all, making my peace with God.' He then took off his gown and doublet and asked the axeman to show him the axe. 'This is sharp medicine...that will cure all my diseases. Let us dispatch. At this hour my ague comes upon me. I would not have my enemies think I quaked from fear.' Ralegh placed his head on the block, forsook the usual blindfold and gave the signal to strike. When the axeman delayed, he cried: 'Strike man, strike!' The axe fell and fell again. His wife took his head home in a leather bag.

Parliament Square

St Margaret Westminster

William Caxton (d. 1491), the pioneering printer who lived locally, is buried in an unknown spot in the church famous for its society weddings, including those of Samuel Pepys and Winston Churchill.

A Protestant fundamentalist by the name of William Flower attacked the priest as he was administering the sacrament on Easter Day 1555, and was imprisoned in the nearby Gatehouse where one of his hands was cut off. He was then burnt alive in the churchyard, crying out three times: 'O Thou Son of God, receive my soul!' The clergy celebrated by holding a feast at which they consumed a sirloin of beef, half a veal, four green geese, three capons, a dozen pigeons and a dozen rabbits.

St James's Square

St James's has been home of the aristocracy and the very wealthy since the earliest medieval times on account of its proximity to the various Westminster palaces. Around St James's Square is some of the most expensive real estate in the world.

Libyan Peoples' Bureau (1980s), *No. 5*
WPC Yvonne Fletcher was killed by an unknown gunman shooting from the window of the Libyan Peoples' Bureau as she policed a demonstration outside on 17 April 1984. Those inside the building remained protected by diplomatic immunity and no one was ever charged with the murder. The spot where Fletcher fell is marked by a memorial and fresh flowers are delivered daily.

No. 18
After Westminster Abbey agreed in 1822 to bury Lord Castlereagh, the unpopular foreign secretary, crowds gathered outside his London home, 18 St James's Square, intent on forcefully reminding the authorities that the Abbey was not allowed to inter suicides.

Castlereagh had infuriated the public by being part of a government intent on implementing the most repressive legislation, even going as far as to suspend *habeas corpus*. By 1822, the year he died, Castlereagh was considered to be insane. He told colleagues: 'I'm mad. I know I'm mad,' and asked his doctor for the precise location of his jugular vein. He then deliberately cut an artery with a small knife and bled to death at his Kent country seat. When his coffin was borne on a gun carriage to Westminster Abbey it was booed in the street.

Lord Byron captured the mood in his epic *Don Juan* (1823):

Of the manner of his [Castlereagh's] death little need be said, except that if a poor radical ... had cut his throat, he would have been buried in a cross-road, with the usual appurtenances of the stake and mallet. But the minister was an elegant lunatic – a sentimental suicide – he merely cut the 'carotid artery,' (blessings on their learning!) and lo! the pageant, and the Abbey! and 'the syllables of dolour yelled forth' by the newspapers – and the harangue of the Coroner in the eulogy over the bleeding body of the deceased – (an Anthony worthy of such a Caesar) – and the nauseous and

atrocious cant of a degraded crew of conspirators against all that is sincere and honourable. In his death he was necessarily one of two things by the law.

Ten years later Shelley's poem 'The Mask of Anarchy' was posthumously published, vilifying Castlereagh further. The poem was a diatribe against the 1819 Manchester Peterloo Massacre in which 11 people died as a direct result, many believed, of Castlereagh's policies. In it Shelley personified Castlereagh as 'Murder'. It begins:

I met Murder on the way
He had a mask like Castlereagh
Very smooth he looked, yet grim
Seven bloodhounds followed him...'

St Margaret Street

Houses of Parliament

The seat of British government has not been plagued by quite as many murders as the parliaments of more volatile countries. However, on 11 May 1812 the prime minister, Spencer Perceval, was shot dead in the lobby of the House of Commons by John Bellingham, a businessman with a grievance against the government. Perceval died very quickly but still had time to state, correctly, 'I am murdered.'

After the murder Bellingham quickly gave himself up to Palace of Westminster officials and was hanged a week later. Perceval's body lay in 10 Downing Street for five days before burial at St Luke's Church, Charlton.

In January 1661 the head of Oliver Cromwell, dug up from his Westminster Abbey tomb, was put on a spike outside Westminster Hall, part of the Houses of Parliament complex. There it remained until 1703 when it was blown down in a storm. A guard picked it up, took it home and hid it in his chimney, revealing the news to his wife only on his deathbed. The head then passed through several owners. It was exhibited in an Old Bond Street shop in 1799, and eventually ended up at Sidney Sussex College, Cambridge, Cromwell's alma mater. Two scientists in the 1950s ascertained that it had been embalmed according to 17th-century practice, the brain having been taken out by the sawing off of the skull-cap.

The three British kings who died in office during the 20th century lay in state in Westminster Hall. A quarter of a million people came to pay their respects to Edward VII in May 1910. After George V died at Sandringham 26 years later gamekeepers and gardeners at the estate kept guard over the body which was then taken by train to King's Cross. As the procession made its way through London the new king, Edward VIII, spotted a bright object 'dancing along the pavement' – it was the Maltese Cross which had fallen from the crown. In Westminster Hall nearly one million people filed past the coffin.

After George VI died, also at Sandringham, on 6 February 1952, the coffin was brought to Westminster Hall, where it was visited over the next three days by 306,806 people. Further huge crowds lined the route from Westminster to Paddington, where mourners took the train to Windsor for the funeral.

The Conservative MP Airey Neave, who had escaped from Colditz prisoner of war camp in Germany during the Second World War, was assassinated here by the Irish National Liberation Army. The INLA planted a bomb under his car which exploded as he drove out of the House of Commons car park on 30 March 1979. Both of his legs were blown off and he died in hospital an hour after being freed from the wreckage.

The INLA told Neave's biographer Paul Routledge that the MP 'would have been very successful at that job [Northern Ireland Secretary]. He would have brought the armed struggle to its knees.' The following

August the organisation issued a statement about the assassination:
'In March, retired terrorist and supporter of capital punishment, Airey
Neave, got a taste of his own medicine when an INLA unit pulled off the
operation of the decade and blew him to bits inside the 'impregnable'
Palace of Westminster. The nauseous Margaret Thatcher snivelled on
television that he was an 'incalculable loss' – and so he was – to the
British ruling class.'

The controversial one-time Tory MP Enoch Powell maintained that
the British security services themselves, in the shape of MI6, not an
Irish terrorist group, had staged the killing to prevent Neave carrying
out his threat to rid the spying agency of 'corruption'. This, apparently
outlandish, theory was indeed more likely, if one bears in mind how
enormously difficult it would be for any outside organisation to carry
out such a complex murder plot in so prominent a place.

The Mall

Buckingham Palace

After Prince Albert, Queen Victoria's consort, died in December 1861 the
monarch went into prolonged mourning and the palace became a mausoleum. She left the rooms and Albert's possessions untouched. A manservant even filled a basin with water for the deceased prince every night.

Edward VII was the first royal to die at the palace (on 6 May 1910). On
his deathbed he asked for his closest adviser, the Jewish diamond merchant Ernest Cassel, whom he told: 'I am very seedy but I wanted to see
you.' Edward lay in state in the purple Throne Room for 11 days before
his coffin was taken to St Stephen's Hall, Westminster.

Former German Embassy, No. 9

No sooner had the German ambassador Leopold von Hoesch died of
heart failure after collapsing in the bathroom of the German embassy
on The Mall in 1936 than rumours spread that the Nazis had eliminated
him for showing insufficient support for National Socialism. Von
Hoesch's coffin was taken on a gun-carriage, led by two companies of
Grenadier Guards, from The Mall to the boat-train at Victoria station
along streets lined with dignitaries – British and German – paying their
respects as the cortège went by. The German contingent was dressed in
full Nazi uniform and liberally gave the Nazi salute as the coffin passed,
in what remains the only instance of overt legitimate Nazi military display in London history.

Tothill Street

Around 1,000 soldiers taken captive in 1651 at the Battle of Worcester (1651) during the English Civil War were buried by the chapel that stood here. A decade later Tothill Fields was used as a plague pit.

When Thomas Blood, the adventurer who almost succeeded in stealing the Crown Jewels in 1671, died nine years later he was buried in the chapel. Some claimed his death was faked as a cover-up to enable him to flee the country. A week after Blood's funeral the coffin was exhumed but found to contain the deceased – to general disappointment.

Whitehall

Daniel McNaughten shot dead Edward Drummond, secretary to the prime minister Robert Peel, on Whitehall on 20 January 1843, mistaking him for the PM.

Cenotaph

At the southern end of Whitehall stands the Cenotaph, designed by Edwin Lutyens for the tomb of the Unknown Warrior in 1920. Lutyens was given two weeks to create a non-denominational shrine, and it was he who suggested it be called the Cenotaph – Greek for 'empty tomb'. Every year on the Sunday nearest 11 November crowds gather at this spot to pay their respects to the fallen in both world wars.

Charing Cross

At the northern end of Whitehall, where the road meets Trafalgar Square, is Charing Cross, the point from which all distances to London are measured, marked by Hubert le Sueur's statue of Charles I. Edward I created a monument, Charing Cross, here in 1294 as a memorial for his recently deceased queen, Eleanor of Castile. It was one of twelve resting-places (others include Waltham Cross) at which her coffin stopped in 1290 on the route from Lincoln, where she died, to Westminster Abbey, the setting for the funeral. The cross stood here from 1294 until 1647, when the Puritans ordered its removal as they considered it to be an idolatrous object. A copy of it – Eleanor's Cross – now stands in front of Charing Cross station.

In his diary, Samuel Pepys describes his visit to Charing Cross on 13 October 1660 to witness the execution of Thomas Harrison, who had been involved in the execution of Charles I eleven years previously:

I went out to Charing Cross to see Maj.-Gen. Harrison hanged, drawn, and quartered – which was done there – he looking as cheerfully as any man could in that condition. He was presently cast down and his head and his heart shown to the people, at which there was great shouts of joy. It is said that he said that he was sure to come shortly at the right hand of Christ to judge them that now have judged him. And that his wife doth expect his coming again. Thus it was my chance to see the King beheaded at Whitehall and to see the first blood shed in revenge for the blood of the King at Charing Cross.'

Whitehall Palace, *east side*

Henry VIII died at Whitehall, English royalty's main late-medieval palace, on 28 January 1547. The Privy Council was immediately invited to inspect the corpse and confirm that the king was no longer alive. According to the historian John Strype, writing in 1721, various apothecaries and surgeons were then called for 'spurging, cleansing, bowelling, searing, embalming, furnishing and dressing with spices'. 'Spurging' was washing the corpse with aromatic water; 'cleansing', the emptying of the bowels and plugging the rectum; 'bowelling', making an incision in the ribcage to remove the soft organs.

Banqueting House

Charles I was executed outside Banqueting House, the newest part of Whitehall Palace, on 30 January 1649. Banqueting House, designed by Inigo Jones from 1619–22, was London's first building in the Italian Renaissance style, and was chosen for the execution because it glorified the institution of monarchy. The execution was watched by tens of thousands in the street below, some clinging to chimneys or perched precariously on walls and most unsure how to behave, embarrassed at being at such an event at all.

There was much delay to the proceedings. After the king attended Holy Communion, he was sent a meal, which he refused to touch until those present urged him to take stock against the cold; and then he was made to wait for four hours while the commissioners argued over signing the death warrant. At 2 p.m. the king was taken to the balcony, accompanied by two masked men wearing false beards (no one wanted to be identified with the regicide), who were probably Richard Brandon and William Lowen, and passed over to Dr Juxon, the Bishop of London. 'I go from a corruptible to an incorruptible Crown, where no disturbance can be. Remember,' Charles told him. The executioner then did the deed, lifted Charles's head up to the onlookers, and cried out: 'Behold, the head of a traitor.'

At this point the crowd surged towards the scaffold. Some tried to climb up and dip their handkerchiefs into the blood of the deceased king, others searched for souvenirs, scraps of hair or clothes. Back in Banqueting House the head was reunited with the body.

But was it even Charles who went to the scaffold? Theories circulating in Masonic circles allege that Charles may not have been executed after all. His place was allegedley taken by the lawyer and astrologer Elias Ashmole, founder of Oxford's Ashmolean Museum, and a loyal follower of the king. Behind this bizarre theory is the idea that as those who ordered Charles's execution were all Freemasons and no Mason would execute his Grand Master, Charles I, the two men swapped over and Ashmole allowed himself to be executed while Charles I lived out the rest of his days as Ashmole. Such a scam would have been easily possible given that the public watching the execution was not familiar with the king's appearance and would not have been able to see the heavily covered victim closely enough to identify him anyway.

Among those watching Charles's execution was the young Samuel Pepys – 11 years before he began his diary. At the time he wasn't particularly upset at the king's untimely death, and seemed quite keen on the idea of the republic, but in the early 1660s Pepys was caught up in the euphoria that swept Charles II to power. By 30 January 1662, the 13th anniversary of Charles's execution, his views had softened and he recorded in his diary:

> Fast-day for the murthering of the late King. I went to church, and Mr. Mills made a good sermon upon David's words, 'Who can lay his hands upon the Lord's Anoynted and be guiltless?' So home and to dinner, and employed all the afternoon in my chamber, setting things and papers to rights, which pleased me very well, and I think I shall begin to take pleasure in being at home and minding my business. I pray God I may, for I find a great need thereof. At night to supper and to bed.

Ironically it was in the palace that Oliver Cromwell died on 3 September 1658 and it was here also that Charles II chose to hold a feast to celebrate the restoration of the monarchy in 1660.

CHAPTER 5

River Thames

RICHMOND to THAMESMEAD

Richmond Palace, south bank

After Elizabeth I died in 1603 at the Thames-side Richmond Palace her body was taken by water to Whitehall, or as the historian William Camden described it:

> At every stroke the oars did tears let fall
> More clung about the barge, fish under water
> Wept out their eyes of pearl, and swam blind after.

Parts of Richmond Palace remain to the north of Richmond Bridge.

Syon House, Brentford, north bank

Soon after Henry VIII died on 28 January 1547 his body was taken to Syon House, Brentford, a former Bridgettine nunnery, where it was lodged overnight. A few years previously, during the Reformation, the Syon House friar had been evicted from the property and in his ire warned that one day the dogs would lick the king's blood. Sure enough, the night after Henry died his coffin burst open, unable to cope with his corpulent frame, and the next morning a servant found the Syon House dogs licking up the royal entrails.

Duke's Meadows, Chiswick, north bank

Early morning strollers out on the meadows on 17 June 1959 found the body of a woman, the prostitute Elizabeth Figg, propped up against a willow tree, her striped blue and white dress torn open. She had been strangled and her knickers forced down her throat. The murder, never solved, was later linked with a series of homicides now said to be the work of the unknown 'Jack the Stripper'.

Kelmscott House, 26 Upper Mall, Hammersmith, *north bank*

When William Morris, the great Victorian poet and polymath, was dying at his Thames-side property in 1896, the physician brought in to treat him was asked what was wrong. He replied: 'Simply being William Morris, and having done more work than most ten men.'

Putney Embankment, south bank

Following a huge nationwide manhunt John Christie, the 10 Rillington Place murderer (☞ p. 276), was finally found by police on 31 March 1953, wandering along Putney Embankment. At his trial Christie pleaded insanity and confessed to all the murders, remarking: 'The more the merrier!'

Grosvenor Road, Pimlico, north bank

When the Thames flooded in January 1928 the embankment just west of Vauxhall Bridge was breached with the sound of an explosion and a torrent of water surged into Grosvenor Road. Thanks to the quick thinking of several individuals who ran down the street urging people to flee, only ten people died.

Waterloo Bridge

In the 19th century gravediggers clearing out overcrowded burial sites near St Clement Dane's church would throw load after load of dirt mingled with human remains into the Thames at this point. Once, when a load fell off the cart into the street, the crowd picked out of it a human skull, which prompted the gravediggers to be more careful thereafter.

In the Sherlock Holmes story 'The Five Orange Pips' (1891), John Openshaw, having been pursued by the Ku Klux Klan and sought Holmes's help, is found drowned in the Thames near the bridge, murdered. 'That he should come to me for my help, and that I should send him away to his death...' cries Holmes, distraught at one of his greatest failures.

The Bulgarian secret service, probably in collusion with the KGB, assassinated a political opponent, Georgi Markov, as he waited for a bus on the bridge on 7 September 1978 (☞ p. 214).

Blackfriars Bridge

After Henry VI died in the Tower in 1471, probably murdered, his body was taken in an open coffin to St Paul's and on to the Blackfriars waterside where it was seen to still be bleeding. It was then transported on a boat to Chertsey Abbey for burial.

Henry's body was later moved to St George's Chapel, Windsor, and plans were announced in the 19th century to transfer the king's remains to Westminster. Nothing happened until 1910, when the coffin was opened and a jumble of bones was found surrounding the dismembered body. The skull had been broken and the right arm was missing. Alongside was a bone of a small pig. Henry was kept in Windsor.

Roberto Calvi, a financier with the Italian Banco Ambrosiano, dubbed by the press 'God's Banker' on account of his links with the Vatican, was found hanged by the river below Blackfriars Bridge in June 1982 after the bank's collapse. Calvi's pockets were filled with stones and straw, and his body was dosed with enough drugs to kill a man. If it were suicide, why hadn't he simply taken an overdose at his Hampstead home, or jumped in the river? many asked. It then emerged that Calvi had belonged to Grand Master Lucio Gelli's secret Masonic lodge, P2, open only to army officers, civil servants, politicians, newspaper editors and businessmen.

Because the body was left hanging by the water, conspiracy theorists believe it was a Masonic punishment, citing the Brotherhood's long-standing warning:

> First, Jubela. O that my throat had been cut across, my tongue torn out, and my body buried in the rough sands of the sea, at low water mark, where the tide ebbs and flows twice in twenty-four hours...

A 1992 inquiry concluded that Calvi had been murdered, and hanged to make it look like suicide. Five years later the Rome police charged a member of the Sicilian Mafia of the crime. In 2003 the City of London police reopened its murder inquiry and in April 2005 charged four people with Calvi's murder. They were all later cleared, so the death remains a mystery – a most intriguing one involving the Mafia, the Vatican and one of the most secretive Masonic lodges in the world.

Baynard's Castle, Blackfriars, *north bank*

Anyone found in the grounds of the medieval Blackfriars palace that filled the riverside south of modern-day Queen Victoria Street would be thrown into the nearby river and left to drown.

Southwark Bridge

Between here and London Bridge Lizzie and her father, Gaffer Hexham, fish for dead bodies in Charles Dickens's *Our Mutual Friend* (1865) so that they can riffle their pockets. At the beginning of the novel the Hexhams find the drowned John Harmon, who has returned from abroad to claim a large fortune, and this discovery sets in motion the events of the novel.

Marchioness *disaster site*

Fifty-one people died when the dredger *Bowbelle* struck the *Marchioness* pleasure vessel under Cannon Street rail bridge on 20 August 1989. Twice the captain of the dredger was charged with failing to keep an adequate lookout and twice cleared.

London Bridge

Until the late 17th century London Bridge was the capital's main site for displaying the heads of traitors who had been hanged, drawn and quartered, which were impaled on long poles so that no passer-by on foot or in a boat could miss them. This transfixed Joseph Justus Scaliger, a foreign visitor to London in 1566, who noted: 'In London there ever were many heads on the bridge; I have seen there, as if they were masts of ships and at the top of them, quarters of men's corpses.'

Those whose first posthumous days were spent on the bridge include the Scottish nationalist William Wallace ('Braveheart') in 1305; Jack Cade who tried to seize control of London in 1450; and Bishop Fisher who refused to back Henry VIII as head of the English church in 1535. After 14 days, not only had the bishop's head avoided deterioration but, as an unnamed commentator claimed, 'It grew daily fresher and fresher; in his lifetime he never looked so well.'

The head of Thomas More, executed for treason on Tower Hill, also in 1535, was displayed on London Bridge. Passing under it on the river one day, his daughter cried out: 'Oh how many times it has lain on my lap; Oh God if only it could now fall into my lap,' Whereupon, so the story goes, the head remarkably left its spike and landed in that very spot in the boat. She then safeguarded the skull and sent it to Canterbury Cathedral, where it remains.

In his epic 1922 poem 'The Wasteland', T. S. Eliot describes the crowd that 'flowed over London Bridge. So many, I had not thought death had undone so many,' drawing a connection between post-war London and Dante's Hell where the streets swarm with the living dead.

Custom House, *north bank*

The ever-depressed late 18th-century poet William Cowper planned to commit suicide by jumping into the river outside Custom House. Cowper, who suffered acutely from suicidal tendencies, had long planned his own death. However, on the day he chose, the tide was too low and he was saved by 'a porter seated on some goods as if on purpose to prevent me'.

Tower Pier, *north bank*

The coffin containing the body of the statesman-poet Sir Philip Sidney arrived at Tower Pier in 1586. Having carelessly discarded his leg armour, he had died fighting in a war in the Netherlands. The coffin was escorted back to England by 1,000 soldiers and he lay in state for three months while the authorities sorted out his affairs.

After the funeral service of Winston Churchill at St Paul's Cathedral on 30 January 1965, the coffin was taken on board the *Havengore* at Tower Pier, just west of the Tower, amid a 19-gun salute. As it passed the docks, the dockers lowered the jibs of their derrick cranes in respect.

Tower of London, *north bank*

Many of those executed at the Tower were brought in by river, entering the complex through Traitors' Gate. Such was the fate of Ann Boleyn in 1536.

Tower Bridge

The torso of a young African boy floating in the Thames was found by a man walking across Tower Bridge in September 2001. It had been in the water for up to ten days. Nearby on the south bank police found seven half-burnt candles wrapped in a white sheet on which was written a name common in the Yoruba area of Nigeria. Police were unable to trace anyone with that name in Britain and believe the boy, whom they named Adam, was probably the victim of a ritualistic 'muti' killing, carried out by witch doctors who use human body parts for medicines.

Town of Ramsgate, 62 Wapping High Street, *north bank*

Judge Jeffreys, James II's unpopular Lord Chancellor, who was responsible for ordering the execution of hundreds of men, was seized here in 1688 while attempting to flee to the continent to avoid the troops of William III, who had taken the throne from James. Jeffreys was sent to the Tower of London, where he tried unsuccessfully to drink himself to death and became unable to eat anything but poached eggs for months.

Execution Dock, *opposite Brewhouse Lane, Wapping, north bank*

Pirates were hanged at Execution Dock in Wapping on a gallows erected on the shoreline at low tide. After execution the bodies were chained to stakes until three tides had washed over them, supposedly to cleanse their souls, their corpses rotting as the birds picked at the flesh. Those who met their fate this way included Thomas Walton (d. 1583), who 'rent his Venetian breeches of crimson taffeta and distributed the same to his old acquaintances', and Captain Kidd (d. 1701) whose ghost supposedly haunts the vicinity. Kidd was considered so important a catch that they moved his corpse to a more prominent location at Tilbury, where it was left swinging for a few years. The last men to be hanged at Execution Dock were George Davis and William Watts, executed for murder and mutiny on 17 December 1830.

Thames Tunnel

Ten workmen died during the construction of the Thames Tunnel, the first to go under the river, in the 1840s, so difficult was the task of shoring up the walls and roof. The tunnel was designed by Marc Isambard Brunel and took 18 years to complete. It was taken over by the East London Railway in 1869 and is now part of the underground network, linking Wapping and Rotherhithe stations.

Deadman's Dock, *east of Grove Street, Deptford, south bank*

So named because when excavated in the 1920s it was found to contain a large number of corpses, probably plague victims from the 17th century. It was also here that prisoners from France, Spain and Holland were executed during the Napoleonic Wars. The site is now covered by the Pepys council estate.

Royal Naval College, *Greenwich, south bank*

After lying in state at the Royal Naval College, Greenwich, for three days following his fatal wounding at the Battle of Trafalgar, Lord Nelson was taken upstream by boat in a half mile-long cortège. The party came to a halt at Charing Cross, so that the coffin could be taken to the Admiralty, and there it stayed overnight before being transferred to a hearse shaped like the *Victory*, and on to St Paul's for the funeral.

Thames Ironworks, *north bank*

Disaster struck when the shipbuilding and engineering company Thames Ironworks, which was situated on both sides of the mouth of the River Lea, launched the *Albion* in 1898. Thirty thousand spectators had turned up to see the ship off, and 200 of them were standing on the slipway bridge, even though it was signposted as dangerous. When the vessel hit the water, the impact created a huge wave which poured over the bridge, smashing it to pieces and throwing those on it into the river. Thirty-seven spectators lost their lives, their cries drowned out by the cheers of those who were applauding the launch.

Princess Alice disaster site, *Tripcock Ness, south bank*

Britain's worst waterway disaster occurred off Tripcock Ness, a headland jutting into the Thames east of Thamesmead, on 3 September 1878, when the *Bywell Castle* coal barge crashed into the *Princess Alice* paddle steamer. Most of the passengers were unaware of the seriousness of the impact, but water quickly filled the breach and the pressure helped break up the vessel.

Hundreds fell into the water just at the point where the south-east London sewer discharges its contents into the river. The few ropes that the crew of the *Bywell Castle* threw down were hopelessly inadequate and saved only 50 people; the women in their billowy dresses and petticoats quickly drowned.

The *Princess Alice*'s companion ship, the *Duke of Teck*, following behind, arrived ten minutes later, but was unable to help. Because children did not need tickets, the authorities were unsure how many died, but around 630 bodies were eventually recovered, including those of the captain, his son, brother and sister-in-law.

CHAPTER 6

East London

ALDGATE/THE EAST END, E1
Alderney Road
Batty Street
Brady Street
Brushfield Street
Cannon Street Road
Commercial Road
Commercial Street
Dorset Street
Durward Street
Garnet Street
Gunthorpe Street
Hanbury Street
Henriques Street
Old Castle Street
Philpot Street
Prescot Street
Princelet Street
Royal Mint Street
Sidney Street
Stepney High Street
Swedenborg Gardens
The Highway
Tower Hill
Vallance Road
Wellclose Square
Whitechapel Road

BETHNAL GREEN, E2
Bethnal Green Road
Cheshire Street
St Matthew's Row

BOW, E3
Bow Road
Grove Road
Southern Grove

CHINGFORD, E4
Old Church Road

FOREST GATE, E7
Cemetery Road
Romford Road
Sebert Road

HOMERTON, E9
Lauriston Road
Victoria Park Road

MANOR PARK, E12
Aldersbrook Road

POPLAR/ISLE OF DOGS, E14
Dolphin Lane
West India Dock Road

STRATFORD/WEST HAM, E15

VICTORIA DOCKS, E16
Barking Road
Butcher Road
Hallsville Road
Thames Road

ALDGATE/THE EAST END, E1

To the Romans the East End was mostly a graveyard, dominated by three main burial sites near the main roads to the west, north and east of what is now the City of London. These may have contained as many as 100,000 graves during the first four centuries AD even though many of the dead were cremated.

To modern Londoners the East End is associated with poverty and violent murder. In this part of the capital the victims tend to be more tragic (the Marr family, Alfie Cohen) and the killers more memorable (the Ratcliffe Highway murderer, Jack the Ripper). Such local deaths are compounded by the large number of state-sponsored executions at the Tower of London over the centuries.

Alderney Road

Jewish Cemetery

The main attraction in what is the second oldest Jewish cemetery in London is the grave of the 18th-century mystic and Kabbalist Chaim Jacob Samuel Falk, an East End figure known as the 'Ba'al Shem of London'. The title 'Ba'al Shem' means 'master of the secret name of God' and refers to his alleged power to use these secret names to perform miracles. For decades after Falk's death in 1782 hundreds of devotees visited his graveside to pay their respects, particularly on key dates in the Jewish calendar. Some still do.

The cemetery opened in 1697 and featured a wheeled sentry-box from which new graves were watched for the first few nights to prevent resurrection men removing the bodies and selling the parts to medical schools. It closed for newcomers in 1852.

Batty Street

No. 16

This small terraced house was the setting for a rare Jewish murder, that of a young woman, Miriam Angel, who was found under a bed with a curious yellow staining around her mouth in June 1887. Also in the room was the semi-conscious Israel Lipski, a 22-year-old Jewish umbrella maker who lived at the same address. He, too, had yellow staining around his mouth.

Once he had been revived, Lipski claimed that he had been attacked by two Jewish hawkers he had invited home to discuss some work and whom he had accosted when he saw them entering Miriam Angel's bedroom. A crucial piece of evidence that militated against him was that the door of the bedroom where he and Angel were found was locked from the *inside*. However, the door was in such poor condition that the key could have been turned from the outside.

After Lipski's conviction, the case was taken up by the crusading journalist W. T. Stead, and public opinion began to turn in favour of Lipski. But before the home secretary was able to recommend commuting the death sentence, Lipski confessed and he was hanged at Newgate on 22 August 1887, one of only two Jews ever hanged in England. His defenders soon claimed that he had been pressurised into confessing by a rabbi who wanted him to take the blame for the crime so that growing anti-Semitism in London would cease.

Brady Street

Brady Street Jewish Burial Ground

Nathan Meyer Rothschild (d. 1836), founder of the Rothschild banking dynasty, is the most famous of those buried at Brady Street, a disused burial ground in the heart of the East End, which is itself surprising given that his remains had to be brought over from Germany.

In the 1970s Lord (Victor) Rothschild, by then head of the British branch of the family, announced that he wished to be buried beside Nathan Meyer, even though the cemetery had closed down in 1858. It needed several years of negotiations involving the Privy Council, the Beth Din, Tower Hamlets council and the environment minister William Waldegrave, a long-standing political ally, to grant him his wish.

When the cemetery became full a four-foot thick layer of earth was spread over the site. Some of the gravestones contain the address of the deceased, a detail provided by those families who wanted to show how far socially the departed had moved from the East End.

Brushfield Street

Intensive recent rebuilding of Brushfield Street to accommodate giant office blocks for the ever-expanding City of London has unearthed a number of Roman burials. The Museum of London now has the remains of a young Roman woman, a typical burial of the fourth century AD, unearthed in 1991, whose body had been wrapped in cloth woven with silk and gold, and placed in a lead coffin which in turn had been put in a limestone sarcophagus. Nearby were found hair decorations, a jar which once probably contained perfumed oil, and a box made of lignite and coal meant to protect the spirit.

In the 18th century Spitalfields became a silk-weaving area. By the 19th century it had become poverty stricken, squalid and overcrowded. The commentator George R. Sims discovered in 1883 that the body of a child who had died at 26 King Street, Spitalfields, had been kept in the house for nine days as his parents were too poor to bury it. 'During that time the body became so offensive that it was necessary to remove it to a shed at the rear of the house. Eventually the father applied to the relieving officer, and obtained an order for the burial of the body.'

Cannon Street Road

Alfie Cohen deathplace (1974)

Cohen, a 69-year-old Jewish kiosk holder, was battered to death outside his premises at the north-west end of the street at four o'clock in the morning on Friday 27 September 1974, only a few hours after the end of Yom Kippur, the holiest day in the Jewish calendar. Seven years previously his brother Mike had been beaten and robbed outside the stall, later dying from his injuries.

The East End underworld was horrified by the murder. 'We will not rest until the guilty are brought to justice,' one villain told the local paper. 'We are all mucking in to try and find Alfie's murderers. We all respected him and this one time we'll be pleased to turn someone over to the law.' What further shocked the public was that while the murderers made off with only a few pounds police searching the kiosk for clues found a total of £105,000 hidden under old boxes and stuffed into various corners, all of which was left behind when the murderers fled. To add to the mystery, at Cohen's feet somebody, possibly the killers, had scattered two brass rings and some coins – just like Jack the Ripper had done at the feet of his second victim, Annie Chapman, in 1888. Two men who had no connections with the area were eventually caught and convicted.

John Williams's grave, *junction with Cable Street*
Some who die are not afforded the luxury of a designated burial site. No space in a cemetery or church graveyard was granted to John Williams, chief suspect for the 1811 Ratcliffe Highway murders (☛p. 125 and p. 133).

After being arrested – on the flimsiest evidence – in connection with the killings, Williams was sent to Coldbath Prison in Clerkenwell (☛p. 38). When he was later found hanged, his death appeared to be suicide, so the authorities arranged for his body to be dragged through the streets and buried at a crossroads. This was usually the case with those who took their own life because it was thought that if the spirit did wish to haunt its former home the choice of the four roads would confuse it. Indeed some East Enders feared there might be reprisals from a spectral Williams, and recalled that in 1784 an Aberystwyth woman who had poisoned her lodger, and killed herself was then buried by the sea to prevent her joining a band of ghosts terrorising a nearby village.

Instead of incarcerating Williams near the scene of the murders the authorities chose the crossroads of Cable Street and Cannon Street Road, then one of the major East End landmarks. On the evening of 30 December 1811 the body was taken from the prison to St George's Watch House, where it was kept overnight in preparation for the ghoulish ceremony the next morning. At 10.30 a.m. on that New Year's Eve the procession left the watch house. Williams was lying almost vertical on a specially constructed cart, his ruddy, freshly scrubbed face with its demonic staring eyes exposed for all to see, his body clothed in blue trousers and white open-necked shirt, his left leg in irons.

The procession moved along a route lined with some 10,000 spectators, past all the sites connected with the murders, and eventually came to a halt at this junction where a hole had been dug deliberately too small so as to give the late Williams as much discomfort as possible.

The corpse was turned out of the cart and one of the party shoved it into the opening, piercing the heart with a long wooden stake. This was to ensure not only that Williams was dead but that his spirit was truly extinguished. The crowd then broke into cries, oaths and jeers. Finally a quantity of lime was thrown over the corpse and the earth smoothed out on top.

A hundred years later workmen digging up the road to lay gas pipes exhumed and mutilated Williams's body. The bones were shared out among forensic scientists looking for clues, and the landlord of the Crown and Dolphin that overlooks the site kept the skull as a souvenir. It was stolen soon after by the French occultist Mina Bergson, who was trying to create a golem, an artificial human being made according to Kabbalist ritual.

Commercial Street

Christ Church

This Nicholas Hawksmoor church, one of the East End's great landmarks, was particularly targeted by bodysnatchers in the 18th and 19th centuries. The coffin of 73-year-old Mary Mason had three iron bands fastened around it after she died in 1814 and another chained to the wall to prevent the resurrection men making off with her. Undertaker William Horne, who died in 1826, was even more careful. He chose for himself three coffins – one of lead, one of iron, one of wool, which were placed one inside the other.

Excavations of the vaults in the 1990s led to the opening of one of the coffins, which revealed the perfectly preserved body of a 14-year-old girl dressed in a white linen dress, bonnet and gloves. Within 24 hours contamination with the air turned her to black dust.

Music hall songs were performed at Christ Church during the 1996 funeral service of the artist Joshua Compston. Some believed he had not died but simply organised the funeral as a publicity stunt.

The church is the setting for the murder of a schoolboy in Peter Ackroyd's time-shifting detective story *Hawksmoor* (1985).

Dorset Street

Location of the fifth Jack the Ripper murder, no. 26

Mary Kelly, supposedly the last victim of Jack the Ripper, was murdered and mutilated in her Dorset Street room – the site now occupied by a multi-storey car park on White's Row – on the night of 9 November 1888. The murderer must have spent considerable time with the corpse for when Kelly was found the next morning she had been completely disembowelled, her entrails draped around the room as if they were decorations.

Experts are divided over whether this was really the last Ripper murder, or whether some later East End murders perpetrated in a similar way were also his work. There are even theories that it wasn't Kelly who was killed that night but an unknown victim; a number of witnesses claimed they had seen her over the next few days before she finally disappeared.

The police failed to arrest anyone for the crime, much to the fury of Queen Victoria, who told the prime minister, the Marquess of Salisbury, 'This new most ghastly murder shows the absolute necessity for some very decided action. All these courts must be lit, and our detectives improved. They are not what they should be.' Subsequently street lighting appeared in the area.

Durward Street

Location of the first Jack the Ripper murder

Mary Ann 'Polly' Nichols, a 44-year-old prostitute, was found murdered at 3.40 in the morning of 31 August 1888 on Durward Street (then Buck's Row). Her throat had been cut from ear to ear, the windpipe and gullet completely severed, and her abdomen had been wrenched open, exposing her intestines. There were two small stabs in the groin area.

Neither the police officers patrolling nearby streets nor the residents in houses alongside Buck's Row had heard or seen anything suspicious. Indeed there were no witnesses, weapon or clues. To add to the mystery, even though her clothes were soaked with blood, there was hardly any blood was on the ground, and if she had been killed here she would surely have bled profusely on the spot. Nichols was identified by her clothing, which contained the mark of the Lambeth Workhouse, where she lived.

At this stage there was little suggestion the police had a series of murders on their hands and the name 'Jack the Ripper' had not been coined. Once again, as after the murder of Martha Tabram (➤ p. 126), locals quickly laid blame for the murder on the Jews, who had been arriving in the area in large numbers. A theory circulated that the murderer must be a Jewish animal slaughterer, as such a man would have the knives and the anatomical knowledge. Two slaughterers were arrested, but both had plausible alibis. Meanwhile, Jewish leaders clarified the religious minutiae: the *khalef*, the implement used to kill an animal according to the kosher method, is single-edged and not pointed – as had been the one used in the murder.

When locals later heard the postman going from house to house crying 'Number 8 Murder Row', they campaigned to have the name changed. Buck's Row became Durward Street.

Garnet Street

Location of the second Ratcliffe Highway murder, no. 81

The second set of Ratcliffe Highway murders took place at the King's Arms pub at the north-west end of what was then New Gravel Lane, on 19 December 1811. The publican John Williamson, his wife, Elizabeth, and an elderly servant, Bridget Harrington, were all butchered by an unknown assailant or assailants. A fortnight previously the Marr family, who lived a mile west at 29 Ratcliffe Highway had been murdered, leaving the East End in fear of the perpetrators' return.

On the evening of Thursday 19 December Williamson noticed a suspicious-looking man wearing a brown jacket listening at the door of the pub. He asked Anderson, a constable, to look out for the man, and Anderson made off along New Gravel Lane. Returning soon afterwards to the King's Arms to tell Williamson that he had found nobody fitting the description, the policeman saw a tremendous commotion in the street outside the pub. A small crowd of people were watching as Turner, the Williamsons' lodger, was frantically making his way out of an upper window, hanging on to knotted sheets crying: 'Murder! Murder!... they are murdering the people in the house!'

As the half-naked lodger dropped to the ground, Anderson rushed into his own house for his truncheon, and with the help of others beat down the door of the King's Arms. Inside they found a chilling sight. Williamson was sprawled out on the stairs, his head beaten to a pulp.

His wife was nearby. Her skull had been bashed in and her throat slashed, blood pouring from the wound. The maid was by the hearth, her skull also smashed and her throat sliced through as far as the bone.

During questioning Turner claimed that he was not the culprit and had escaped the house in panic as the murderer or murderers were carrying out the killings. He explained that after he had gone to bed he had heard a loud bang at the front door and the servant cry: 'We are all murdered!', followed by the sound of two or three blows and Williamson shouting: 'I'm a dead man!', whereupon he had fled. It soon became clear that Turner was not the murderer.

John Williams, who was later apprehended for both sets of murders, committed suicide before he could be tried (p. 121).

Gunthorpe Street

On 8 August 1888 the body of prostitute Martha Tabram was discovered on the landing of George Yard Buildings, a block of flats on Gunthorpe Street, near Aldgate East station. She had been stabbed 39 times. Earlier that evening Tabram had been socialising with a friend, Pearly Poll, and two soldiers. All soldiers stationed at the Tower were put on an identification parade, but Pearly Poll failed to identify a possible culprit and the two soldiers had alibis anyway.

Suspicion fell on the Jews – convenient scapegoats. No gentile could have perpetrated such a crime, locals asserted, disregarding the fact that only two Jews had been hanged for murder since the return of the Jews to England in the 1650s. *The Times* recalled how a few years previously a Polish Jew had been arrested near Cracow for murdering and mutilating a non-Jewish woman in a ritualistic killing. The chief rabbi had to explain that such practices had no place in Judaism.

This was the second similar attack on a prostitute in what became the year of Jack the Ripper, but experts exclude Tabram from the list of five 'canonical' victims as her throat was not cut in the manner of later victims, nor was she disembowelled.

Hanbury Street

Location of the second Jack the Ripper murder, No. 29

Annie Chapman, a 47-year-old East End prostitute known as 'Dark Annie', was found at the back of 29 Hanbury Street on 8 September 1888 murdered and disembowelled, her head almost severed from her body. She was a victim of Jack the Ripper, so it is believed, and it was only a week after the similar murder of Mary Ann Nichols on Buck's Row, Whitechapel (➤ p. 124).

Early the following morning a huge crowd gathered outside. Some paid to be taken to an upper window of a nearby block to gain a better view of the spot where the body had been found. The murder had taken place on the second day of the Jewish New Year – the Day of Judgement – and was not the first similar killing to have taken place that year on a date significant in the Jewish calendar. Word soon spread through the East End that the slaying must have been the work of a deranged Jew enacting some arcane chronological biblical ritual to rid the East End of sin. Jews defended their reputation, pointing out that the murders could equally as likely have been the work of a disturbed gentile steeped in Judaic knowledge intent on humiliating East End Jewry.

Jewish leaders braced themselves for a fresh murder a week later, for 15 September was the Day of Atonement, the holiest day of the Jewish year, when the worshipper begs forgiveness for all sins. It is the day when in biblical times the high priest conducted a special Temple ceremony to clean the shrine, slaying a bull and two goats as a special offering. Perhaps there would be a human slaying this time?

When no murders occurred that day the theory that the killings were linked to the Jewish calendar seemed to be dashed. Or maybe the murderer was interrupted while about to commit a fresh atrocity? *The Times* reported that on the evening of 14 September, as the Day of Atonement was being ushered in at synagogue, police arrested a Jew, Edward McKenna, of 15 Brick Lane, on suspicion that he was the man who had emerged from the Tower Subway and asked the attendant: 'Have you caught any of the Whitechapel murderers yet?' He had then produced a foot-long knife with a curved blade and remarked: 'This will do for them' before running away. McKenna was unable to provide an explanation for his behaviour, but had to be released because of the lack of any more substantial evidence against him.

Chapman's funeral had been held in secret the previous day with only her family present, and no curious members of the public in attendance.

Subsequent Ripper murders took place on dates without significance in the Jewish calendar.

Henriques Street

Known as Berner Street in the 19th century when it was caught up in the Jack the Ripper murders, it was later renamed Henriques Street after the local philanthropist Sir Basil Henriques.

Location of the third Jack the Ripper murder, No. 40

Elizabeth Stride, a 45-year-old Swedish prostitute, was found by the International Working Men' Club on what is now Henriques Street, her throat cut, the blood still pouring from the wound, at one o'clock in the morning of 30 September 1888. Louis Diemschutz, the steward of the club, told police that he felt that the murderer was still in the yard when he discovered the body. The nature of the attack on Stride led the authorities immediately to associate it with earlier similar murders now believed to be the work of Jack the Ripper. Crucially, two days previously, a note had been sent to the Central News Agency which read:

> Dear Boss, I keep on hearing the police have caught me but they won't fix me just yet. I am down on whores and I shan't quit ripping them till I do get buckled. Grand work the last job was. I gave the lady [Annie Chapman] no time to squeal. How can they catch me know? I love my work and want to start again. You will soon hear of me and my funny little games. The next job I do I shall clip the lady's ears off and send to the police officers

just for jolly...Keep this letter back till I do a bit more work, then give it out straight. My knife is nice and sharp. I want to get to work right away if I get a chance. Good luck. Yours truly, Jack the Ripper

This time there was a witness, Israel Schwartz, a Jewish Hungarian immigrant, who saw a woman being attacked at 12.45 a.m. and walked away but to his horror found himself being briefly followed by one of the attackers.

Some Ripperologists believe that Stride was not a Ripper victim but was killed by her common-law husband, Michael Kidney, because, unlike the other victims, she had no mutilations other than a cut throat.

Police found no weapon for Stride's murder, and no one was ever apprehended.

Stride wasn't the only local murder victim that night. A few hours after her death another prostitute, Catherine Eddowes, was killed, possibly by Jack the Ripper, on Mitre Square, near Aldgate station, about half a mile away (p. 20).

Old Castle Street

Alice M'Kenzie, a prostitute, was found murdered and mutilated, her throat cut and abdomen sliced open, on 17 July 1889, on what was then Castle Alley, a passageway between Middlesex Street and Commercial Street described in 1889 by *The Times* as 'one of the lowest quarters in the whole of east London'. At the inquest a verdict of murder 'by a person or persons unknown' was reached. A drunk named William Wallace Brodie later confessed to murdering M'Kenzie and claimed responsibility for all the murders associated with Jack the Ripper the previous year. Scotland Yard dismissed Brodie as being of unsound mind, and it later transpired that he had been in South Africa when most of the murders had taken place.

Philpot Street

York Minster

The pub was the setting for a showdown in 1902 between two sets of early 20th-century Jewish gangsters, the Bessarabians and the Odessans, which resulted in murder. As the pub's clientele were being entertained by a group of Russian dancers one night, a mass brawl broke out, result-

ing in the death of an Odessan, Henry Brodovich, who stumbled out of
the premises one hand on his own knife, the other on his stab wound,
and collapsed in the street.

The Bessarabians included Charlie 'Kid' McCoy, the boxer known as
the Real McCoy, who killed wife number 7 in America. He escaped a
murder rap by pleading insanity caused by his boxing injuries, but committed suicide in Detroit in April 1940.

Prescot Street

Late 20th-century excavations uncovered evidence of more than 600
Roman burials and around 120 cremations on or near this street. There
were also jars filled with coins supposedly used by the souls of those
departed to pay Charon, the ferryman, to take them across the Styx.

Princelet Street

Hebrew Dramatic Club (late 19th century), Nos. 6–10
Seventeen people were crushed to death after a false cry of 'fire' was
shouted out during a performance of an operetta at this cramped
theatre in January 1887. *The Jewish Chronicle* blamed the tragedy on
Yiddish-speaking Jews keeping themselves in 'persistent isolation', and
warned fellow Jews to 'avoid such performances of strolling minstrels
acting in the jargon [and] hasten the process of "Anglicising"'.
Unsurprisingly the crowds failed to return after the tragedy. There is a
relief of a cello in the pavement outside the house to mark the site.

Royal Mint Street
opposite northern end of Cartwright Street

Frances Coles, a prostitute, was found dying under the railway arch to
the north of Royal Mint Street some 18 months after the last East End
murder now attributed to Jack the Ripper. Police arrested Thomas
Sadler, a merchant seaman who had consorted with Coles, believing,
understandably, that they had caught the Ripper. Sadler vehemently
denied any involvement. He explained that after being discharged from
his ship on 11 February he had visited the Princess Alice pub and spotted Coles, whom he had picked up in Whitechapel a year previously. He
had left with her and the following day they went on a pub crawl

through Spitalfields. During the afternoon, while Frances Coles was in a shop, Sadler was mugged, something she might have arranged given her quick disappearance. Sadler went to hospital to get treatment for his injuries, and when he returned to his doss house he was arrested for murdering her.

Although Coles's throat was cut, it was with a blunt knife unlike the canonical Ripper slayings, there was no evidence that she had been strangled, and no mutilations on the abdomen. Witness statements later claimed that Sadler was so drunk at the time of the crime that he could not have been the murderer. The jury returned a verdict of 'Willful Murder by some person or persons unknown'. The crowds who had gathered outside the magistrates' court to lend Sadler their support were delighted and cheered uproariously. The murder has remained unsolved and there were no further killings in the style of Jack the Ripper.

Sidney Street

Sidney Street Siege, No. 100

One of the most famous events in East End history, the siege took place when a small band of east European anarchists staged a shoot-out from the property that then stood on this site on New Year's Day 1911 and died in the fire that later engulfed the house.

No. 100 Sidney Street, located a few yards south of Whitechapel station, was the home of Betsy Gershon, mistress of one of the gang which had been involved in the robbery of a jeweller's on Houndsditch (☛ p. 18). Once police discovered that the robbers had taken refuge here they waited overnight in the snow and at first light tried to gain entry, only to be met with a volley of shots. One of these hit Detective Sergant Leeson, who fell to the ground and spluttered to his superior, Detective Inspector Wensley: 'Mr Wensley, I am dying. They have shot me through the heart. Goodbye. Give my love to the children. Bury me at Putney.' He survived.

In need of reinforcements, the police contacted the home secretary, Winston Churchill, who sent in the Scots Guards and appeared at the scene himself, wearing a top hat and a fur-collared overcoat. More shots rang out and, after a couple of hours of stalemate, the house caught fire and collapsed. Police later found the bodies of two men inside.

Stepney Green

When the Black Death hit the East End in 1348 Pope Clement VI
devised an imaginative antidote. He sent to London a group of 120
holy men, who walked through the East End, their faces hidden, chant-
ing Pater Nosters and Ave Marias.

When they arrived at Stepney Green they stopped marching,
stripped to the waist and formed a large circle. Their leaders passed
around heavy leather scourges, tipped with metal studs, which the men
used to beat each other while the master of the holy men prayed for
God's mercy.

They repeated this ceremony twice during the day and once at night
for thirty-three and a half days, some of the men dying in the process.
The Black Death subsequently abated, but it was unlikely to have done
so because of these dramatic activities.

No one knew what had caused the plague until 1905 when scientists
reasoned that fleas in the woollen goods that Edward III imported
from France brought the disease, and were then carried around by rats.

Stepney High Street

St Dunstan and All Saints

William Jerome, the vicar of what is the East End's oldest surviving
church, was burnt alive in 1540 for preaching an Anabaptist sermon at
Paul's Cross outside St Paul's Cathedral. Two hundred years later, in
1736, Thomas Jenkins, a St Dunstan's gravedigger, was found to have
been selling dead bodies in the churchyard to a Pall Mall surgeon, and
was sentenced to be publicly whipped. He was tied to a cart by a group
of sailors and chimney sweeps. The hangman lashed Jenkins 100 times
as the cart made its way along the road.

Swedenborg Gardens

In what is now one of the East End's most depressing slums no trace
remains of what was a smart Georgian square, site of the Swedish
church where the scientist-turned-mystic Emanuel Swedenborg
was buried in 1772. When the church was demolished in 1908,
Swedenborg's body was exhumed so that it could be taken to Sweden
to be placed in a marble sarcophagus in Uppsala Cathedral. By that

time, however, the corpse was missing its skull, which had been removed by a Swedish sailor who hoped to sell it as a relic. It was later recovered and returned to London, to be exhibited with other skulls in a phrenological collection. In a bizarre mix-up the wrong skull was returned to Swedenborg's body, while the genuine one went on sale in an antiques shop. In 1978 it was auctioned at Sotheby's in London for £2,500.

The Highway
(former Ratcliffe Highway)

One of London's oldest routes, dating back some 2,000 years, the Highway was originally a Roman Pretorian Way connecting the lake fort, Llyndin, with the gravel spur by the river at Ratcliffe ('red cliff'). In 1811 the road's reputation as a centre of depravity was reinforced by what became known as the 'Ratcliffe Highway Murders', the most notorious London killings of the early 19th century.

Location of the first Ratcliffe Highway murder, No. 29,

The first set of Ratcliffe Highway murders took place on the night of 7 December 1811 when four members of the Marr household at No. 29, a draper's shop, were butchered by an unknown assailant. Just before midnight the householder and shop-owner, Timothy Marr, sent out his maid, Margaret Jewell, to buy oysters. Unable to find any, Jewell returned home and to her surprise found the house in darkness. She enlisted the help of the nightwatchman to break in and there they found Marr, his wife, baby and assistant dead, their throats cut. Nearby was a heavy ship's mallet covered with blood and hair.

Twelve days later another similar killing spree took place a little further east on New Gravel Lane (p. 125). The police eventually arrested a sailor, John Williams, who had been a shipmate of Marr, but despite the lack of substantial evidence, he was charged with the murders. Williams committed suicide in Coldbath prison (p. 38) before he could be tried. He was then buried in a ghoulish ceremony at a nearby crossroads (p. 121).

The gory details of the case and the mystery surrounding the true identity of the culprit have continued to fire the imagination of writers. In his essay 'Murder Considered as One of the Fine Arts' (1827) Thomas de Quincey ironically commented: 'If once a man indulges himself in

E1

murder, very soon he comes to think little of robbing; and from robbing he comes next to drinking and Sabbath-breaking, and from that to
incivility and procrastination.'

A hundred years later P. G. Wodehouse mocked the murders in
Ukridge:

> 'The Canning Town 'Orror,' he would announce.
>
> 'Yes, dearie?,' his mother cast a fond glance at him and a proud one at
> me.
>
> 'In this very 'ouse, was it?'
>
> 'In this very 'ouse', said Cecil, with the gloomy importance of a con
> firmed bore about to hold forth on his favourite subject.
>
> '"Jimes Potter"' is nime was. 'E was found at seven in the morning
> underneaf the kitchen sink wiv 'is froat cut from ear to ear. It was the
> landlady's brother done it. They 'anged 'im at Pentonville.'

In 1990 P. D. James and T. A. Critchley published *The Maul and the
Pear Tree*, an eerily dispassionate account of the case, based on newspaper and court reports.

Tower Hill

Local ancient tribes buried the head of Bran, a Celtic god king, under Tower Hill, which they held as holy. They believed the head of Bran possessed magical powers and had remained alive after his death. It was buried facing France to ward off invaders.

England's major beheadings took place in public on Tower Hill from 1485 to 1747, for the nearby Tower of London was where traitors were imprisoned. There were 75 beheadings over the years and they were carried out when the government wanted to make an example of someone. The occasion would end with the executioner picking up the severed head and proclaiming to the crowd: 'Behold the head of a traitor!'

A hundred years before the executions began, rebels taking part in the Peasants' Revolt of 1381 broke into the Tower, dragged out Sir Robert Hales ('Hobbe the robber'), the official responsible for enforcing the poll tax, and took him to Tower Hill, where they killed him by hacking away until 'being mangled with eight several strokes in the neck and head, he fulfilled most worthy martyrdom'.

EXECUTED ON TOWER HILL

‖ The first execution on Tower Hill was that of **Simon de Burley**, Richard II's tutor, for treason, in 1386.

‖ Before going to the scaffold in 1535 for refusing to accept the Act of Supremacy which made Henry VIII head of the English church, **Thomas More** told the governor of the Tower: 'I pray you, see me safe up, and for my coming down let me shift for myself.' He then said to the executioner: 'Pluck up thy spirits, man. My neck is very short!', and on the block moved his beard away with the quip: 'It were a pity it should be cut off, it has done no treason.' More was buried in the Royal Chapel of St Peter ad Vincula, one of London's oldest churches, which stands in the precincts of the Tower.

‖ Much interest was taken in the execution of the Puritan **Christopher Love** on 22 August 1651, condemned for plotting to return Charles II to the throne during the Commonwealth. In his final speech Love announced: 'I am exchanging a pulpit for a scaffold and a scaffold for a throne. I am exchanging a guard of soldiers for a guard of angels, to carry me to Abraham's bosom.' Some considered Love a martyr and saint. On hearing his final words and prayer, one man began to repent of his sins, and was 'born again' as Love died.

II **Algernon Sidney**, a Republican who plotted against Charles II, was
executed here on 7 December 1683. On the scaffold he failed to make
the expected signal to the executioner, who bent down and asked
him if he were going to rise again. 'Not until the resurrection,'
Sidney retorted, 'Strike away.'

II Prior to his execution on Tower Hill in 1685, the **Duke of Monmouth**
told the notoriously unreliable executioner Jack Ketch: 'Pray do your
business well. Do not serve me as you did Lord Russell. I have heard
you gave him three or four strokes – if you strike me twice I cannot
promise not to move.' Nevertheless Ketch's first blow caused only a
slight wound, and after his second the duke's head refused to budge.
Eventually the executioner had to call for a knife to complete the
decapitation.

When the headless Duke was taken to the Tower, the authorities
realised that no official portrait of him existed, and so they asked the
royal surgeon to stitch the head back on and tie a white cravat
around the neck to make him look more appealing while the por-
traitist did his work before the body began to decay. The picture now
hangs in the National Portrait Gallery.

II In August 1746 huge crowds gathered on Tower Hill to witness the
executions of the Jacobites **Lord Kilmarnock** and **Lord Balmerino**.
Some climbed on to rooftops and balconies, others even mounted
the rigging of ships in the Thames. When the executioner, John
Thrift, dressed in his white suit, stepped forward to wield the axe he
was so overcome with the excitement of the occasion that he fainted.
Revived with a glass of wine, Thrift burst into tears when he saw
Lord Kilmarnock before him. The farce ended when the condemned
Kilmarnock gave Thrift a purseful of guineas. Then the executioner
dispatched him with one blow.

II The last Tower Hill execution took place in 1747 when **Simon, Lord
Lovat**, was beheaded for supporting the Jacobite attempt to seize the
throne of England.

Tower of London

It has been a palace, prison, mint, armoury, menagerie, and is now a
major tourist attraction, but no London location has witnessed as much
official killing as the Tower. Traitors were put to death in medieval
times on Tower Green within the Tower's precincts, as well as on Tower
Hill, or in later years were shot within the walls. Those murdered in

cold blood here include two kings: Henry VI (May 1471) and the young
Edward V 12 years later. No one has been killed in the Tower – as far as
anyone knows – since Josef Jakobs, a German spy, during the Second
World War.

ACCIDENTAL DEATHS AT THE TOWER

‖ **Elizabeth of York**, daughter of Edward IV, was the last royal to
choose the Tower as a palace. She died here in childbirth in 1502.

‖ In medieval times the Royal Mint was inside the Tower precincts.
When in 1560 a number of Germans invited to London to help with
the refining of some base coins at the Mint fell ill from the arsenic
fumes emitted in the process, they were told to drink out of the skull
of a dead man to recover. Some of the rotting heads being displayed
on spikes on London Bridge were taken down and handed to them
so that they could sup. After drinking, some of the men felt better,
but most of them died soon after nonetheless.

EXECUTIONS AT THE TOWER

‖ After decreeing in the 1280s that all Jews must wear a yellow patch in
the shape of a star attached to their outer clothing, so that they could
be identified in public (an idea that Hitler adopted 650 years later),
Edward I had the heads of all Jewish households arrested. Over 300
were taken to the Tower and executed, while others were murdered
in their homes.

‖ After falling in love with Jane Seymour, Henry VIII had **Anne Boleyn**
arrested on charges of treason, adultery and incest (with her brother
George Boleyn), and put to death in 1536. He decided that the queen
would be executed with a sword, rather than the usual axe, and was
obliged to hire a Frenchman to carry out the act for there was no
English executioner able to manipulate a sword so dextrously. After
the deed was done the head was placed next to the body, which itself
was put in a narrow chest in the Tower's Chapel Royal of St Peter ad
Vincula. The next day Henry married Jane Seymour.

‖ When **Margaret Plantagenet** was taken to the gallows for execution
in 1541 after refusing to support Henry VIII's break with the Roman
Church, she refused to lay her head on the block and ran manically
around the platform screaming that she was no traitor. The executioner ran after her and killed her by hacking away at her head with
his axe.

‖ **Catherine Howard**, the fifth wife of Henry VIII and cousin of Anne
Boleyn, had an affair with Thomas Culpepper amongst others, news
of which vexed the king so much he had her executed in 1542. She
was imprisoned in Hampton Court and taken to the Tower by river,
past the heads of her executed lovers impaled on London Bridge.
Howard asked for a rehearsal the day before her execution to make
sure the executioner didn't botch the job. Her last words were: 'I die
a queen, but would rather die the wife of Culpepper.' When the
Chapel Royal was renovated in 1876 she was re-interred formally.

‖ The 15-year-old **Lady Jane Grey** was executed, six months after taking the throne according to the wishes of her predecessor, Edward
VI, whose will pushed her claims at the expense of his half-sister,
Mary Tudor. Jane lasted as queen only nine days. On 12 February 1554
she watched as her husband, Lord Dudley, was led to his execution,
and continued watching as his headless body was taken away. Later
that day she met the same fate.

‖ **Robert Devereux** was the Earl of Essex, one of Elizabeth I's favourite
courtiers, who after rebelling against her was executed on Tower
Green in February 1601. Some years previously the Queen had given
him the Essex Ring and told him that if he were ever in trouble he
should send it back to her and she would save him. He tried to do
so from the Tower, but either it did not reach the Queen or she
ignored it.

‖ **Carl Friedrick Muller**, a German agent shot on 23 June 1915, was
unmasked when British secret agents uncovered a spy ring operat-
ing from 201 Deptford High Street. After Muller's execution British
Intelligence continued to supply his German paymasters with (false)
information and take his £6 a week salary so as not to arouse the suspicions of his contacts. Having amassed £400 the agents bought a
car which they called 'the Muller' in memory of the executed spy.

MURDERED IN THE TOWER

‖ **Henry VI** is believed to have been murdered in the Wakefield Tower
on 21 May 1471 as he knelt at the altar, stabbed with a dagger wielded
by the Duke of Gloucester, who later became Richard III. Every year
on the anniversary of Henry's death, the provosts of Eton College
and King's College, Cambridge, lay roses and lilies on the altar.

‖ **Edward IV**'s brother, the Duke of Clarence ('false, fleeting, perjured
Clarence', according to Shakespeare), was sent to the Bowyer Tower

Last execution at the Tower

On 15 August 1941 Josef Jakobs, a German spy, became the last individual to be executed at the Tower of London. He was tied to a
Windsor chair, a white lint was pinned on his chest over his heart,
and at 7.12 a.m. he was shot by an eight-man firing squad. Later that
day, the Home Office's leading pathologist, Bernard Spilsbury, conducted a post-mortem and found that one shot had hit Jakobs in the
head, the other seven around the target area. He was buried in an
unmarked grave at Kensal Green.

after being accused of high treason and in 1478 drowned here in a
butt of malmsey wine.

II The Princes in the Tower – **Edward V** and **Richard, Duke of York** –
were put to death here in 1483. The 12-year-old Edward was taken to
the Tower while awaiting his coronation – not unusual in itself given
that the place was occasionally used as a royal residence as well as a
prison – and was joined there by his younger brother, Richard. They
were then removed to the prison section of the complex and after a
few days never seen alive again.

History popularly claims that Richard, Duke of Gloucester, driven
by the desire to smooth through his passage to the throne (as Richard
III), was the culprit, but some experts maintain that there is no proof
the princes were murdered here and that Henry, Earl of Richmond,
who became Henry VII, was just as likely to have been the offender as
Richard.

In 1674 workmen repairing a stairwell in the White Tower found
the skeletons of two boys in an elm chest. They were sent to
Westminster Abbey where they were reburied. In 1933 George V had
the remains exhumed for scientific examination. They were found to
be the bones of two children of around 11 years, and that one of the
skulls had bloodstains consistent with death by suffocation.

Vallance Road

Hughes Mansions

The last Second World War V2 rocket to fall on London destroyed this block of flats on 27 March 1945, killing members of 130 families, nearly all of them Jewish. The Nazis had deliberately targeted Hughes Mansions as it was home to a large number of Jews. William Joyce, the one-time British Union of Fascists propaganda chief, who broadcast for German radio throughout the war, had told his listeners that the Luftwaffe would 'smash' Stepney and that 'those dirty Jews and Cockneys will run like rabbits into their holes'. They had also chosen that specific date for 27 March was the day before the Jewish Passover began. In a cruel irony, the V2s were manufactured by slave labour that included a number of Jews.

Whitechapel Road

The Whitechapel area has long been characterised by poverty, deprivation and violence, much of it directed at the various immigrants – Irish, German, Jewish and more recently Bengali – who have colonised the area over the centuries. The local Jack the Ripper murders, which took place in 1888, are often described as the 'Whitechapel Murders', and George Lusk, chairman of the Whitechapel Vigilance Committee, played an unfortunate role in the drama. He received a gruesome package in the post on 16 October, a few weeks after the Ripper murdered Catherine Eddowes, which contained a rancid kidney and an atrociously spelt note claiming to be sent 'From Hell' that read:

> Mr. Lusk
>> Sir
>>> I send you half the Kidne I took from one women prasarved it for you tother piece I fried and ate it was very nise. I may send you the bloody knif that took it out if you only wate a whil longer.
>> Signed
>>> Catch me when you can
>>>> Mishter Lusk.

Lusk and colleagues took the kidney to the London Hospital, where a doctor ascertained that it was not only human, but part of a left kidney, and therefore could have come from the body of Catherine

Eddowes, for hers was missing from the corpse. The police were making no assumptions and opened a fresh investigation to track down the owner of the missing kidney. As with the rest of their Ripper enquiries, it came to nothing. Interestingly, it is the Lusk letter, which does not mention Jack the Ripper, that many Ripper experts believe to be the most genuine.

Altab Ali Park, *east of Whitechapel Lane*

The park is named after a local Pakistani, Altab Ali, murdered in 1978 by members of the National Front who chased him along Brick Lane and across Whitechapel Road to this spot. It covers the site of the long-demolished St Mary Matfelon church whose white chapel gave the area its name, and whose churchyard contains the Martyrs' Monument, dedicated by the local Bengali community to those killed in Pakistan for refusing to give up their own language and speak Urdu.

Blind Beggar, *No. 337*

The pub is best known for Ronnie Kray's gangland murder of George Cornell on 9 March 1966, but it had long attracted extreme violence. In the 1920s the Blind Beggar was home to a gang of pickpockets responsible for murdering a commercial traveller in the pub. The gang regarded his presence as an intrusion and told him to leave. When he refused, one of their number, Wallis, poked the ferrule of an umbrella through the man's eye. He later died in the London Hospital.

At the inquest it was disclosed that the ferrule had been driven into the eye with such force that a piece of wood from it had embedded itself in the victim's brain. Nevertheless Wallis was acquitted of the murder at the Old Bailey, after which, in celebration, he was hoisted aloft on the shoulders of his supporters, placed in a horse-drawn carriage and cheered back to the pub.

On 9 March 1966 George Cornell, an associate of the south London Richardson gang, walked into the Blind Beggar for a beer after visiting a fellow villain in the London Hospital opposite. The previous evening, during a brawl in a Catford nightclub, one of the Richardson gang had murdered a member of the Krays, so the latter were seeking revenge. When Ronnie Kray heard that a Richardson acolyte had ventured north of the river, he was livid. He left for the pub, tooled up, with an accomplice, Ian Barrie. As they entered, Cornell looked at Kray and exclaimed what were to be his last words: 'Well, look who's here.' Barrie fired a shot into the ceiling, but Kray aimed his gun between Cornell's eyes and shot him dead. The needle of the jukebox, which was playing the Walker Brothers song 'The Sun Ain't Gonna Shine Anymore', stuck on the word 'anymore' and played it repeatedly until it was put out of its misery. Kray was later convicted and sentenced to a minimum of 30 years in jail – mainly for this murder.

London Hospital, *east of New Road*

Emma Smith, the first prostitute to be attacked in 1888, the year of Jack the Ripper, died here on 7 April, four days after a group of men followed her from Whitechapel Church, beat her up, raped and mutilated her, and left her for dead at the corner of Wentworth Street and Osborn Street.

Smith somehow managed to make her way back to her lodgings, where her housemates found her. They rushed her off to the London Hospital – against her will. She was able to describe her attackers, but fell into a coma and died four days later. No one was apprehended, but crime experts believe she was a victim of the Old Nichol gang of villains rather than the Ripper.

A year later Joseph Merrick, the so-called 'Elephant Man', who suffered from neurofibromatosis, a disorder of the lymphatic system that severely disfigured his face, died in the hospital, which still retains his skeleton.

Wellclose Square

What was until the early 20th century the most desirable address in east London, its history tying in with a number of East End mysteries, legends and tragedies, is now a windswept, ravaged site dominated by inhospitable tower blocks and dead ends. Those in charge of rebuilding the capital after the Fire of London created Wellclose Square at the end of the 17th century as an enclave for intellectuals and free-thinkers. In the mid-18th century these included Chaim Jacob Samuel Falk, an expert in Kabbalism known as the 'Ba'al Shem of London', who fled to England penniless in the 1750s after being sentenced to death for sorcery in Westphalia, Germany, but was soon living in extreme comfort in Wellclose Square.

Falk had many detractors including Elias Levy, a prominent member of the Great Synagogue congregation and the previous owner of Falk's Wellclose Square villa. After the two men fell out, Falk supposedly

placed a Kabbalistic curse on Levy, who died a few months later despite having no history of illness. Falk was also deemed to be responsible, from beyond the grave, for the strange death of a former friend, Aaron Goldsmid, who had stumbled across sealed papers among Falk's effects which the latter had instructed to be 'securely treasured up, but never opened, nor looked into'. Not possessing the necessary willpower, Goldsmid opened them after months of psychological torment, removed a piece of paper covered with Kabbalistic figures and hieroglyphs, and died 'mysteriously' later that day.

In 1828 the Brunswick Theatre on Wellclose Square collapsed during a rehearsal, killing a dozen people. That year the Danish church in the middle of the square was let to the Anglo-Catholic movement and became a mission hall, St Saviour's. One night in 1862 the missionaries were woken by a distraught woman. Her daughter had died, and she was frantically seeking help. Two of their number, Joseph Redman and his colleague Father Ignatius of Llanthony, headed to the deceased girl's house armed with a fragment of what they claimed was the True Cross – the Cross of Golgotha on which Jesus Christ was crucified. They laid the relic on the dead girl's breast, and when Father Ignatius proclaimed: 'In the name of Jesus Christ I say unto thee, "arise!", the girl's right hand moved slowly, tracing a cross in the air. The shocked Redman quietly breathed: 'Father, what have you done?', to which Father Ignatius replied: 'I have done nothing, but our Lord has done a great thing indeed.'

Some Jack the Ripper experts believe that the Danish church was where the Duke of Clarence, wayward son of Edward, Prince of Wales and heir to the throne, married a shop girl some time in the 1880s watched by a group of prostitutes who later tried to blackmail the royal family over the scandal. The prostitutes were murdered in revenge, so the story goes, by a team hired by the Duke who tried to make it look like the work of a lone killer – Jack the Ripper.

Christchurch Hall

A demand by Jewish anarchist Benjamin Feigenbaum that God kill him on the spot to prove His existence went unanswered at a public meeting in the hall in autumn 1889. Jewish anarchists had called the meeting to coincide with the Day of Atonement, the holiest day in the Jewish calendar, which they abhorred. The main speaker was Feigenbaum, discoursing on the topic 'Is There A God?'. He thundered: 'What is God? It is a prejudice handed down from father to children. If there is a God, and if he is as Almighty as the clergy claims he is, I give him just two minutes to kill me on the spot so that he may prove his existence!' Two minutes elapsed during which God, being sought for forgiveness at synagogues across the world, failed to respond. Feigenbaum then turned to the room and exclaimed: 'See! There is no God!', to considerable applause and the strains of the 'Marseillaise'.

BETHNAL GREEN, E2

The western edge of Bethnal Green – the Old Nichol – had the worst crime rate in London in the 18th and 19th centuries, and a death rate twice the capital's average. One reason why this was so high was because Old Nichol villains would often bring about the premature deaths of their fellow men. For instance in 1831 two Old Nichol residents, John Bishop and his brother-in-law, Thomas Head, abducted Carlo Ferrari, a local 14-year-old Italian boy who made his living exhibiting performing mice. They forced him to drink rum laced with laudanum, which swiftly brought on unconsciousness, and then drowned him in a nearby well. When the pair tried to sell Ferrari's body to surgeons at King's College, the police were called and arrested them. At that time surgeons were only permitted to dissect bodies of executed criminals. Bishop and Head were found guilty of murder, and were hanged at Newgate in front of a crowd of 30,000. Ironically, their corpses were then sent to the very surgeons they had been dealing with.

E2

Bethnal Green Road

At the eastern end of Bethnal Green Road, at its junction with Cambridge Heath Road, stands the Salmon and Ball pub, long associ-ated with the casual violence that has beset the area. In 1768, in an atmosphere of industrial turmoil, members of the weavers' union met in the tavern. When the authorities raided it there was gunfire, and one of the silk cutters killed a soldier. In turn the soldiers shot at the windows of the rooms where the cutters were assembled, killing two of the customers. A third man had his hat destroyed by a bullet which tore through both sides, just missing his head.

On 6 December 1769 two Irishmen, John Doyle and John Valline, accused on the flimsiest evidence of involvement in these so-called 'Cutters' riots', were arrested and sentenced to be hanged. As the gallows was being erected outside the pub a mob pelted the builders with bricks, tiles and stones. Doyle and Valline were brought before the crowd and the former proclaimed: 'I John Doyle do hereby declare, as my last dying words in the presence of my Almighty God, that I am as innocent of the fact I am now to die for as the child unborn. Let my blood lie to that wicked man who has purchased it with gold, and them notorious wretches who swore it falsely away.' They were hanged.

Bethnal Green station, *junction with Cambridge Heath Road*

One of the worst East End wartime incidents occurred at Bethnal Green tube station on 3 March 1943 when 178 people died on the stairs and 62 were injured during an air-raid warning. The station had been turned into one of east London's main shelters, with room for 5,000 bunk beds, but was accessible only through one narrow entrance which led to a staircase dimly lit by a 25-watt bulb.

An air-raid warning sounded at 8 p.m. and hundreds made for the station. A little while later there was a thunderous noise. Given that bombs didn't make that kind of sound, it had to be landmines, many surmised. In fact it was an anti-aircraft salvo, but some of those at the top of the station panicked, which led to a stampede. At the bottom of the steps a girl stumbled. Someone fell on top of her, and someone else on top of them. Those at the surface feared they wouldn't get in and that they were in danger outside so they pushed, which only increased the crush at the bottom. Soon the entire stairway was a heaving mass of gasping, breathless, dying bodies. Within minutes more than 100 had died, mostly from suffocation. Only muted news of the disaster appeared in the press, and the place and number of casualties were kept secret for fear of giving encouragement to the enemy.

W. English & Son, *No. 464*

W. English is the East End's best-known funeral parlour, for this was the company which conducted the arrangements for all three deceased Kray brothers at the end of the 20th century. Each funeral took place nearby at St Matthew's Church (➤p. 147).

Cheshire Street

Carpenters Arms, *No.73*

Ginger Marks, an East End villain, was shot dead on 2 January 1965 outside this pub, then owned by the Kray twins, by Freddie Foreman, the south London hitman known as 'Brown Bread Fred' ('Don't mess with Brown Bread Fred, or you're dead').

Marks was killed by mistake. Foreman had intended to shoot his companion, Jimmy Evans, a renowned safe-breaker who had shot

Foreman's brother. Knowing that Evans and some fellow villains were on their way to rob a jeweller's in the East End, Foreman drove around looking for them. Eventually he spotted the group walking along Cheshire Street. He drove up in his Jaguar, leaned out of the window and aimed his .38 revolver. Evans grabbed Ginger Marks and used him as a human shield to protect himself from Foreman's bullets. Marks died instantly, while Evans and the others ran off.

Freddie Foreman now had to get rid of a dead body – and not the right dead body either. He did so, but no one knows for certain how. Some believe he threw Marks into the Thames near Staines, the legs encased in concrete, others that he dumped Marks in a gravel pit in Kent. There were also rumours that Marks had been dumped in a cement-mixer and then into the concrete piers holding up Hammersmith flyover. One plausible theory is that a compliant undertaker put the corpse into an already filled coffin, as in the Sherlock Holmes story 'The Disappearance of Lady Frances Carfax'.

The police knew that somebody – they didn't know who at first – had been shot and that the victim had been shot in the stomach, for they found a potato chip embedded in the wall of the pub. It took them some time to connect the shooting with the simultaneous disappearance of Ginger Marks. In his book *Respect*, Foreman confessed to the murder, attributing his violent behaviour to the 'respect' that he craved 'at any cost'. He was however acquitted of the crime and told reporters that his only regret about the affair is that he 'didn't shoot the two of them that night'.

St Matthew's Row

St Matthew

In the 18th century the church graveyard was at the mercy of resurrectionists commissioned by the local hospitals, in particular the gang led by Ben Crouch, which used to pay gravediggers to hand them a fresh body as soon as mourners had left the graveside. In 1754 a watch house was built at the corner of St Matthew's Row and Wood Close, and a reward of two guineas paid to anybody preventing the theft of a corpse.

The funerals of the Kray twins, Ronnie (29 March 1995) and Reggie (11 October 2000), and in between of their elder brother, Charlie (19 April 2000), were all held here. Tens of thousands lined the streets around the church for Ronnie Kray, London's best-attended funeral since the death of Winston Churchill 30 years previously.

Kray's coffin, enclosed in a glass-sided hearse, carried by six black-plumed horses florally decorated with the words 'Ron' and 'Colonel', was at the head of a procession of 25 limousines. Among the mourners were the gangsters Frankie Fraser and Freddie Foreman (☛p. 146), and, of course, Reggie Kray, who had been allowed out of jail where he was serving time for the twins' escapades, and was handcuffed to a woman officer.

Charlie Kray, the twins' older brother, died of heart trouble on 4 April 2000 while serving a 12-year prison sentence for drug smuggling. His funeral was a much less ostentatious affair than Ronnie's. Nevertheless thousands of people crowded the streets to watch the cortège make its way to St Matthew's. The most striking sight was the flowers in the shape of a broken heart which Charlie's girlfriend Diane Buffini had sent. The card read: 'To my darling Charlie, with my eyes wide open. Am I dreaming, can it be time?' Again Reggie Kray, now the last surviving brother, was there, this time handcuffed to a female prison warder.

For the funeral of Reggie Kray in October 2000 there were fewer spectators lining Bethnal Green Road, and for the first time a Kray

funeral had no living Kray gangster in attendance. Six black-plumed horses carried the coffin from the undertakers to St Matthew's Church ahead of 18 limousines carrying family and friends. The number of policemen in attendance was augmented by some 400 'security' men in long leather jackets or Crombies, wearing red armbands and lapel badges emblazoned 'RKF' (Reg Kray Funeral). After the service the coffin was carried out of the church to the strains of Frank Sinatra's 'My Way'.

BOW, E3

The original stone bridge across the River Lea separating the area from Essex was bow-shaped. Bow developed through the river's industries, particularly tanning, which involved boiling blood for making dye, and fulling in which woollen cloth was pounded with water and fullers earth to clean and thicken it.

Bow Road

Bow station (19th century), *opposite Tomlin's Grove*

Passengers boarding a train at the station on 9 July 1864 found one carriage empty save for a black bag, a walking stick, a hat and a huge pool of blood. The blood was that of one Thomas Briggs, who had just become the first individual to be murdered on a railway. The 70-year-old Briggs had taken a train on the new line that went from Fenchurch Street to Hackney Wick and found himself in a carriage with Franz Muller, a 25-year-old German tailor. Muller killed Briggs and threw his body on the line. He also stole Briggs's watch, which he later sold to raise funds for buying a ticket to America.

Police traced the chain that once linked the watch to a Cheapside jeweller, John Death [*sic*], who remembered the German customer, and further enquiries led to a London address. Muller had fled, but a fellow tenant revealed that the German had taken a passenger ship headed for New York. Police rushed to Southampton and boarded a faster ship, which beat Muller's by two weeks. When the German arrived, they searched his luggage and found the gold watch and Briggs's hat, which the killer had mistakenly snatched up instead of his own as he fled the carriage. Muller was hanged on 14 November 1864.

Bow Flyover, *at the River Lea*

Confusion reigns over whose body parts are buried in the concrete supports of the flyover, disposed of there by members of the Krays' gang when it was being built in the 1960s. One theory says they belong to Ginger Marks, a minor jewel thief who was accidentally killed by Freddie Foreman outside the Carpenters Arms in 1965 (p. 146). But they are more likely to be those of Frank 'The Mad Axeman' Mitchell, a violent but genial giant whom the Kray twins sprang from Dartmoor prison in 1966 and then killed when his presence became a threat to their safety (p. 159). Ronnie Kray's funeral cortège in 1995 made a detour to cross the river Lea here, presumably to point out the flyover's nefarious associations, on its way to Chingford Cemetery where Kray was to be buried.

Grove Road

The first German V1 rocket fell on Grove Road, at 4.25 a.m. on 13 June 1944, killing six people. It was one of ten V1s – Vergeltungswaffe guided missiles – launched in that first wave, of which five crashed at once, one fell in the Channel, and three in Kent, causing little damage. Only one got through – the one that landed on Grove Road – which some described as 'looking like a burning enemy aircraft crossing the sky with a sword of flame emanating from its tail'.

It hit the railway bridge which carries the Great Eastern Railway across Grove Road. Nearby Kathleen Williams was lying in bed in her sister's house. She later recalled hearing a plane above and the noise of the engine suddenly cut out. The next second, she explained: 'I could see the house falling in on me.' Williams lay under the rubble for three hours but survived. The couple who lived upstairs weren't so lucky: 'They got killed outright, they had their head blown off.'

Southern Grove

Tower Hamlets Cemetery

A company of local merchants including a corn merchant, a ship owner, and a timber merchant, and the Lord Mayor of London opened what was originally the City of London and Tower Hamlets Cemetery in 1841. It soon became the most working class of London graveyards, aimed at those who could not afford a plot and funeral and had to make do with a pauper's grave. By the 1890s nearly a quarter of a million people had been interred here, but the cemetery soon became overcrowded and neglected. The GLC bought Tower Hamlets in 1966 and closed it down, intending to the turn the land into a public park, but was dissuaded by public opposition.

Graves include those of Alex Hurley, the comedian married to Marie Lloyd, who sang 'The Lambeth Walk', and Alfred Linnell who died in the 'Bloody Sunday' demonstration at Trafalgar Square in 1887. The procession from the Soho undertaker's which dealt with the late Linnell was so long that it took three-quarters of an hour to pass any one spot. By the time the throng reached the cemetery it was raining and getting dark. As *The Times* wrote, not too sympathetically, 'the crowd which sprawled over the tombs, and graves and monuments made no pretence of being animated by any feeling of respect. In the darkness which was illuminated for a few seconds now and then fitfully by matches being struck, evidently by smokers, the Burial Service of the Church of England was read, but it was heard by few for the others were talking more or less loudly.' After the band finished the 'Dead March' from *Saul* the polymath William Morris gave a eulogy at the graveside.

CHINGFORD, E4

The area began as a hamlet by the River Lea and has no notable features other than its cemetery.

Old Church Road

Chingford Mount Cemetery

The entire Kray gangster family is buried in this cemetery, which was developed by the Abney Park company. Alongside Ronnie (d. 1995) and Reggie (d. 2000) is the latter's wife, Frances, who died of a drug overdose in 1967 when she was only in her 20s.

Frances Kray was buried in her wedding dress, a possibly unsuitable choice as it is unlikely the marriage was consummated. Her death shattered Reggie who declared: 'We had the wedding of the year and I made sure we had the funeral of the year.' He also asked an associate, Albert Donoghue, to make a note of all those who had not sent flowers 'for future reference'. When visiting the grave Reggie would often become maudlin, and once, spotting a robin nearby claimed: 'It's Frances reincarnated as a bird.'

FOREST GATE, E7

With more room in the suburbs than in the nearby East End as London grew during the 19th century, cemeteries were soon being opened. There are three in Forest Gate: Manor Park, West Ham and Woodgrange Park.

Cemetery Road

West Ham Cemetery

Elizabeth Stride, the third 'official' victim of Jack the Ripper, is buried at West Ham in a grave without a headstone or marker.

The adjacent walled-off – open only by arrangement – Jewish Cemetery, west of the main burial ground, , was created after Brady Street Cemetery in the East End became full. It contains the elaborate circular Rothschild mausoleum designed by Matthew Digby Wyatt for

Evelina de Rothschild, who died in childbirth in 1866. Her husband, Ferdinand de Rothschild, spared no expense on the structure and had Wyatt carve the initials "E R" into the monument.

Also buried here is Sir David Salomons, who in 1851 became the first Jew to speak in Parliament. Like Lionel de Rothschild he refused to take the oath 'on the true faith of a Christian', but broke the rules by speaking regardless and was ejected by the Sergeant-at-Arms.

In 2005 vandals desecrated the cemetery, defacing headstones with swastikas and damaging the door of the Rothschild mausoleum with an iron bar.

Romford Road

Woodgrange Park Cemetery

Newham council sold off some of the site for new houses in 2000. This led to much debate about the morality of razing the graves of those killed in the Blitz. A 20-foot pit had been dug here to accommodate the many local victims.

Sebert Road

Manor Park Cemetery

Annie Chapman, the Ripper's second victim, was murdered on
Hanbury Street, Spitalfields in 1888 (p. 127) and buried here 12 feet
down in a communal public grave which has since been re-used.

The cemetery is the Small Faces' 'Itchycoo Park' in the song of that
name.

HOMERTON, E9

Barely separable from Hackney, Homerton developed from the late Middle Ages through industries such as gunpowder manufacturing, paint production and brick-making.

Lauriston Road

Royal Inn On The Park

Gangster Jimmy Moody was shot dead by an unknown gunman while drinking a pint of bitter in the Royal on 1 June 1993. A member of the powerful south London Richardson gang, Moody had been on the run for over a decade since escaping from Brixton Prison. He was shot probably in revenge for a gangland hit he had carried out a few months previously.

Victoria Park Road

Harry Stanley was shot dead by police on Victoria Park Road while walking home from the pub on 22 September 1999. Police suspected he was an Irish terrorist armed with a sawn-off shotgun. In reality he was a 46-year-old decorator with no criminal associations, carrying a mahogany coffee-table leg in a bag. Stanley was targeted only because a worried pub-goer had phoned the police. When they accosted Stanley he held the bag up to them, presumably to explain it was only a chair-leg, but was gunned down instantly. The Crown Prosecution Service chose not to prosecute the officers involved on the grounds of 'insufficient evidence', but an inquest in 2004 concluded that Stanley had been unlawfully killed by two officers, Constable Kevin Fagan and Inspector Neil Sharman. However the jury's verdict was later quashed by a High Court judge. The Crown Prosecution Service ruled out prosecuting the two officers for murder.

MANOR PARK, E12

A dreary suburb near Ilford with little interesting history but containing one of Europe's largest cemeteries.

Aldersbrook Road

City of London Cemetery
The cemetery opened in June 1856 on land that had been Aldersbrook Farm, and was meant to have its own railway station, though that was cancelled due to lack of funds. The City of London does however contain seven miles of curving paths and chestnut-lined avenues, Gothic chapels, mausoleums and a catacomb valley. More than half a million bodies have been buried here including some of those associated with East End tragedies. There are two Jack the Ripper victims – Mary Ann Nichols (☞p. 124) and Catherine Eddowes (☞p. 129), the latter's name being wrongly spelt as 'Eddows' – and the policemen Charles Tucker and Robert Bentley, shot dead during the Houndsditch jewel robbery of December 1910 (☞p. 18).

POPLAR/ISLE OF DOGS, E14

Now home to the dazzle and wealth of the Canary Wharf skyscrapers, near some of East London's bleakest council estates, Poplar is dominated by the Isle of Dogs, where gibbets for hanging criminals in public were dotted in medieval times.

Dolphin Lane

Dolphin House, No. 13
John Childs conducted a spate of gruesome killings in this block in the 1970s as part of his 'Dial H for Murder' sting, which even offered its services to the mother of the fugitive peer Lord Lucan, insisting it would 'do' anyone who tried to harm or even find the missing peer.

His first victim was Terry Eve, a business partner, to whom he wanted to teach a lesson. Childs and an associate bought a large butcher's mincing machine, went to Eve's factory and strangled him with a piece of rope. Childs put the body in his Jaguar and took it to Dolphin House, where he fed it into the machine. When it jammed he tried to dispose of the rest of the flesh down the lavatory. That also proved a problem, so he chopped up the remains and burned bit by bit in the flat over the next 24 hours.

Next Childs targeted a business associate, Fred Sherwood, who ran a nursing home in Herne Bay. On 31 July 1978 he pretended to be interested in buying Sherwood's car, lured him to a bungalow and hit him with a hammer. Sherwood was finished off not by Childs, but by an associate, Harry 'Big H' MacKenny, the 'H' of 'Dial H for Murder', the courts later heard.

Next Childs and MacKenny murdered a father and son at their Dagenham factory. But forensic scientists wouldn't accept that they spent 24 hours incinerating the bodies in their living-room grate, and to test the story they got an 11-stone pig and burned it. It took them 13 hours. Childs received six life sentences, and in 1998 confessed to five more killings. However, in 2003 MacKenny appealed against his convictions and won. He became the first prisoner serving a whole life tariff to have his conviction quashed, and sought compensation.

Some worrying circumstances surrounding Eve's 'murder' then came out. No murder weapon or corroborating witnesses had been found. There was no forensic evidence. In fact Childs's testimony was the prosecution's sole evidence that *anybody* had been murdered. And as for Eve, there was no body for he had not been killed. He was alive for years after his 'murder', living in west London under an assumed name.

West India Dock Road

Railway Tavern/'Charlie Brown's'

The funeral of the tavern's landlord, Charlie Brown, in 1932 was London's best attended of the 20th century until that of Winston Churchill in 1965. Thousands came to pay their respects to Brown, who ran one of the most unusual pubs in the capital, every corner stuffed with a collection of eccentric curiosities gathered from around the world. There was a half-fish half-baby mummy, a two-headed calf, poisoned arrows, opium pipes, busts, statues, totems and trinkets. After his death the collection went to the pub opposite (also now demolished), but after a family row it was mostly lost.

STRATFORD/WEST HAM, E15

More than 400 people were killed on Saturday 7 September 1940, the first day of the Second World War Blitz, when wave after wave of bombers targeted the area the Germans called '*Zielraum*': the loop of the Thames around the Isle of Dogs.

The first bombs began to fall in the early afternoon, and as thousands fled through the debris their clothes were ripped off them in the compression that followed the explosions. When the bombers returned after dusk, they were guided back by the fires that blazed along the Thames, and dropped another 300 tons of explosives and thousands of small incendiary bombs. The river, which provided the firemen with vast amounts of water, prevented the flames spreading. In this wave of bombing 430 people died, many found lying in their gardens or in the street.

VICTORIA DOCKS, E16

Many of London's most noxious industries were based here in Silvertown, just outside the jurisdiction of the more stringent metropolitan regulations in the 20th century. Factories made caustic soda, sulphuric acid, manure, and petrol, and the workers lived nearby in tightly packed terraced houses. The dangerous closeness of plant and people resulted in a tragedy in 1917 that became known as the 'Silvertown Explosion'.

Barking Road

No. 206a

The Krays' callous disregard for human life becomes apparent in the story of how they disposed of Frank 'The Mad Axeman' Mitchell. A giant psychopathic simpleton, Mitchell was in prison at Dartmoor until the Krays, needing a new henchman, decided to spring him a few weeks before Christmas 1966. They helped Mitchell flee and took him from Devon to London, while reports of his escape dominated the news, and secreted him in a hideaway at 206a Barking Road, Canning Town.

Mitchell didn't take too well to being treated like a caged animal, especially given that he expected to be paraded round the West End's leading nightspots and fêted by the Krays as an underworld hero. Nor was he impresed by the call girl brought in to service him. With the police on his trail and the tabloids describing him as 'Britain's most wanted man', he was struck by cabin fever, threatening to shoot the Krays if he wasn't allowed out.

At that point Ronnie Kray decided Mitchell had to be eliminated. On Christmas Eve the Krays' henchmen bundled the Mad Axeman into a van and shot him dead as it was being driven along Barking Road. They then dumped Mitchell's body, possibly in the sea off Newhaven or in the foundations of Bow flyover, which was being built.

Butcher Road

Ronan Point

The worst housing disaster in London's history occurred on 16 May 1968 when a section of the newly built 22-storey Ronan Point tower block

collapsed, killing three people. At 5.45 in the morning Ivy Hodge, a tenant in an 18th floor flat, struck a match by her cooker and accidentally caused an explosion that blew out the panels on the side of the building, which collapsed like a pack of cards. Remarkably, Mrs Hodge survived. Ronan Point was rebuilt but demolished in 1986.

Hallsville Road

A tragic Second World War incident took place at Hallsville Road school during the first wave of the Blitz in September 1940. Coaches meant to arrive at the school to take hundreds of mothers and their children away from the bombed East End to countryside towns failed to turn up. There was increasing panic and the children who were growing impatient begged to be allowed to play in the crater a bomb had opened in the playground. There were over a hundred still taking refuge when bombs dropped on the building at 3.45 a.m. the next day, killing nearly everyone. The children who had been playing in the crater the day before were now buried in it. It later transpired that the coaches had mistakenly gone to Camden Town, ten miles away, instead of Canning Town.

Thames Road

London's biggest ever blast killed 73 people on 19 January 1917 in what became known as the 'Silvertown Explosion'. Just before 7 a.m. 50 tons of high explosives detonated at the Brunner Mond works, recently adapted for the production of TNT for the war. Part of the factory was instantly destroyed, as were several nearby buildings and streets. A gas holder exploded on the other side of the river and electric lights flickered across London. The blast was heard as far away as Cambridge.

It took three days for the story to hit the censored newspapers, and even then reports merely stated that a 'munitions factory in the neighbourhood of London' had exploded with 'considerable loss of life and damage to property'. The inquiry that followed stated that Silvertown, despite its high concentration of noxious industries, was unsuitable for a TNT plant, and condemned Brunner, Mond & Co. for negligence. The report remained secret until the 1950s.

E16

CHAPTER 7

North London

ANGEL/ISLINGTON, N1

One of the most fashionable addresses in London at the end of the 20th century, thanks to its associations with New Labour, Islington has seen its exclusiveness diminish in the 21st century with the opening of the N1 shopping centre and the decline of the Camden Passage antiques market.

Eagle Wharf Road

A grimy street bordering Regent's Canal, Eagle Wharf Road was built on the site of Hogsden Fields, where the Elizabethan playwright Ben Jonson killed the actor Gabriel Spenser in a duel on 22 September 1598. Jonson was imprisoned in Newgate, and expected to be hanged, but was saved following his conversion to the Church of Rome, which allowed him to escape the gallows on the grounds of 'benefit of clergy' – that he could read the Bible in Latin. In prison Jonson's left thumb was branded with the letter 'M' (for murderer). He remained a Catholic for 12 years.

Euston Road

King's Cross station

Following George V's death at Sandringham in January 1936 his coffin
was watched over by the estate gamekeepers and then taken by train to
King's Cross where the Imperial Crown was fixed to it. As the funeral
cortège made its way through London the new king, Edward VIII,
noticed something bright 'dancing along the pavement'. It was the
Maltese Cross, which had fallen from the crown. It was retrieved.

Thirty-one people died in King's Cross underground station on
18 November 1987 when fire ripped through the concourse at half
past seven in the evening. The blaze, which began in a machine room
beneath a wooden escalator, may have been started by a discarded match
and took more than two hours to get under control. Following the
King's Cross tragedy smokers were banned from lighting up anywhere
in the station. The last victim to be indentified – in January 2004 –was
Alexander Fallon; he had been sleeping rough in London and had not
been reported as missing.

In an eerie premonition, a few months before the fire the Pet Shop
Boys released the song 'King's Cross', which contains the verse:

> Only last night I found myself lost
> By the station called King's Cross
> Dead and wounded on either side
> You know it's only a matter of time.

Noel Road

Joe Orton's death place (1967), *Flat 4, No. 25*

The *Entertaining Mr Sloane* playwright was beaten to death with a hammer on 9 August 1967 by his lover, Kenneth Halliwell, in the flat the
couple shared. An hour or so after the murder a chauffeur knocked to
take Orton to a TV studio and on getting no response summoned help.
A party of men broke in. The first body they found was not Orton's but
Halliwell's. He had committed suicide by swallowing 22 Nembutal pills
after killing the playwright.

Upper Street

Old Pied Bull, *No. 100*

During the 1665 bubonic plague outbreak that killed nearly 100,000 Londoners one man close to death fled from his house on Aldersgate Street in the City, which had been boarded up to stop the infection spreading, and took lodgings here overnight, hoping to escape into the countryside the next morning. When he failed to come down for breakfast, staff broke down the door of his room and found him stretched out on the bed, dead, stiff and cold, his clothes pulled off, his jaw dropped and, according to Daniel Defoe in *A Journal of the Plague Year*, 'his eyes open in a most frightful posture, the rug of his bed being grasped hard in one of his hands'. At that time the epidemic hadn't reached Islington, but within a week 14 locals were dead from the plague.

EAST FINCHLEY, N2

An early 20th-century suburb, to the north-east of Golders Green, East Finchley stands on land that was too hilly to be of interest to the Romans or Saxons, but was where the Bishops of London established a hunting park of over 1,000 acres in the 13th century. The coming of the railway in the mid-19th century rendered the northern heights ripe for development, including the building of huge cemeteries. In the late 1920s the North Circular Road was cut through, bringing further suburban sprawl.

East End Road

St Marylebone Cemetery

'A retired and rural spot', as the *Builder* described it in 1854, before which the site was farmland, St Marylebone is easily identifiable by its large Gothic lodge and decorated Gothic chapel. The cemetery has catered mostly for the wealthy of Finchley and Hampstead. One of its most remarkable sights is the massive grey and pink tomb of the Australian colonist Thomas Skarratt Hall (d. 1903), modelled on Napoleon's in Paris.

BURIED AT ST MARYLEBONE

II **Quintin Hogg** (d. 1903) was an Eton-educated philanthropist who
founded the first 'ragged school' to help the poor in Of Alley, off the
Strand, and later established The Polytechnic (now the University of
Westminster) near Oxford Circus. He also captained Scotland in
their early football internationals.

II **Lord Northcliffe** (d. 1922), the newspaper magnate born Alfred
Harmsworth who at one time owned *The Times*, *Daily Mail* and *Daily
Mirror*, died in dramatic circumstances on the roof of Carlton
Gardens, Westminster (➨p. 95).

II **Austen Chamberlain** (d. 1937) was one of the few Tory party leaders of
the modern era not to become prime minister.

II Police constable **Keith Blakelock** (d. 1985) was the officer murdered
in gruesome circumstances during the 1985 Broadwater Farm riots
(➨p. 188).

II **Kenneth Williams** (d. 1988) the comic legend, suffered from depression throughout his life and died from an overdose of barbiturates.
The inquest recorded an open verdict. (His father had committed
suicide by drinking a bottle of disinfectant in 1962.)

Finchley High Road

St Pancras and Islington Cemetery

London's first municipal cemetery, its vast spaces filled with a variety
of mature trees, was formed from the Horseshoe Farm in 1852 and
takes up 180 acres of land by what is now the North Circular Road. Ford
Madox Brown (d. 1893), the Pre-Raphaelite painter, and Henry Croft
(d. 1930), the original pearly king, are among those buried here. The
cemetery's most remarkable feature is the Mond mausoleum, a granite
and stone classical memorial created for Ludwig Mond, a philanthropic
German industrialist.

Winnington Road

Peter Rachman's address (1959–62), *Bishopstone*

When Peter Rachman, the 1950s slum landlord, died suddenly of a
heart attack in November 1962 his luxury mansion, Bishopstone, was
besieged by creditors, but most of them came away with nothing,
thanks to his refusal to commit his business dealings to paper.
Rumours then abounded that Rachman hadn't died, but that his body
had been switched at Edgware General Hospital so that he could lie

low while his affairs were sorted out. He never reappeared. In July 1963 burglars disguised as police officers raided Bishopstone and made off with Rachman's jewellery. Rachman has acquired the dubious notoriety of having a word – 'Rachmanism' – posthumously coined from his name to describe the exploitation and intimidation of tenants by an unscrupulous landlord.

HIGHGATE, N6

A picturesque suburb occupying a lofty position at the edge of Hampstead Heath which is best known for the much-visited Highgate Cemetery, burial place of Karl Marx.

South Grove

Francis Bacon, science pioneer, philosopher and early 17th-century Lord Chancellor, died in March 1626 from pneumonia at Arundel House (since replaced by the Old Hall at No. 17), which he caught after stuffing a chicken with snow as part of a refrigeration experiment on Highgate's Pond Street.

St Michael's

The church is built on the site of the banqueting hall of Arundel House (see above) and contains the tomb of the poet Samuel Taylor Coleridge, which was moved here from Highgate School chapel in 1961. A stone on the floor of the nave is inscribed with the epitaph the poet himself wrote:

> *Stop Christian passer-by!*
> *Stop child of God*
> *And read with gentle breast.*
> *Beneath this sod*
> *A Poet lies or that which once seemed he*
> *O lift one thought in prayer for S-T-C-*
> *That he who many a year with toil of breath*
> *Found death in life may here find life in Death!*
> *Mercy for praise to be forgiven for Fame*
> *He ask'd and hoped through Christ*
> *Do then the same!*

Swain's Lane

Highgate Cemetery

London's most famous cemetery – resting place of Karl Marx, George Eliot and Michael Faraday – features huge catacombs, Egyptian columns, stone angels, and ivy-covered vaults in one of the capital's wildest settings, a hillside site on the edge of Highgate. The cemetery was designed by Stephen Geary and built in the 1830s by the London Cemetery Company over the garden and park of [g]Ashurst House, in what was then part of the Forest of Middlesex.

Highgate opened in 1839 with the burial of Elizabeth Jackson of Golden Square in the West End. There were 204 interments in that first year, and it soon became a fashionable place for burials. The wealthy commissioned some of the grandest Gothic and romantic effects in the capital, particularly the Circle of Lebanon, the centrepiece of the western section, with its ring of excavated vaults surrounding a huge cedar tree considerably older than the cemetery. Nearby is the Gothic gloom of the Egyptian Avenue and the huge Julius Beer mausoleum, the businessman's revenge on a society that refused to take him seriously. In 1854 the cemetery company bought an adjacent site to the east, such was the demand, and a tunnel was cut through to link the two sites enabling coffins to be transferred discreetly.

The cemetery fell into decline during and after the two World Wars but, over the past decades, Friends of Highgate Cemetery Trust have rescued and revived the area. Highgate is once again an active burial ground, but access for visitors to the Western cemetery is limited to guided tours. The sensitive conservation of the Grade II*-listed park means Highgate has retained its romantic and historic appeal. Mark Girouard describes Highgate in *Country Life* as a 'vast army of Victorian merchants, officers, widows and judges gently [crumbling] into anonymity beneath ivy and saplings and lushly sinister mare's tails'.

BURIED AT HIGHGATE

A survey of Highgate once recorded at least 850 notable people buried within, most of whom appear in the *Dictionary of National Biography*. These include six Lord Mayors of London, 48 Fellows of the Royal Society and the founders of well-known firms such as Maples and Foyles, alongside the very famous, such as Karl Marx.

‖ The death of **Elizabeth Siddal** in 1862 from laudanum poisoning left her husband, the poet and artist Dante Gabriel Rossetti, so grief-stricken that he buried a book of new poems in her grave. Seven years of poverty forced on Rossetti the need to publish the poems, and he sought permission from the authorities to dig up the coffin to extract the book. The exhumation was conducted at night by the

light of a great bonfire. Unfortunately the pages had become entangled in Siddal's red-gold hair, which had continued to grow wildly after death. After being carefully removed, each page had to be soaked with disinfectant before the book could be published.

‖ **Thomas Druce** (d. 1864) was a furniture salesman on Baker Street who died of heart failure at the age of 71 and was buried in the family vault at Highgate. There was no reason to suspect anything unusual until 32 years later, when his daughter-in-law, Anna Maria Druce, astounded London by claiming Druce had never existed – that he was the alter ego of the wealthy and eccentric late 5th Duke of Portland.

The Duke had allegedly created the shopkeeper persona so that he could lead an ordinary life whenever he wished, travelling between his house and Druce's Marylebone shop via a tunnel that linked the two premises. Druce's daughter-in-law maintained that the coffin would be empty of a body and filled with lead weights, and that consequently the Duke's fortune should go to her.

A lengthy court case ensued, and Anna's son, G. H. Druce, continued the campaign after his mother's death. In 1907 a judge ordered the authorities to open the coffin and settle the matter. Unsurprisingly, it was found to contain the body of Thomas Druce.

‖ One of the best publicised funerals of the mid-Victorian period was that of the fighter **Tom Sayers** in 1865. At the head of the cortège of mourners was a brown dog occupying its own mail-phaeton, its collar bound in black crape, and along the route of the procession tavern landlords raised flags and held parties.

‖ The mausoleum of **Julius Beer** (d. 1880), proprietor of the *Observer*, who died of apoplexy in his early 40s, is one of the cemetery's most remarkable sights. It was designed by J. Oldrid Scott in the style of the tomb of the Greek king Mausolus at Halicarnassus, one of the seven wonders of the world, and stands on the highest point of the western section. Inside, a marble angel stoops to kiss a life-sized child whose face was modelled on the death mask of Beer's own daughter.

‖ **George Eliot** (d. 1880), the great Victorian novelist, born Mary Ann Evans, could not be buried in Poets' Corner, because she was an agnostic, and so was interred at Highgate instead.

‖ **Karl Marx** (d. 1884) – The founder of communism, born Jewish, was buried in unconsecrated ground. His grave, marked with a monument that reads 'Workers of All Lands Unite', is one of the most visited in Highgate. On the first anniversary of his death some 3,000 supporters gathered, including the designer and campaigner

William Morris, who was himself unable to get near to the grave and had to pay his respects at a nearby patch of ground, where the crowd sang 'The Internationale'. Every 14 March, the day Marx died, the Marx Memorial Library holds a memorial by the grave.

|| The novelist **Marguerite Radclyffe Hall** who died in 1943, earned instant notoriety after her novel The Well of Loneliness (1928) was lambasted by the critics for its promotion of 'sexual inversion' – lesbianism. Her epitaph, 'And if God choose, I shall but love thee better after Death', was chosen by a girlfriend, Una Troubridge, who had hoped to be buried alongside Radclyffe Hall but died in Rome and was never returned to Britain.

|| **Douglas Adams**, the creator of The Hitch-Hikers' Guide to the Galaxy, died suddenly in May 2001 in California. A year later his ashes were buried at Highgate.

|| In 2006 the former Russian spy **Alexander Litvinenko**, was poisoned at a hotel in the West End (➤p. 76) and died an agonising death at University College Hospital (➤p. 44). His burial service at Highgate that December was interrupted by a Muslim imam who claimed that Litvinenko had converted to Islam just before he died. His wife, however, maintained that her husband had wanted a non-denominational service.

The Grove

Samuel Taylor Coleridge death place (1834), No. 3

Samuel Taylor Coleridge, the poet whose 'Kubla Khan' and 'Rime of
the Ancient Mariner' are among the best-known poems in the English
language, moved to Highgate when his fortunes were at a low ebb in
1823 and he was trying to cure himself of his addiction to laudanum.
But his habit actually increased, and he rarely left the house except to
sit occasionally on Highgate Hill looking down on the smoke of
London. He died here in 1834.

Waterlow Road

'Brides in the Bath' murder place, No. 14

When Margaret Lloyd died in her bath at 14 Bismark (now Waterlow)
Road in Highgate in December 1914, it appeared to be a tragic accident
– if rather unusual. However, Lloyd's obituary was spotted by the relative of another woman who had died in similar circumstances.
Suspicions aroused, the relative went to the police. It soon came to light
that the other victim's husband – George Joseph Smith – was also the
husband of the Bismark Road victim, masquerading under the name
John Lloyd. He was also Oliver George Love, Charles Oliver James and
Henry Williams – married nine times and responsible, it turned out, for
murdering several of his wives in the bath as well as robbing each one
of her money or life insurance.

   On the afternoon of 18 December 1914 Lloyd had encouraged his
wife to visit her solicitor in Islington to make a will in his favour. Later
that evening he mentioned to the owner of the Bismark Road house
that he was going out to buy tomatoes for his wife's supper while she
took a bath. According to his story, when he returned he had been
unable to gain a response from his wife in the bathroom and had broken down the door, to find her dead. The inquest recorded a verdict of
accidental death. At the funeral Lloyd told the undertaker: 'I don't want
any walking, get it over as quick as you can.'

   Once suspicion about Mrs Lloyd's demise was aroused the leading
pathologist of the 20th century, Bernard Spilsbury, persuaded several
young women to dress in bathing suits and sit in water-filled bathtubs
while a detective tried to 'drown' them. Repeated failures suggested
that it was not possible for someone to drown in this way, until one

member of the investigating team suggested that Lloyd had killed the women by grabbing their feet and pulling so that the head quickly hit the water inducing helplessness, which made drowning easier. They tried this on one of the volunteers who soon became unconscious. Smith's lawyer claimed that his client had induced the women to kill themselves by 'hypnotic suggestion'. Nevertheless he was convicted and executed in 1915.

HOLLOWAY, N7, N19

Holloway was built on land owned in medieval times by the Dean of St Paul's, which later passed to St John's Priory and St Mary's Nunnery in Clerkenwell. The name first appeared in the 15th century to describe the muddy hollow way – what is now Holloway Road, its main thoroughfare – and the area grew with the arrival of the railways in the mid-19th century. As the home of two major London prisons – Holloway and Pentonville – it has witnessed a large number of official executions.

Caledonian Road

Pentonville Prison, *at Wheelwright Street*

Pentonville was built in 1842 as a model prison for men between 18 and 35. Prisoners were initially kept in solitary confinement in light, airy cells, which was an improvement on the overcrowding of traditional prisons, even though inmates could be sent to the basement if they made contact with others.

A number of Britain's most famous prisoners have been among the 120 executed at Pentonville on a gallows beam brought from Newgate, including Dr Crippen and John Christie. Pentonville was also used as a training centre for new hangmen. They used a dummy, 'Old Bill', on which they would practise putting on the hood and noose, then taking out the safety pin and pushing the lever for the drop until they became proficient.

HANGINGS AT PENTONVILLE

‖ The poisoner **Dr Crippen** was hanged at Pentonville in 1910 a few months after being convicted of murdering his wife in their north London flat. Crippen was visited shortly before his execution by the librettist W. S. Gilbert, researching what became his final play, *The Hooligan*.

‖ **Sir Roger Casement**, the Irish patriot who was indicted for treason during the First World War after spying for the Germans, was hanged here in August 1916. The prison authorities threw the corpse into a pit which they covered with quicklime – a treatment they didn't mete out to most victims. Casement's body was exhumed from the prison cemetery in 1965 and reburied in Dublin.

‖ Eighteen-year-old **Henry Jacoby**, convicted of murdering an elderly woman in her hotel room, was so unconcerned about his impending doom he played cricket with one of the warders in the exercise yard on the afternoon before his execution in 1922.

‖ During the Second World War six German spies were hanged at Pentonville for treachery. In October 1946, a year after the war ended, five Germans were executed here for the murder of a fellow prisoner, Wolfgang Rosterg, a German anti-Nazi who had been sent to the camp for SS officers in Wiltshire by mistake and revealed the men's escape plan to the authorities. The foiled PoWs had beaten him up in the toilets and hanged him. They were tried before a military tribunal at the 'Cage' – London's only German PoW camp – on

---

Albert Pierrepoint – hangman extraordinaire

Pierrepoint, the most prolific hangman of the 20th century, executed 433 men and 17 women between 1932 and 1956, a number boosted during the Second World War, when he worked abroad as well as in Britain and hanged some 200 Nazis. Pierrepoint began his unwholesome career assisting his uncle Tom hang Patrick McDermott at Mountjoy Prison in December 1932. His first execution was that of gangster Antonio 'Babe' Mancini, responsible for a murder in Soho's Wardour Street, who went to the drop at Pentonville on 17 October 1941.

Among Pierrepoint's victims were the traitors John Amery, who told the hangman that he had always wanted to meet him; and William Joyce, aka 'Lord Haw-Haw', who had spent the war broadcasting Nazi propaganda from Germany. Another was John George Haigh, the 'Acid Bath Murderer' (☛ p. 243), who met his end at Wandsworth on 10 August 1949. Four years later Derek Bentley was also hanged there amid considerable controversy, for his part in the murder of Constable Miles. Bentley had shouted out to his partner in crime 'Let him have it', but whether this was an injunction to kill or to hand over the gun is not known.

Pierrepoint is credited with the quickest hanging on record, that of James Inglis, in only seven seconds, on 8 May 1951 at Strangeways, Manchester. He resigned from his post in 1956 after a row over fees.

Kensington Palace Gardens and sentenced to death. Two more German prisoners of war were executed at Pentonville a month later for the murder of a fellow German at their Sheffield camp.

‖ In 1946 **Theodore William John Schurch** became the last person to be executed in Britain for an offence other than murder. His crime was treason – working for Italian and German intelligence in the Second World War despite enlisting in the British army as a driver.

‖ **Timothy Evans** was hanged at Pentonville in March 1950 for supposedly murdering his wife, Beryl, and daughter, Jeraldine, at 10 Rillington Place, Notting Hill (☛ p. 278). When it later became apparent that the real murderer was John Christie, the landlord, the public realised a major miscarriage of justice had taken place. The case was one of the most influential in the subsequent abolition of the death penalty.

‖ **John Christie**, who committed the murders at 10 Rillington Place (☛ p. 276), was himself hanged here in July 1953 by the famous hangman Albert Pierrepoint 'in less time than it took the ash to fall off a cigar I had left half-smoked in my room'.

‖ The last Pentonville hanging was that of 21-year-old **Edwin Bush** on 6 July 1961. He had murdered a shop assistant, Elsie Batten, when stealing a sword from her antiques shop.

Highgate Hill

𝔄ndrew 𝔐arvell's address (1670s), *opposite No. 112*

An obscurely sited plaque marks the site of the cottage where the 17th-century poet Andrew Marvell died, either of an overdose of opium, a drug he took to relieve ague, or, as claimed more dramatically by the biographer Aubrey after being poisoned by Jesuits for attacking the idea of returning a Catholic to the throne. Three years after Marvell's death his poems were published by his housekeeper, Mary Palmer, who claimed they had been married, and that it was she who had written his poems and should therefore pick up the cheque for £500 due to him. It wasn't until around 100 years after his death that Marvell was confirmed as the author of his own poems.

The cottage was demolished in 1867.

Hilldrop Crescent

Dr Hawley Harvey Crippen murder place, *No. 39*

For nearly 100 years Dr Hawley Harvey Crippen was believed to have poisoned his wife, Cora, a music-hall performer, in their Hilldrop Crescent flat (since replaced by a council block) in 1910 for reasons unknown. Crippen told friends she had died in America while visiting relatives, but when his secretary, Ethel Le Neve, was spotted wearing his late wife's clothing and jewellery, suspicions were aroused. Police questioned Crippen, and he told them Cora had eloped with a lover, a fact he had withheld out of embarrassment. The police were satisfied, but Crippen panicked and left for the United States with Le Neve.

Once he was gone, officers searched 39 Hilldrop Crescent. Somehow they found nothing, not even the loose brick leading to a coal hole where headless remains were buried. However, on a later search they discovered human flesh wrapped in a pyjama top. Now they had to find Crippen. Word reached the police that a Mr and *Master* Robinson (Ethel Le Neve dressed as a boy) were on board the SS *Montrose*. Satisfied it was the absconding pair, officers gave chase on a faster vessel and arrested them – one of the first instances of a criminal being captured through radio telegraphy.

Crippen was hanged at nearby Pentonville in November 1910. Nevertheless many were concerned that there was insufficient evidence to be certain that the remains belonged to Mrs Crippen. In 2002 the slides used by the forensic scientist in the case, Bernard Spilsbury, were re-examined and found to be inconclusive. But in 2007 DNA tests proved that the remains were not those of Mrs Crippen.

Holloway Road

Joe Meek's deathplace, *No. 304*

British rock music's first great producer, Joe Meek, shot his landlady on 3 February 1967 during an argument at No. 304 and then turned the gun on himself. It was in the small cramped studio Meek converted from two bedrooms above the shop here that he cut a number of the most successful records of the early 1960s, including Johnny Leyton's eerie 'Johnny Remember Me' and the Tornados' space-race tribute instrumental 'Telstar'. But Meek was a troubled man. Paranoid about rivals stealing his work, he would incessantly search the building for bugs and lose his temper at the slightest thing, even going as far as to threaten drummer Mitch Mitchell with a shotgun for playing the wrong rhythm. In 1966 police questioned him about the so-called 'Suitcase Murder', in which a rent boy was cut up and dumped in a suitcase in a Sussex field. That must have exacerbated his neuroses, and led to the fateful double shooting.

Parkhurst Road

Holloway Prison, *at Camden Road*

More famous than nearby Pentonville, on account of its modern-day role as a women's prison, Holloway was built as a House of Correction for men and women in 1849–51. It was regularly used as a remand prison; Oscar Wilde awaited trial here after his arrest for gross indecency in 1895. It was set aside for women exclusively in 1902, and it was here that Ruth Ellis became the last woman to be hanged in Britain on 13 July 1955.

HANGINGS AT HOLLOWAY

Women expecting the death sentence were occasionally treated more leniently than men. Of the 47 women who spent time in Holloway's condemned cell, more than half of whom had killed their children or a sibling, 40 were reprieved. One of those was Dorothy O'Grady who, in 1941, early in the Second World War, having been caught in a prohibited part of the Isle of Wight, was accused of cutting an army telephone line and possessing a defence document. She was convicted at the Old Bailey of treason, for which the death sentence was mandatory. However, after an appeal the sentence was commuted, and she spent 14 years in jail here instead.

‖ **Amelia Sachs** and **Annie Walters** were the first women hanged at Holloway. Their crime was baby-farming and the possibility that they had murdered as many as 20 infants. They were hanged together in 1903 –Britain's last female double hanging.

‖ At the same time as **Edith Jessie Thompson** was taken to the Holloway gallows on 9 January 1923, her lover, **Frederick Bywaters**, was hanged at Pentonville for the murder of Edith's husband, Percy.

‖ **Ruth Ellis** was the last woman to be hanged in Britain. Convicted of murdering her lover in Hampstead (☞p. 203), she went to the drop at 9.01 a.m. on 13 July 1955. The hanging was a minute later than scheduled, delayed by a hoax telephone call made to the governor by someone claiming to be working for the home secretary.

When Holloway was rebuilt in 1970 the bodies of the executed women were moved to Brookwood Cemetery, Surrey. They were put into unmarked graves as their families could not be traced or did not want the remains. However, Ruth Ellis was reburied at St Mary's, Amersham.

HORNSEY, N8

Better known since 1980s gentrification as Crouch End or Crouch Hill, the area features in Will Self's *North London Book of the Dead* (1992), in which the narrator meets his mother – after her death – carrying a bag of groceries from the local Waitrose. He is puzzled: 'Mother, what are you doing in Crouch End? You never come to Crouch End except to take the cat to the vet. You don't even like Crouch End.'

MUSWELL HILL, N10

Situated on high ground overlooking the capital, Muswell Hill, named after a pilgrim's well, is a popular neighbourhood, dominated by attractive Edwardian houses and offering spectacular views over central London.

Cranley Gardens

Location of Dennis Nilsen's second set of murders, No. 23
Dennis Nilsen, a civil servant and former policeman, killed three men at No. 23 in the early 1980s, having murdered twelve others at his previous address in Cricklewood (➤p. 197) in the late 1970s.

Victim 13, John Howlett, March 1982
Nilsen met Howlett, 'John the Guardsman', whom he already vaguely knew in the Salisbury pub in St Martin's Lane, Covent Garden, sometime in March 1982. The two men returned to Cranley Gardens, where Nilsen cooked a meal, and they then went to bed separately.

In the early hours Nilsen decided Howlett's presence in the house was no longer required and attacked him with an upholstery strap. Howlett fought back but passed out when he hit his head on a hard part of the bed. Nilsen took the opportunity to drag the unconscious man into the bathroom, and held his head under water until he died.

Victim, 14, Graham Allen, September 1982

Archibald Allen became Nilsen's 14th victim after the two men met and went back to Cranley Gardens. There Nilsen cooked him an omelette. Halfway through the meal, according to Nilsen, Allen fell unconscious, possibly through choking, at which point Nilsen strangled him.

Victim 15, Stephen Sinclair, 26 January 1983

Nilsen killed his 15th and last victim, Stephen Sinclair, whom he met in the Royal George pub, Goslett Yard, off Charing Cross Road, by strangling him with a tie. He kept the corpse in the wardrobe for a week and then retrieved it, cut off the head, put it in a pan, and left it simmering on the stove while he went out for a bottle of Bacardi. The next day Nilsen dismembered the rest of the body.

Nilsen's murderous activities were curtailed after fellow tenants, early in February 1983, complained about blocked toilets. Workmen lifted the manhole covers, which let loose a terrible stench. In the sludge they also discovered what looked like specks of blood, and pieces of rotting flesh and hair attached to skin. The police were called, searched the manhole, and found what looked like human remains.

They questioned each tenant individually, and when one officer asked Dennis Nilsen, jokingly, 'Where's the rest of the body?', Nilsen replied: 'In two plastic bags in the wardrobe next door. I'll show you.' At Hornsey police station Nilsen explained that he had got rid of 'fifteen or sixteen bodies since 1978. I'll tell you everything. It's a relief to get it off my mind.' He was found guilty at the Old Bailey of six counts of murder and two of attempted murder, and was sentenced to life imprisonment.

N10

STOKE NEWINGTON, N16

Long popular with writers, radicals, artists and musicians, despite – or possibly because of – its inaccessibility from central London, Stoke Newington grew around the Romans' Ermine Street, now Stoke Newington High Street, and attracted wealthy merchants once the man-made New River was cut through early in the 17th century.

By then the area had become a haven for dissenters and radicals such as the author Daniel Defoe, whose tombstone can be found in the library on Stoke Newington Church Street even though he is buried in Bunhill Fields near the City. Appropriately, one of London's main dissenters' cemeteries – Abney Park – was built here in 1840.

Stoke Newington was the first area of London to be bombed from the air – by Zeppelin in the First World War on 31 May 1915. The first house to be hit was 16 Alkham Road in a raid that took five lives.

Evering Road

Jack 'The Hat' McVitie murder place, *No. 97*

The gangster Reggie Kray murdered Jack 'The Hat' McVitie, a small-time villain who always wore a hat to hide his baldness, at 97 Evering Road in one of the most infamous gangland killings in London's history.

McVitie had annoyed the Krays by failing to shoot an associate in their Regency club and by wiping a bloody knife on a woman's dress in the basement of the club after a stabbing. On 28 October 1967 the Kray twins' aide-de-campe, Tony Lambrianou, ferried Jack McVitie to Evering Road for a 'quiet word'. McVitie had been told there was going to be a party, so when he entered the room and found things weren't as animated as he had expected he wailed: 'Where's all the birds, where's all the booze?'

Reggie Kray pointed a gun at McVitie's head, but when he fired the gun jammed. As Jack tried to escape through the closed window his hat fell off. He was hauled back in whereupon. Kray picked up a carving knife and jabbed McVitie below the eye. He then stabbed him in the throat with such force that the knife stuck to the wall behind and had to be wriggled around in McVitie's throat before it could be removed.

Now came the problem of disposing of the body. As it would not fit into the boot of the Krays' car, it was placed upright on the back seat – the hat firmly secured on dead Jack's head – and driven on a long tortuous route through London (to lose possible pursuers and confound potential witnesses), before being dumped outside St Mary's church in Rotherhithe (p. 227).

Stamford Hill

Abney Park Cemetery

Built as a cemetery for dissenters in 1840, when Bunhill Fields in Moorgate became full, Abney Park takes up a wild 32-acre site that was the grounds of two long-demolished 17th-century mansions, Fleetwood House and Abney House. Some elements of the demolished houses remain, such as the ornamental Egyptian influenced ironwork over the Church Street entrance which come from the entrance to the latter.

It was the first cemetery built in the European garden style, with reception buildings, landscaping and a non-denominational and ecumenical chapel; there were no divisions in the cemetery along religious lines and no consecrated ground except as chosen by individuals for their plot. All its 2,500 trees and shrubs were labelled and arranged

N16

around the perimeter alphabetically from A for Acer (maple) to Z for Zanthoxylum (American toothache tree).

There are Celtic crosses, austere Welsh slate memorials and hieroglyphs over the lodges which read 'The Gates of the Abode of the Mortal Part of Man', but as the resting-place of Baptists, Methodists and other Non-conformists the cemetery is relatively free of the intensity of Gothic ornamentation that fills Highgate and Kensal Green, and contains only one mausoleum. Nevertheless the abandoned Gothic chapel at the centre is one of the most terrifying sights in London. It has no religious significance as the ground is not consecrated and is used now mostly as a backdrop in horror films.

The Abney Park Cemetery Company made some effort to attract the working class – a significant move given the closure of the traditional City graveyards in 1852 – unlike the other major new garden cemetery companies which sought to maximise income for the best plots. The company abandoned the cemetery in the 1970s. Mature woodland and unusual plant life including around 2,500 species covers the site, which is also rich in wildlife. Hackney council bought the cemetery for one pound in 1978 and it is now run by the Friends of Abney Park.

BURIED AT ABNEY PARK

|| **William Allen** (d. 1843) was a local anti-slavery campaigner who founded the African Institution that set up a colony in West Africa for freed slaves.

|| **Dr Isaac Watts** (d. 1748), the great hymn-writer who lived in Abney House, has just a memorial here as he was buried at Bunhill Fields. Nearby is Dr Watts's Mound, a small granite memorial to his favourite island heronry in Hackney Brook.

|| **William Booth** the founder of the Salvation Army, was visited by 150,000 people as he lay in state at the Congress Hall, Clapton, after his death on 20 August 1912. His memorial service, held at Olympia, was attended by 35,000 people, including Queen Alexandra, who came incognito. Before the funeral the body rested at the Salvation Army's Queen Victoria Street headquarters. Five thousand Army volunteers then met at the Embankment to escort Booth to Abney Park for a funeral attended by 7,000 members of the Salvation Army and 40 bands.

|| **Albert Chevalier** (d. 1923), one of the top music-hall stars of the early 20th century, born Albert Onesime Britannicus Gwathveoyd Louis Chevalier, popularised the costermonger song and two classic London numbers, 'My Old Dutch' and 'Wotcher (Knocked 'Em in the Old Kent Road)'.

|| **William Bramwell Booth** (d. 1929), the son of Salvation Army founder William Booth, ran the organisation after his father's death. He also led the campaign against child prostitution in London. Thousands filled Abney Park for his funeral, for which a special platform was built in the cemetery. The service was led by his daughter, Catherine, who went on to live to the age of 104, dying in October 1987.

|| Around 170 locals perished after a German bomb fell in 1940 on a shelter in Stoke Newington's Coronation Avenue which had been constructed below a terrace of 15 shops. Many of the victims drowned in the water that quickly filled the site and were buried here.

Stoke Newington High Street

Police station, *No. 33*

Five black people died in mysterious circumstances in the police station towards the end of the 20th century. Of these the best known was Colin Roach, who was shot dead in the foyer on 12 January 1983. The police claimed Roach walked in and shot himself in the mouth. However the man who drove Roach to the police station saw no gun, and investigations proved that the weapon could not have been concealed in Roach's bag. The inquest nevertheless ruled that he had committed suicide.

In December 1994 Oluwashiji Lapite, a Nigerian asylum-seeker, died in custody at the station. He had suffered severe head injuries during a struggle with up to eight policemen. At the inquest Stoke Newington officers admitted that they had kicked and bit Lapite, and applied a neckhold that police guidelines warned against.

In August 1999 Sarah Thomas, an architecture student, was arrested by Stoke Newington police for 'acting suspiciously'. While she was being led away, witnesses heard her screaming: 'Help me, help me, they're trying to kill me.' She lost consciousness and stopped breathing in the station. Officers claimed that her collapse was drug related.

TOTTENHAM, N17

Totta's village in Saxon times was the surrounded by forest which was gradually cleared. In the 1870s, following the construction of the Enfield-Liverpool Street railway, which offered cheap tickets for workmen, thousands of poor-quality houses were built to create a mostly working-class district.

Broadwater Road

Broadwater Farm

Constable Keith Blakelock was attacked and killed, stabbed 40 times with a bread knife which was rammed into his neck and left with the handle protruding, by unknown assailants during riots which took place in this decrepit maze of a 1960s housing estate on Sunday 6 October 1985.

The riots followed the death of a black resident, Cynthia Jarrett, during a police raid on the South Tottenham home of her son, Floyd. According to community leaders, when police entered the property an officer pushed over Mrs Jarrett, who was in poor health, and she died soon after as a result. While the Jarrett family was in the police station lodging their complaint, the small crowd that had gathered outside became unruly and broke the station windows. Around the same time that afternoon two constables patrolling the Broadwater Farm Estate were attacked and injured, and a police van answering a 999 call was surrounded by youths.

Officers in riot gear were sent to deal with the disturbances but a mob of black youths armed with knives, machetes, iron bars and hammers gathered and using blazing cars to form barricades looted shops, broke into houses, attacked pedestrians and assaulted the drivers of passing vehicles. When police went to deal with a fire in a newsagents on the Tangmere block at 9.30 p.m., PC Blakelock became separated from his colleagues, and was attacked and killed. His killers tried to remove his head to place it on a pole but were unable to do so. When news of the murder spread, the violence abated. Three men, including Winston Silcott, who was on bail for murder at the time, were arrested and charged with Constable Blakelock's murder. Silcott was convicted, but later had his sentence quashed on appeal.

Chesnut Road

Two Latvian anarchists, Jacob Lepidus and Paul Hefeld, staged a wages snatch at a rubber factory at the corner of Chesnut Road and Tottenham High Road on 23 January 1909 and shot dead a policeman in what came to be known as the 'Tottenham Outrage'.

The drama began when a chauffeur-driven car carrying the wages drew up. Lepidus and Hefeld seized the bag containing the cash, and shot at the driver and a passing stoker who tried to restrain them. Officers in the local police station heard gunfire and gave chase after the fleeing robbers.

In the mêlée that followed the anarchists fired some 400 shots at their pursuers, and shot dead a ten-year-old boy who was passing by. They then hijacked a tram by forcing the driver at gunpoint, and were pursued by police in a horse and cart. Though the robbers understandably soon gained ground on the officers, they decided to shoot the horse and continued their escape on a (slower) milk-float, which they later swapped for a horse-drawn van. During the chase they shot PC William Tyler dead, but were eventually cornered at the River Ching by policemen who had followed them on bicycles.

Lepidus and Hefeld were no ordinary robbers. They were trying to raise funds for a Russian revolutionary organisation. Lepidus was the brother of an anarchist who had blown himself up when a bomb he was carrying in his pocket in order to assassinate the president of France exploded before he could plant it. At the end of the drama Hefeld told Lepidus to flee and the latter locked himself in a nearby cottage. As officers tried to break in and shoot him, he killed himself with his last bullet. Hefeld shot himself in the head. He died in hospital three weeks later after cryptically announcing: 'My mother is in Riga.'

CHAPTER 8

North-West London

CAMDEN TOWN/REGENT'S PARK, NW1

One of the liveliest centres in the metropolis thanks to the music venues, bars, cafés and markets of Camden Town, NW1 also includes picturesque Regent's Park and the desirable suburb of Primrose Hill.

The area was developed in the middle of the 19th century following the construction of the London and Birmingham Railway. In the 1840s, locals clashed violently with Irish labourers brought over to help build the line. Fighting began when a group of Irish navvies attacked some English workmen who, they claimed, had provoked them. The brawl raged for about an hour, hundreds were injured and one person died in what became known as the battle of Camden Town. The man who died wasn't even involved; he had merely gone to see what the fuss was about, and had been beaten to death amid cries of 'Kill the f—— Protestant.' The next day scores of labourers appeared in court, but proceedings turned to farce when one man was called to be a witness to his own murder, and another, allegedly dead, rose to prove his continued existence.

Agar Grove

The 1907 'Camden Town Murder' was the slaying of prostitute Phyllis Dimmock, found with her throat cut at 29 St Paul's Road (now Agar Grove) on 12 September. Dimmock had been living a supposedly respectable life with Bert Shaw, a chef on the London–Sheffield train, but while he was at work she reverted to her old ways, dallying with a postcard salesman, Robert Wood.

When Dimmock's body was found, two of Shaw's razors were by the wash bowl near a bloodstained towel and her postcard collection was scattered around the room. One of these had been sent by Wood and read: 'Phyllis darling. If it pleases you to meet me at 8.15 at the [here he had drawn a rising sun]. Yours to a cinder.' He had signed it 'Alice' so as not to arouse Shaw's suspicions.

Wood was charged with the murder but cleared at the Old Bailey in a landmark case in which he became the first defendant in a murder trial to give evidence on his own behalf. Because no one – Wood, common-law husband Shaw, or any of her other suitors – was ever convicted of Dimmock's murder the case soon became linked with the equally unsolved Jack the Ripper murders of prostitutes of nearly 20 years earlier, even though Dimmock's body was not mutilated. Ripperologists have since made more connections, not least because of a series of paintings – 'The Camden Town Murders' – made by the locally based artist Walter Sickert, who some experts believe was, or was involved with, the Ripper.

Fitzroy Road

Sylvia Plath's death place (1963), *No. 23*

The American poet Sylvia Plath committed suicide at this address on 11 February 1963 a few months after splitting up with the poet Ted Hughes. He had left her, their two-and-a-half-year-old daughter and nine-month-old son for another woman. The suicide was not really a surprise. Ten years previously, when Plath's mother noticed scars all over her legs, Sylvia told her she wanted to die. Psychiatric help was sought, but in August 1953 Plath pretended to run away from home, hid in the cellar of her mother's house and took 40 pills.

That February 1963 morning, Plath threw open the windows of the children's bedroom, taped up the doors in the kitchen, turned on the cooker's gas jets and stuck her head inside the oven. Helpfully, she left a note containing her doctor's phone number, asking whoever found her to call him. After her death Hughes, the cause of most of her new woes, destroyed her journals.

Six years later Hughes' latest lover, Assia Wevill, copied Plath and also committed suicide by turning on the gas oven and lying down on the mattress to die with their daughter, Shura.

Hanover Terrace

No. 13

The novelist and science-fiction writer H. G. Wells died at his Regent's Park address in 1946, nine years after telling the previous owner as he bought the property that he was dying. By the end of the Second World War Wells's fears were at last being realised. Disillusioned with life, he painted a mural in one of the rooms depicting man's evolution and wrote beneath the modern section 'Time to go (for man)'.

Macclesfield Bridge

In 1874 a barge travelling along Regent's Canal carrying sugar, nuts, barrels of petrol and five tons of gunpowder detonated as it went under the bridge. The barge sank, the bridge was destroyed and all three crew were killed by the blast, probably the greatest explosion witnessed in London before the First World War. One individual lucky not to die in the blast was the painter Laurence Alma-Tadema, whose house in the vicinity was destroyed, but who was out that night.

At the outset of the Second World War chloroform was used to kill the poisonous snakes in the nearby Regent's Park Zoo, where the aquarium was drained, and many of the fish eaten. When a bomb fell close by in September 1940 no one died but a zebra escaped from its cage and ran off across Regent's Park, closely followed by the zoo's secretary, Professor Julian Huxley.

Pancras Road

St Pancras Old Cemetery

One of the oldest Christian sites in England, named in honour of Pancras, a fourth-century Christian martyr, in medieval times this was a pleasant rural spot by the River Fleet but it is now hemmed in by railway lines.

In 1725 Old St Pancras briefly became the burial place of Jonathan Wild, 'King of Thief-Takers'. Wild was hanged at Tyburn in 1725 after being accused of criminal activity and was brought here, but after a few days resurrectionists dug up the corpse. The body of an unknown man was soon washed up on the bank of the Thames near Whitehall, his hairy chest leading some to claim it was Wild, but there was no formal identification. The skeleton is now on display at the Royal College of Surgeons.

Charles Dickens, who was familiar with the problem of the cemetery and bodysnatchers, created a character, Jerry Cruncher, who robs tombs and snatch bodies from Old St Pancras in A Tale of Two Cities (1859).

In the early 19th century Old St Pancras became the resting-place of French refugees fleeing the revolution, their number including many clerics who refused to sign the oath of allegiance to the civil constitution of the clergy, and feared deportation to French Guiana. Among them was Arthur Richard Dillon, Archbishop of Narbonne and Primate

of Languedoc, who was exhumed when his grave was later moved. He was found to have a set of porcelain dentures, a French innovation that never enjoyed much acceptance in Britain.

In 1814 the poet Shelley declared his love for Mary Wollstonecraft over the grave of her mother, Mary Wollstonecraft Godwin, author of *A Vindication of the Rights of Woman* (1792), who had died in childbirth. In 1822 St Pancras New Church was built further south. Fifteen years later the old cemetery became the burial site of Sir John Soane, architect of the Bank of England. His grave is marked by an ostentatious mausoleum designed by him for his wife in 1816, on which Giles Gilbert Scott later based the red telephone kiosk. It is one of only two Grade I listed monuments in London, the other being Karl Marx's tomb in Highgate.

The cemetery closed in 1854 with the passing of acts to build new vast cemeteries in the suburbs. A decade later there was an outcry when thousands of graves were disturbed for the construction of the Midland Railway line leading into nearby St Pancras station. One of the surveyors engaged in the work was the young Thomas Hardy, who in his poems 'The Levelled Churchyard' and 'In The Cemetery' entreats passengers who use the line to remember the 'piteous groans/Half stifled in this jumbled patch/Of wretched memorial stones'. Similar activity – and controversy – took place at the beginning of the 21st century due to the resiting of the Channel Tunnel rail terminus.

Regent's Park Road

Primrose Hill

One of the highest points in London at 200 feet and once part of Middlesex Forest, Primrose Hill was where in 1678 the body of Sir Edmund Berry Godfrey, a well-known London magistrate and friend of the diarist Samuel Pepys, was found.

Godfrey had been stabbed with his own sword, and the inquest returned a verdict of wilful murder. There was much speculation about who could have murdered him and why, and it soon emerged that a few weeks previously Godfrey had been approached by two men, Dr Israel Tong, a Presbyterian minister, and Titus Oates, an unfrocked priest, and told of a Catholic plot to massacre Protestants like himself, overthrow the government, and replace Charles II with the Catholic sympathiser the Duke of York (later James II). Godfrey began to conduct investigations into a Catholic conspiracy but was killed soon after, possibly in Somerset House on the Strand.

When one commentator noted that the murdered Godfrey's name was an anagram of 'Died by Rome's revenged fury' panic spread; obviously there *was* a Catholic plot to take over the country, many concluded. A cutler even made a special Godfrey dagger with the words 'Remember the murder of Edmund Berry Godfrey' on one side and 'Remember religion' on the other, and sold 3,000 in one day. A Catholic silversmith named Prance later confessed that he had been hired to murder Godfrey.

In 1820 Primrose Hill was chosen to be the setting for a vast new cemetery which could hold 5 million corpses, but locals set up a campaign to keep it as a public park instead.

CRICKLEWOOD, NW2

A cosmopolitan area either side of the busy A5 (Edgware Road) where the mass murderer Dennis Nilsen lived and killed in the late 1970s and early 1980s.

Melrose Avenue

Location of Dennis Nilsen's first set of murders, *No. 195*

Dennis Nilsen, a civil servant and former policeman, killed twelve men while living here from 1976–81. Nilsen began turning his violent fantasies into reality in 1978 when he met three men in Kilburn High Road and invited them home for a drink. When they fell asleep, Nilsen closed all the doors and windows, covered the stove with a jacket sprinkled with water, and lit the gas. Smoke quickly filled the room. When one of the men woke and began shouting for help, Nilsen burst in to 'rescue' them.

At the end of the year, filled with despair and overcome with loneliness, he committed his first murder. He was later caught at his new address, 23 Cranley Gardens, Muswell Hill, where he had committed more murders. After Nilsen confessed, police officers searched Melrose Avenue, which had been renovated since he moved out, and found fragments from about a thousand charred bones.

II **Victim 1, Stephen Holmes, 30 December 1978**

Not till 2005 were the authorities able to identify Nilsen's first victim as Stephen Holmes, whom the killer met at the Cricklewood Arms, a rough Irish pub, on 29 December 1978. Nilsen took Holmes back to Melrose Avenue, where they went to bed but did not have sex. In the morning Nilsen woke and decided that he wanted Holmes to stay with him over New Year, whether the latter liked it or not, so he wrapped his tie around the man's neck while he slept. Holmes woke, and began violently resisting Nilsen's strangulation, but soon fell limp.

A few minutes later Nilsen realised the man was still conscious and thrust his head in a bucket of water to kill him. He unsuccessfully tried to have sex with the corpse, then buried it under the floorboards. The following August he burned the remains in a bonfire. No one ever reported a missing person fitting Holmes's description.

The following October Nilsen brought a Chinese student home, and after the two men tied each other up, Nilsen attempted to strangle the Chinaman with a tie. The latter freed himself and called the police, but no charges were brought because the Chinaman was unwilling to proceed. Nilsen himself later admitted that he should have been arrested.

Victim 2, Kenneth James Ockenden, 3 December 1979

Nilsen met Kenneth James Ockenden, a 23-year-old Canadian tourist, in the Princess Louise pub, High Holborn. There they chatted for a few hours before returning to Melrose Avenue, where Nilsen strangled him with headphone wire. After clearing up the mess, he spent the night with the corpse, then put it in a cupboard and went off to work. When he returned, he rested the dead body on top of himself in bed while he watched TV. Over the next few weeks the odd couple – Nilsen, the occasionally naked civil servant and two times murderer, and Ockenden, the dead, decaying, unburied Canadian – would often sit together in the living room in front of the television. Nilsen eventually buried the body under the floorboards.

Victim 3, Martyn Duffey, 17 May 1980

Duffey, a troubled 16-year-old Liverpudlian, left his home city after telling his parents he was going to the library, slept rough, then headed for London. There he met Nilsen and went back with him to Cricklewood, where the latter tried to strangle him in bed. When Nilsen realised that Duffey was not dead, he carried him into the kitchen and put his head under water until he stopped breathing. Later he buried him under the floorboards.

Victim 4, William Sutherland, August 1980

Nilsen met Sutherland, a 27-year-old hard-drinking Scotsman from Edinburgh and a male prostitute, in a West End pub. After the night's drinking they parted at Leicester Square tube, but as Nilsen bought his tube ticket Sutherland told him he had nowhere to go. Nilsen invited him back to Cricklewood and there strangled him.

Victim 5, unidentified Filipino man, October 1980

Nilsen met a Filipino in the Cricklewood Arms, took him back to Melrose Avenue and strangled him.

‖ **Victim 6, unidentified Irishman, autumn 1980**

An Irishman Nilsen met in the Cricklewood Arms sometime in autumn 1980 went back to Melrose Avenue, where Nilsen strangled him, burying the body under the floorboards.

‖ **Victim 7, unidentified tramp, autumn 1980**

Nilsen met a tramp at St Giles's Circus in the West End, took him back to Melrose Avenue in a taxi, strangled and dismembered him, and once again buried the remains under the floorboards. Soon after the murder he removed the bodies of the earlier victims and burned their remains on waste ground near his house.

On 10 November that year Nilsen took Douglas Stewart, whom he met in the Golden Lion pub on Charing Cross Road, back to Cricklewood and tried to murder him. Stewart escaped and contacted the police, who dismissed the incident as a homosexual tiff.

‖ **Victim 8, unidentified man, late 1980**

Nilsen met an unknown man in the West End sometime in late 1980, took him back to Melrose Avenue where, in the usual manner, he strangled him and hid the body under the floorboards.

‖ **Victim 9, unidentified man, January 1981**

An unknown man whom Nilsen met in January 1981 at the Golden Lion went back home with him. Nilsen strangled him with a tie, hiding the body under the floorboards.

‖ **Victim 10, unidentified man, February 1981**

Nilsen met an unknown man in the West End in February 1981, took him home and strangled him with a tie. He disposed of the body in the usual way.

‖ **Victim 11, unidentified skinhead, April 1981**

In Leicester Square in April 1981 Nilsen met a skinhead, whom he took back to Cricklewood, where he strangled him. (The victim helpfully had a tattoo around his neck with the words 'cut here'.) Once again, he buried him under the floorboards.

‖ **Victim 12, Malcolm Barlow, 18 September 1981**

Barlow, an epileptic and occasional male prostitute, made the mistake of being taken ill outside 195 Melrose Avenue in the morning of 17 September and was spotted by Nilsen who called an ambulance. When Barlow was discharged the next day he returned to Melrose

NW2

Avenue and waited for Nilsen, who invited him in, and cooked a meal. Barlow had a few Bacardis, which mixed uneasily with the pills he was taking for his epilepsy, and fell into a deep sleep on the couch. Unable to wake him, Nilsen strangled him to death and left the body overnight. The next morning he temporarily stuffed the dead Barlow under the sink and went to work, later burying him under the floorboards – the last Melrose Avenue victim.

On 4 October 1981 Nilsen removed the bodies of the last five victims from their subterranean lair, took them to wasteground and burned them. The next day he moved to Cranley Gardens, Muswell Hill (☞p. 182), where he murdered three more men before being apprehended.

HAMPSTEAD, NW3

One of London's most picturesque and romantic settings, Hampstead is dominated by exquisite domestic architecture and the wild heath. It is on the heath that children are found 'with tiny wounds in the throat' in Bram Stoker's *Dracula* (1897). In the Sherlock Holmes story 'The Adventure of Charles Augustus Milverton' (1904) Holmes and Watson flee across the heath after the murder of the hero. In Dorothy L. Sayers's *Unnatural Death*, the lawyer, Tripp, tells the police a story about being lured to a house on Hampstead Heath to prepare the will of a woman who then tries to murder him.

Church Row

St John

Bram Stoker was probably thinking of St John's burial ground when he wrote in his vampire classic, *Dracula* (1897), of a 'lonely churchyard, away from teeming London, where the air is fresh, and the sun rises over Hampstead Hill, and where wild flowers grow of their own accord'.

Among those buried at St John is the Victorian novelist and cartoonist George du Maurier (d. 1896), whose tombstone is inscribed with the closing lines from *Trilby*:

> *A little trust that when we die*
> *We reap our sowing! and so – good-bye.*

There is also the gravestone of Hugh Gaitskell (d. 1963), the Labour Party leader, who may have been assassinated by the Soviets at their Notting Hill embassy (☛ p. 268), not that anyone outside espionage circles would have realised this at the time. After his death the House of Commons adjourned for 24 hours, something usually reserved for former premiers.

Downshire Hill

No. 9

Allan Chappelow, an eccentric local writer who had published an acclaimed biography of George Bernard Shaw, was murdered in his overgrown Downshire Hill mansion at the age of 86 in 2006. His battered body was found weeks later under a mountain of debris which took 48 hours to remove. The corpse was only discovered because staff at his local bank became suspicious when more than £10,000 was withdrawn from his account and he failed to make his usual weekly deposit. Officers suspected that an intruder beat Chappelow into divulging his bank details and then battered him to death.

Chappelow was known for riding a 1940s motorbike around the area – the same motorbike which he had ridden to the Hertfordshire home of George Bernard Shaw in 1950 to photograph the playwright just before he died. In his later years Chappelow refused to let anyone inside 9 Downshire Hill, or repair the property, to the consternation of locals anxious to maintain the tone of the area.

No. 47

One of a number of Hampstead properties with strong associations with the art world, it was home from 1914–36 to Richard Carline, whom Stanley Spencer used as a model for a corpse in his famous painting *Resurrection*, Cookham. He later became Unesco's first art consultant.

Keats Grove

Originally Albion Grove, it was renamed after its most famous resident, the poet John Keats, in the 19th century. Shortly before expiring at No. 20 in 1964 the writer Edith Sitwell told a friend: 'I am dying but otherwise quite well.'

John Keats's address (1818–20)/Keats House, *south side*

A small museum dedicated to the poet was originally two properties, in one of which Keats lived from 1818–20 when he was ill with consumption. In October 1819 Keats staggered home, not drunk, as his landlord, Charles Brown, believed, but ill, and made his way upstairs to lie down. Keats was coughing up blood and asked Brown to bring him a candle. Once he saw that the blood was bright red and therefore must be from an artery, the poet told Brown: 'I cannot be deceived in that colour – that drop of blood – it is my death warrant – I must die.' Die he did soon after, aged 25, in February 1821, in Italy, where he had gone to recuperate.

Maitland Park Road

Karl Marx's death place, No. 41

Karl Marx died at No. 41 in March 1883, aged 65, without making a will. His estate was valued at £250. His letters, notes and manuscripts passed to his patron, Friedrich Engels.

New End

On the north side of the road is the innovative New End Theatre, previously a mortuary, where the body of Karl Marx was laid out on a slab, before being buried at Highgate Cemetery. So too was that of David Blakely, murdered by Ruth Ellis outside Hampstead's Magdala pub (see below). The mortuary was converted into a theatre in 1974.

South Hill Park

Ruth Ellis, a 28-year-old nightclub hostess, was the last woman to be hanged in Britain. Ellis had shot dead her lover, racing driver David Blakely, as he left the Magdala pub in South Hill Park, Hampstead, on 10 April 1955, and went to the drop at Holloway Prison on 13 July that year.

In a remarkable coincidence the penultimate woman to hang, Styllou Christofi, was executed for murdering her daughter-in-law at a house on the same street.

KILBURN, NW6

Kilburn was Kyle Bourne (cold stream) and the community grew around the Roman Road of Watling Street (now the A5). There was little development until the arrival of three main railways in the 19th and early 20th centuries. To the east is the more middle class West Hampstead, so renamed by estate agents after the Second World War.

Fortune Green Road

Hampstead Cemetery

Opened in 1876 and the setting for some of the most glorious memorials in London, Hampstead is the final resting-place of Joseph Lister (d. 1912), the pioneer of antiseptic surgery, and music-hall star Marie Lloyd (d. 1922). A stone angel allegedly looks like Mattie, wife of the Italian restaurateur Cesare Bianchi, who died shortly after giving birth in 1936. Nearby a splendid stone organ commemorates Charles Barritt, landlord of the Blue Posts pub on Tottenham Court Road. The seat was stolen in 1997 but has since been replaced.

BURIED AT HAMPSTEAD

⫶ **Julia Frankau** (d. 1916) was a Jewish writer who wrote anti-Semitic books under the pseudonym Dr Phillips. A review of one of her works ran: 'It should never have been written. Having been written it should never have been published. Having been published, it should not be read.'

⫶ **Dennis Brain** (d. 1957), a child prodigy French-horn player, became principal in the BBC Symphony Orchestra. His love of fast cars proved the death of him, as many had feared, for he lost control of his sports car on his way to London and died in the crash.

⫶ **Peter Llewellyn Davies**, the inspiration for J. M. Barrie's Peter Pan, committed suicide in 1960 at the age of 63 by throwing himself under a train at Sloane Square tube station. Two of his brothers also died tragically: George Llewellyn Davies was killed in action in Flanders in 1915, and Michael drowned in the Thames six years later.

⫶ **Joseph Rotblat** (d. 2005) was a Nobel Peace Prize winner who worked on the wartime Manhattan Project to build the first atomic bomb but quit, claiming that the Germans were not doing the same. He was then banned from entering the USA and became a vociferous anti-nuclear campaigner along with Bertrand Russell and Albert Einstein.

ST JOHN'S WOOD, NW8

One of the capital's most desirable suburbs, St John's Wood was developed in the early 19th century with large detached villas in a woodland setting to tempt the middle classes to move away from the smoke and congestion of central London.

Queen's Grove

Joseph Sieff's address (1970s), No. 48

One of the most fortunate Londoners to escape an assassination attempt was Marks & Spencer's chief Joseph Sieff, a leading contributor to funds for Zionist groups, who was targeted on Sunday 30 December 1973 by the hitman Carlos 'the Jackal'. The Jackal knocked at the door and, when the butler opened it, produced a gun and demanded to be taken to the M&S executive. Sieff was in the bath.

Carlos burst into the bathroom and shot the tycoon in the mouth, but the bullets bounced off Sieff's teeth. The Jackal stepped forward, aimed the pistol at Sieff's head, and pulled the trigger a second time. The gun jammed. The Jackal fled the scene, cursing his first failure as a professional killer.

Wellington Road

St John's Wood Cemetery

This is the resting-place of Joanna Southcott, the early 19th-century millennial prophetess. After her death her disciples refused to believe she had expired and kept the body, awaiting her resurrection. Once the corpse began to decompose, however, she was taken to St John's Wood and buried.

WILLESDEN, NW10

Lying between the River Brent and the no-man's land surrounding the Great Western Railway, Willesden was a hamlet before the railway arrived but grew into a prosperous suburb by the end of the 19th century as street after street of small, almost featureless houses were erected. The district has three main faces: the industrial estate of Park Royal to the west, Harlesden, home of a substantial black working-class community in the centre, and middle-class Brondesbury Park to the east.

Glebe Road

Jewish Cemetery

Various Rothschilds and two chief rabbis are buried in this major Jewish cemetery, founded in 1873. They include Meyer de Rothschild (d. 1874) whose horse Favonius won the 1871 Derby; Anthony de Rothschild (d. 1876), first president of the United Synagogue; and the great natural historian Lionel Rothschild (d. 1937). The cemetery also contains the graves of the chief rabbis Nathan Adler (d. 1890) and Israel Brodie (d. 1979), and of the financier Charles Clore (d. 1979), who owned Selfridges in the mid-20th century.

GOLDERS GREEN, NW11

There was no Golders Green before the Northern Line arrived in 1907. Despite considerable 20th-century growth it has remained one of the most pleasant London suburbs, with quick access to Hampstead Heath and excellent transport links and shops, many of which cater for the large, local middle-class Jewish population.

Hoop Lane

Golders Green Crematorium

London's first crematorium opened in 1902 after the authorities realised that Brookwood in Surrey would not be able to take all those who wanted to be cremated. It has been continually popular with figures from the arts and media, including the architect Charles Rennie Mackintosh (d. 1928), the novelist H. G. Wells (d. 1939), and the comedians Sid James (d. 1976) and Peter Sellers (d. 1980). The crematorium contains luscious memorial gardens and two mausoleums: the Smith, which looks like a Wren church, and Lutyens's work for the Philipson family, which has a domed roof.

CREMATED AT GOLDERS GREEN

‖ When the Potteries novelist **Arnold Bennett** was dying of typhoid at his luxurious Baker Street apartment in 1931, the council spread straw on the road to reduce the noise. Unfortunately it rained overnight and by the morning the surface was so slippery a milk cart overturned and scores of bottles were smashed.

‖ The pioneer of psychology, **Sigmund Freud**, died in September 1939 of cancer of the mouth, which he may have contracted from a life of smoking cigars. Freud had undergone more than 30 operations and had his jaw removed, but when he could no longer endure the pain of the cancer he asked his private doctor to administer a morphine overdose. His ashes were placed in his own Greek urn.

‖ Fittingly the ashes of **Havelock Ellis**, a pioneer in sex education and birth control, who also died in 1939, are at Golders Green.

‖ **Ken 'Snakehips' Johnson** was a black Guyanan bandleader who perished in the dramatic bombing of the Café de Paris nightclub (☞p. 80) in 1941.

NW11

‖ **Tubby Hayes** was one of Britain's few credible jazz musicians. He died in 1973 during a heart operation.
‖ **Paul Kossoff**, the gifted rock guitarist, died on board a Los Angeles to New York flight in 1976 from drug-related heart problems.
‖ **Marc Bolan**, frontman of T. Rex, died in a car accident in Barnes (☛ p. 250) in 1977. His plaque is often stolen by fans and is constantly being replaced.
‖ The great comedian **Peter Sellers** (d. 1980) paid a visit to the crematorium a few days before he died.
‖ **Matt Monro**, the only British crooner who can be favourably compared to Frank Sinatra, died of lung cancer in 1985.
‖ The acclaimed novelist **Shiva Naipul** died suddenly of a heart attack at the age of 40 in 1985. His funeral was held according to Hindu rites.

CHAPTER 9

South-East London

SOUTHWARK, SE1
Cathedral Street
Great Dover Street
Harper Road
Jacob Street
Lambeth Road
Lynton Road
Old Kent Road
Redcross Way
Southwark Bridge Road
Waterloo Bridge
Waterloo Road
Westminster Bridge Road

CHARLTON, SE7
Cemetery Lane

DEPTFORD, SE8
Deptford Green

ELTHAM, SE9
Well Hall Road

GREENWICH, SE10
Blackwall Tunnel Approach
Greenwich Church Street
Romney Road

KENNINGTON, SE11
Kennington Park Road

NEW CROSS, SE14
New Cross Road

PECKHAM, SE15
Blakes Road
Linden Grove

ROTHERHITHE, SE16
St Marychurch Street

UPPER NORWOOD, SE19

HONOR OAK, SE23
Brenchley Gardens

SYDENHAM, SE26
Jews Walk

WEST NORWOOD, SE27
Norwood High Street

SOUTHWARK, SE1

Because the land on the south side of the Thames opposite the capital's most important buildings was swampy, London developed mostly on the north bank until the mid-19th century. Southwark is, however, one of the capital's oldest settlements, dominated by prisons and religious buildings until industrialisation brought the railway and with it some of London's most intensely urbanised working-class areas such as Bermondsey and Elephant & Castle.

Cathedral Street

Southwark Cathedral

Originally St Mary Overie – 'St Mary over the river' – the cathedral contains the tomb of John Gower (d. 1408), often described as 'the first English poet' as he wrote in English, rather than French or Latin. Edmund, the actor brother of William Shakespeare, was buried here in 1607. In another grave are buried two of Shakespeare's contemporaries: John Fletcher (d. 1613), who collaborated with the Bard on *Henry VIII*, and Philip Massinger (d. 1640), who once observed 'Death hath a thousand doors to let out life.'

Great Dover Street

When land alongside Great Dover Street was excavated in 1996 a 2nd-century walled cemetery was uncovered. It yielded evidence of a cremation in which a young woman's remains had been burnt on a pyre over the pit in which the ashes were later found. There were also lamps, incense burners and the remains of a funeral feast of figs, almonds and chicken, implying that the deceased must have been a person of some social standing.

Harper Road

Horsemonger Lane Gaol

During the 19th century 133 people were hanged at Horsemonger Lane Gaol which stood where the Newington Recreation Ground now meets

Harper Road. The first executions took place on 4 April 1800 when five men were hanged for coining, highway robbery and burglary.

Three years later, in February 1803, Colonel Despard and his gang were executed here for high treason. They had been part of a group of 40 conspirators arrested at Lambeth's Oakley Arms pub, ten of whom were convicted of conspiring to capture and kill the king, and overthrow the government. In sentencing them, Lord Ellenborough ordered them to be

> taken from the place from whence you came, and from thence... to be drawn on hurdles to the place of execution, where you are to be hanged by the neck, but not until you are dead; for while you are still living your bodies are to be taken down, your bowels torn out and burned before your faces, your heads then cut off, and your bodies divided each into four quarters, and your heads and quarters to be then at the King's disposal; and may the Almighty God have mercy on your souls!

Surprisingly the authorities eventually relented and simply hanged the men, following which they were decapitated. Despard was buried near the north door of St Paul's Cathedral.

When Maria and Frederick Manning were hanged at Horsemonger Lane on 13 November 1849 there was an outcry in *The Times*, led by Charles Dickens, who was mortified by

> a sight so inconceivably awful as the wickedness and levity of the immense crowd collected at that execution could be imagined by no man, and could be presented in no heathen land under the sun. The horrors of the gibbet and of the crime which brought the wretched murderers to it faded in my mind before the atrocious bearing, looks, and language of the assembled spectators.

The article became instrumental in the change in public attitude towards public executions.

Before being hanged for the murder of his girlfriend in September 1860 William Godfrey Youngman told the hangman: 'Strap my legs tight and be sure to shake hands with me before I go,' which hangman Calcraft duly did.

Perhaps the worst felon hanged at Horsemonger Lane was Margaret Waters, the baby farmer. She was paid to take care of the babies of unmarried mothers but killed them instead, possibly as many as 20. The newspapers of the time were filled with the details of how she had poisoned them, wrapped the bodies in old rags and dumped the corpses in deserted streets. She was hanged in 1870.

One of the last two people to be hanged at Ḣorsemonger Ĺane Ġaol was 23-year-old Isaac Marks, for shooting dead a man he had fallen out with over a failed business deal. Marks was a Jew, one of only two ever hanged in Britain, the other being Israel Lipski (☛p. 119).

Jacob Street

Jacob's Island
A small tract of land between the Thames, the River Neckinger and tidal ditches, Jacob's Island was a foul rookery in Victorian times, described in 1849 by the London chronicler Henry Mayhew as 'the very capital of cholera [where] the very stench of death [rises] through the boards, human beings sleep night after night, until the last sleep of all comes upon them years before its time'. In Charles Dickens's *Oliver Twist* (1838) Jacob's Island is where the arch-villain Bill Sykes accidentally hangs himself at the end of the novel.

The area was cleaned up in the late 19th century.

Lambeth Road

Imperial War Museum/Bethlem Hospital (19th century)
The building that is now the Imperial War Museum was formerly part of the Royal Bethlem Hospital, commonly known as Bedlam, from 1815 to 1930, after it moved from its long-standing home in Moorfields. Nineteenth century patients included Mary Nicholson, who tried to assassinate George III in 1786 and died here in 1828, having been confined throughout that time. Dragoon James Hadfield was imprisoned here in 1802 for shooting at the same king. He died in Bedlam in 1841.

Other would-be assassins who spent their last years in Bedlam included Edward Oxford, who came close to killing Queen Victoria, and Daniel McNaughten, who murdered the secretary of the prime minister Robert Peel, thinking it was the premier himself. The poet and painter Richard Dadd was imprisoned in Bedlam after killing his father in 1843. While incarcerated, he painted for the hospital steward *The Fairy Teller's Master Stroke* (1855–64), a meticulously executed but chaotic vision of Victorian society.

Lynton Road

George Francis murder place, *No. 304*

Francis, an associate of the Kray twins, was gunned down in an under-world execution outside his haulage company business, Signed, Sealed and Delivered, in May 2003. He was the latest in a long line of villains to fall prey to the so-called 'Brinks Mat curse' whereby those connected with the infamous 1983 gold bullion heist have ended up at best betrayed and imprisoned, at worst prematurely dead. Francis, who had also been linked with some 20 gangland killings, may have ripped off jailed Brinks Mat gang members who had entrusted him to look after their stash. In May 1985, two years after the job, a hooded man ran into Francis's pub in Kent and fired a volley of shots at him. Francis survived. But he didn't survive the second attempt on his life. He was shot in the face, back and arm as he leaned into his car in Lynton Road. Two hitmen in their fifties, John O'Flynn and Terence Conaghan, were convicted for the killing in August 2007.

Old Kent Road

A road synonymous with many of the least attractive aspects of south-London life – poverty, blight, decrepit housing and casual violence – it was traditionally the major route from Southwark into Kent, where pub-lic gallows were built to dissuade potential miscreants from crime. In 1836 James Greenacre, an Old Kent Road grocer, murdered a 50-year-old woman and left parts of her body in various locations across south London. Once the story became public knowledge local pie-sellers renamed their meat pies 'Greenacres'.

Redcross Way

Skull and Bones graveyard

A builder's yard covers the burial site for the 'Winchester Geese' – medieval prostitutes licensed by the Bishop of Winchester's London base who operated from legal brothels, or stews, but were forbidden the rites of the church. After the Palace of Winchester burned down in 1814 the site became a paupers' burial ground. It was full by the mid-19th century and closed in 1853. A warehouse was built on the site. During excavations for the Jubilee Line extension in 1999 the graveyard was uncovered, revealing the remains of thousands of bodies, many of whom had died from smallpox or tuberculosis.

Southwark Bridge Road

A vast expanse of land on both sides of the modern-day road was covered before industrialisation by St George's Fields, where demonstrations against injustices in the capital were often held until the mid-19th century. Seven people died at a rally at St George's Fields on 22 March 1769 following the Battle of Fleet Street in which supporters and opponents of the radical politician John Wilkes clashed.

Waterloo Bridge

Northbound bus stop

One of the most remarkable political assassinations in London history took place at the northbound bus stop at the southern end of Waterloo Bridge on 7 September 1978. While waiting for a bus to take him to work at the BBC World Service Georgi Markov, a 49-year-old Bulgarian exile, was stabbed in his right thigh with the sharpened end of an umbrella by a man who apologised and fled in a taxi. By the time Markov arrived at work a small red pimple had formed where he had been stabbed and it was causing him a stinging pain.

That evening, Markov developed a high fever and was admitted to hospital, where he died three days later. Doctors found in his thigh a 1.7mm platinum-iridium pellet filled with ricin, a poison for which there is no known antidote. It transpired that Markov had been deliberately targeted by the Bulgarian secret service, which was planning with the KGB to eliminate troublesome opponents as a birthday present to Bulgarian president Todor Zhivkov. Ten days before Markov's murder, a fellow Bulgarian, Vladimir Kostov, had been assassinated in Paris by the same method.

Markov's wife, Annabel, refused to believe that anyone could be stabbed thus in England. 'I've been brought up in this country. I can't believe people go round stabbing other people with umbrellas,' she told the BBC.

Waterloo Road

Great Train Robber Buster Edwards hanged himself in his lock-up garage by Waterloo station on 28 November 1994, convinced that the police were closing in on a counterfeit cash scam with which he may have been involved, and unable to bear another term in jail. Southwark Crown Court recorded an open verdict at a hearing attended by two surviving members of the gang that had robbed the Euston–Glasgow mail train in one of the biggest heists ever, as well as Charlie Kray, the twins' elder brother, during a rare spell out of prison.

Westminster Bridge Road

Necropolis Railway terminus (1902–39), No. 121
From 1854 the Necropolis Railway Company ran a funeral service on its own trains from Waterloo, taking corpses and mourners to Brookwood Cemetery in Woking, Surrey. Trains displaying the company logo of a skull and crossbones were divided into compartments for the different classes (1st, 2nd and 3rd) and for the different shades of Christianity (Anglican and Nonconformist). After leaving Waterloo they passed

through what the authorities hoped was scenery that would be 'comforting' to mourners: Battersea Park, Wimbledon Park, Richmond, and the Surrey countryside.

Among those who used the service was the late Charles Bradlaugh, the Victorian free-thinker, for whose funeral in 1891 some 5,000 well-wishers (the term mourners would be inappropriate), none wearing black, turned up at Waterloo Necropolis station to board the train with his coffin. In 1902 the Necropolis terminus moved from Waterloo station to 121 Westminster Bridge Road. The service was discontinued after the Second World War.

CHARLTON, se7

Perched on high ground near the Thames to the east of Greenwich, Charlton still retains some village charm.

Cemetery Lane

Charlton Cemetery

Founded in 1855 as a 'Gentleman's Cemetery', Charlton features typical Victorian effects such as a Church of England chapel in the Early English style and a Roman Catholic chapel in the decorated style. There are many memorials to military figures connected with the nearby Royal Arsenal. The most famous monument is that of Thomas Murphy, owner of Charlton greyhound track, who died in 1932 at the age of 39. His tomb is guarded by life-size stone greyhounds at the foot of Corinthian columns supporting entablature emblazoned with his name.

DEPTFORD, se8

Once a great maritime centre, thanks to its shipbuilding and the naval yard founded by Henry VIII, Deptford is now an industrialised sprawl blighted by slum estates.

Deptford Green

St Nicholas Churchyard

The revered Elizabethan playwright Christopher Marlowe was buried in an unmarked graveyard in St Nicholas's churchyard after being murdered in Deptford on 30 May 1593 at the age of 29.

Scholars are still unsure whether his death was an accident, planned murder or part of a political conspiracy. At the beginning of that month Marlowe's colleague Thomas Kyd was arrested in possession of a heretical tract. Under torture Kyd claimed it belonged to Marlowe. The playwright, already in trouble with the authorities on account of his unorthodox religious views, was hauled before the Privy Council on 20 May. Ten days later he was stabbed above the right eye, dying instantly, during a fight at a Deptford tavern with three other men, Ingram Frizer, Nicholas Skeres and Robert Poley, all of whom had links to the intelligence service. There is a plaque to Marlowe on the west wall of the churchyard.

ELTHAM, se9

An attractive suburb with older royal links than nearby Greenwich, Eltham is now infamous as the setting of the 1993 murder of black youth Stephen Lawrence, which has had far-reaching consequences on methods of policing.

Well Hall Road

Location of Stephen Lawrence's murder, at Dickson Road

Stephen Lawrence, a black architecture student, was stabbed by a gang of five or six white youths as he and a friend, Duwayne Brooks, waited for a bus on Well Hall Road at around 10.30 p.m. on 22 April 1993.

Brooks went to phone for an ambulance when a police car appeared on the scene, but officers decided that the injured youth did not need further assistance. Two main arteries had been severed and Lawrence was probably already beyond help. He later died in hospital.

Stephen Lawrence's parents complained of police insensitivity to their son's plight, and that officers did not take seriously crucial information which might have led to the quick apprehension of the culprits. Four local youths were charged with various offences, but the Crown Prosecution Service decided there was insufficient evidence to prosecute them for murder. Scotland Yard then put a different officer in charge of the case. His team installed a hidden camera into a flat used by the main suspects and filmed them making racist comments including threats to kill black people and policemen. However at Stephen Lawrence's inquest the youths refused to answer questions and the case collapsed. The *Daily Mail* took the unusual step of naming the five white youths believed to be the murderers and challenged them to sue the paper if the allegations were untrue. They did not. The Lawrences brought a private prosecution against the five, but this failed on insufficient evidence supplied by Duwayne Brooks.

In 1998 the Home Office set up the Macpherson Inquiry to investigate the policing of the case. Its report, published in February 1999, found that the failure to arrest the five main suspects was a mistake, criticised actions taken at the scene of the crime, the surveillance on the home of two of the suspects and the failure to follow up various clues. It also criticised police stereotyping of black people. But still no one has served time for the murder.

GREENWICH, SE10

One of the capital's great tourist destinations, home to the Old Royal Observatory, the National Maritime Museum, the Royal Naval College, the Cutty Sark tea clipper and Greenwich Park.

Blackwall Tunnel Approach

Millennium Dome

Rumours are still current in the London underworld that the body of Gilbert Wynter, an associate of the all-powerful Adams Family, was buried in the foundations of the dome when it was being built in the late 1990s. Wynter disappeared in 1998 after being cleared at the Old Bailey of murdering Claude Moseley, a former high-jump champion, whom he stabbed in the back with a samurai sword.

Greenwich Church Street

St Alfege

The first recorded murder in London history was that of Archbishop Alfege, killed by a group of Danes on this site, now marked by St Alfege church, in April 1012. The Danes seized the archbishop in Canterbury Cathedral and kept him in near-starvation on a ship on the Thames for seven months. They demanded a ransom – 3,000 pieces of silver. When that was not forthcoming, they killed him after a drunken feast, the mortal blow coming, ironically, from a Dane named Thrum whom Alfege had confirmed as a Christian only the previous day.

The first church was built on the site soon after Alfege's death, rebuilt in the late 13th century, and then again by Nicholas Hawksmoor in 1712–14. It is the burial site of Thomas Tallis (d. 1585), the 16th-century church musician commemorated in music by Vaughan Williams. The body of General James Wolfe, who died in action in Quebec in September 1759, was buried here in the family tomb.

Romney Road

Greenwich Palace

Henry VIII's successor, the ailing boy-king Edward VI, used to sit in the window of the palace in the 1540s so that locals knew he was still alive. He died in 1553, slowly poisoned to death, accidentally, by a doctor who administered arsenic. By the time Edward died his body was too disfigured to be shown to mourners. His last words were: 'Oh my Lord God, defend this realm from papistry and maintain Thy true religion.'

Greenwich Park

Martial Bourdin, a West End tailor and anarchist, blew himself up on Thursday 15 February 1894 when the bomb he was carrying to the Royal Observatory at the southern end of the park accidentally exploded. Bourdin wanted to destroy the Observatory because of its status as the 'capitalist' home of Time.

He survived the premature explosion but was severely injured. His guts were hanging from his stomach, and a finger had landed in a

SE10

nearby tree, where it was found a few days later. He pleaded to be allowed to go home, but instead was taken to the nearby Naval Hospital, where he died. Bourdin was identified through his membership card for the Autonomie anarchist club at 6 Windmill Street, Fitzrovia.

A week later, as Bourdin's funeral cortège passed through Fitzrovia, some 15,000 anti-anarchist protesters gathered, some smashing the windows of the club. The story inspired Joseph Conrad to write *The Secret Agent*, a convincing study of the terrorist mind, in which an anarchist known only as 'The Professor' wanders around London with a bomb and detonator strapped to his waist.

KENNINGTON, SE11

The name Kyning-tun comes from the 'place of the king' as the area was an occasional home to royalty in medieval times.

Kennington Park Road

Kennington Common (Kennington Park)

Before 19th-century development the area was dominated by Kennington Common, a public execution site, where 129 people were hanged on the Surrey gallows in late medieval times. On 30 July 1746 the victims included 17 Jacobites who had joined the Young Pretender (Bonnie Prince Charlie) in Manchester in preparations to seize the English throne. One of their number, an Andrew Wood, was fearless in facing death and even drank a glass to the Pretender's health on the scaffold. Another, a Colonel Towneley, retained signs of life after execution. The axeman struck him violently on the breast so that he wouldn't suffer during the next part of the punishment: the drawing and quartering (➥p. 65). When this didn't work, the executioner cut the colonel's throat. Once Towneley was dead his heart was extracted and bowels thrown on the fire.

On 3 August 1795 the highwayman Jeremiah Abershaw was hanged on the common. He had murdered David Price, a Bow Street Runner, at the Three Brewers inn in Southwark, having vowed to 'murder the first who attempted to deliver me into the hands of justice'. When a Bow Street team discovered that Abershaw was spending his takings at the Three Brewers they raided the tavern. Price found himself staring down the barrel of the highwayman's pistol while a fellow villain urged the other officers to stand clear. When they refused to do so Abershaw fired, killing Price instantly. Abershaw's trial took place at Croydon, the journey from prison taking the party through Kennington Common where Abershaw stuck his head out of the window and asked those in charge of him whether they 'did not think that he should be twisted on that pretty spot by next Saturday'.

NEW CROSS, SE14

The ancient Southwark to Canterbury road, which the pilgrims take in Chaucer's *Canterbury Tales*, meets the road to Vauxhall at New Cross Gate.

New Cross Road

Woolworth's, corner with Goodwood Road

A German V2 rocket fell on the store just before Christmas 1944, killing as many as 168 shoppers, some in the adjacent Co-op. Many passers-by were flung great distances, an army lorry overturned, killing its occupants and a double-decker bus spun round violently, causing more deaths. It took 48 hours to remove the victims from the premises. The bodies of 11 people who may have died in the tragedy were never found.

Site of the 1981 New Cross Fire, No. 439

After 13 young black people died in a fire that swept through No. 439 in January 1981, 15,000 locals marched to central London demanding an end to racist murders, even though the cause of the blaze was uncertain.

For years many suspected it had been started by racists and that officers failed to take the matter seriously on account of the skin colour of the victims.At the coroner's inquest doubt was cast over the integrity of the investigation and the police's professionalism, but matters became confused when witnesses admitted making false statements. All this resulted in the jury returning an open verdict.

In October 2002 the High Court agreed to hold a fresh inquest after lobbying from families. However, the second inquest, in May 2004, also returned an open verdict. There has since been a growing belief that the fire was an accident.

PECKHAM, SE15

Few London locales now bear as invidious a reputation as Peckham, setting for a succession of recent casual murders, in particular that of 10-year-old Damilola Taylor in 2000. Peckham's ever-worsening reputation as an area where all sense of morality has withered away was reinforced in the first decade of the 21st century when 17-year-old Roberto Malasi shot a 35-year-old woman in the head while she held her friend's baby at the child's christening on the Wood Dene Estate on Peckham High Street. Two weeks later Malasi stabbed to death an 18-year-old woman whom he had dragged out of her car after she had supposedly 'disrespected' him. Malasi was sentenced to life with the recommendation that he serve at least 40 years.

Blakes Road

Damilola Taylor murder place, North Peckham Estate

Ten-year-old Nigerian-born Damilola Taylor was murdered for reasons unknown on 27 November 2000 in the stairwell of the North Peckham Estate as he returned home from Peckham Library. He was stabbed in the left thigh, possibly with a broken bottle, and lay bleeding for half an hour before dying in the ambulance taking him to hospital.

There was profound shock at the callousness of the murder and the age of the victim. A high-profile investigation was set in motion, but it ran into several obstacles – silence from some of those involved or their refusal to take proceedings seriously. Two years later four juveniles went on trial at the Old Bailey for murder but all were acquitted after the judge ruled that the prosecution's key witness, a 12-year-old girl, was unreliable.

Police kept the investigation open and made new arrests in 2005. Again a trial ended without any convictions. At their re-trial for manslaughter in 2006, two brothers, Ricky and Danny Preddie, were convicted despite the defence's insistence that the fatal wound could have been caused by Damilola falling on a broken bottle, and that blood-stains on the Preddie brothers' footwear and clothing had been planted by the police. As the verdict was given Ricky Preddie was dragged away by prison service officers swearing 'You're all going to pay for this.'

Linden Grove

Nunhead Cemetery

There was a young man at Nunhead
Who awoke in his coffin of lead
It is cosy enough
He remarked in a huff
But I wasn't aware I was dead.

limerick, anon., 1908

The Cemetery of All Saints, begun in 1840 on the site of the Nun's Head tavern, was the London Cemetery Company's second after Highgate. It was built to ease the problem of overcrowded City churchyards, where as S. Haden noted, 'the soil had become so saturated and supersaturated with animal matter it could no longer properly be called soil'. Nunhead occupies a huge, overgrown expanse to the east of Peckham Rye Common that was surveyed by James Bunning, architect of the extravagant but now demolished Coal Exchange and Caledonian Market, and is characterised by its avenue of towering limes amid the Gothic gloom.

The first Nunhead burial was that of Charles Abbott, a 101-year-old

Ipswich grocer; the last, in 1998, that of a volunteer soldier who became a canon in Lahore Cathedral. Also buried here are Sir Wallis Budge (d. 1934), head of the Egyptian and Syrian antiquities collection at the British Museum, who translated the *Egyptian Book of the Dead* into English, and Robert Abel (d. 1936), the England test cricketer who made 357 runs in one innings at the Oval in 1899, a record that stood for several decades.

The best-known memorial in Nunhead is the 30-foot granite obelisk dedicated to five 18th-century political reformers now known as the Scottish Martyrs who were sent to Botany Bay, Australia, in 1793 for advocating granting the vote to the working class. Their case inspired Robert Burns to write the poem 'Scots Wha Hae' (1793) which closes the Scottish National Party conference every year.

In 1865 it was discovered that the cemetery's first superintendent had defrauded the cemetery company of thousands of pounds. Around 100 years later a property company bought Nunhead and planned new houses on the site until public outcry scotched the scheme. At the end of the 1960s the owners decided to close the cemetery, which by then was in an alarming state of neglect. The Nonconformist chapel had been demolished, the Anglican chapel vandalised and the vaults plundered for jewellery. In 1975, shortly after stories of sightings of a white-robed figure among the graves made the newspapers, Southwark council bought Nunhead for £1. Part of the cemetery is now a nature reserve, dominated by maple, oak, yew and ivy.

‖ Gwynplaine MacIntyre's 1994 sci-fi novel *The Woman Between the Worlds* depicts the 1898 Nunhead funeral of a female extra-terrestrial.

ROTHERHITHE, SE16

A land of market gardens, pastures and shipbuilding yards known as Redriff until the 18th century, it later acquired the name Rotherhithe – 'landing place for cattle' – which were brought here to be fattened up before being taken by boat to central London.

St Marychurch Street

St Mary

After Reggie Kray murdered Jack 'The Hat' McVitie in Stoke Newington in 1967 (☛ p. 184) associates charged with disposing of the body wrapped it in an eiderdown and bundled it into the back seat of a car, intending to dump the corpse somewhere in south London so that the rival Richardson gang would get the blame. They drove the car on a circuitous route through London (to lose any possible pursuers) and left it outside St Mary's church in Rotherhithe. When the Kray twins were told, they were livid and sent henchmen to the church to move the body before anyone found it. In the meantime a wedding had taken place at St Mary's and the car was strewn with confetti – with Jack still on the back seat wrapped in the eiderdown. The corpse has never been found.

UPPER NORWOOD, SE19

The world's first recorded fatal car accident occurred in Upper Norwood on 17 August 1896 when Bridget Driscoll was hit by a vehicle in the grounds of the Crystal Palace while walking to a folk-dancing display. She died within minutes from head injuries. Although the driver, Arthur Edsel, claimed he had been doing only 4 mph, witnesses said he had been travelling at 'reckless pace'. At the inquest the coroner announced, somewhat optimistically, that he hoped such a thing would never happen again.

HONOR OAK, SE23

The oak is the tree by which Elizabeth I picnicked on May Day 1602 and was originally known as the Oak of Honor.

Brenchley Gardens

Camberwell New Cemetery

Two well-known 1960s figures connected to the Kray gang are buried in the cemetery. Freddie Mills, light-heavyweight world champion in the 1940s, was found dead in his car in the West End on 22 July 1965. He may have killed himself after carrying out the so-called 'Jack the Stripper' murders (☞p. 81). According to another theory he was murdered by the Krays as part of a gangland feud. Also in the cemetery is the South London villain George Cornell, famously shot by Ronnie Kray in the Blind Beggar pub in the East End on 9 March 1966 (☞p. 141), the killing which led to Kray's conviction.

SYDENHAM, SE26

Sydenham was where the Crystal Palace was relocated after the 1851 Great Exhibition.

Jews Walk

Eleanor Marx death place, *No. 7*

Eleanor Marx, daughter of Karl Marx, poisoned herself at her Sydenham house on 31 March 1898 at the age of 43 after discovering that her lover, Edward Aveling, had secretly married an actress. When the maid entered her mistress's bedroom at 11 a.m. she found her dead on the bed dressed entirely in white, a bottle of prussic acid by her side and a note which read: 'Dear ——. It will soon be over now. My last word to you is the same that I have said during all these long sad years – love.'

An alternative theory claims that she was poisoned by Aveling. At the inquest it was revealed that on the morning Eleanor died the maid had handed a local chemist a note which read: 'Please give the bearer chloroform and a small quantity of prussic acid for the dog – E. A.' Aveling's card was enclosed with the note, but the court heard that he was journeying to London when the note was handed in.

The coroner ruled that Marx had taken her own life in a state of temporary insanity, a suicide modelled on that of Emma in Flaubert's *Madame Bovary*, the book she had been the first to translate from French into English. Some years later the socialist leader Henry Hyndman claimed that Aveling had told Marx that another woman was trying to force him to marry her and that he and Eleanor arranged a suicide pact, which he failed to keep to.

WEST NORWOOD, SE27

In Victorian times this was Lower Norwood, one of a number of similarly-named places created by the enclosure acts which divided up the Great North Wood.

Norwood High Street

South Metropolitan Cemetery

Better known simply as Norwood, the country's first Gothic Cemetery is a typical example of the Victorian fascination with death, and is resplendent with urns, catacombs, angels, broken columns, monuments and memorials. Indeed Norwood vies with Highgate as London's grandest burial site, even if it is now run down.

Norwood was built in 1837 as one of the big seven commercial graveyards, the work of the South Metropolitan Cemetery Company, and set in 41 acres of land in Lambeth Manor, with the plots on the central higher ground sold originally as prime locations. The design was carried out by William Tite who created a hydraulic lift or catafalque to transport the coffins from the chapel to the vaults below, built the Gothic Anglican chapel in the style of King's College Chapel, Cambridge, and created the Nonconformist chapel at the top of the hill at the east end of the cemetery. Both chapels were damaged in the Second World War and demolished, the latter reworked as a crematorium. The only remaining example of Tite's work is his monument for the banker J. W. Gilbart, in the spandrels of which a carved squirrel gathers nuts, a reference to Gilbart's banking interests.

One of the most impressive memorials is the Greek-style Ralli chapel which Stephen Ralli built in 1872 for his son, Augustus, who died of rheumatic fever at Eton. George Edmund Street, architect of the Royal

Courts of Justice on the Strand, designed a mausoleum for another member of the Ralli family, John, which skilfully uses different types of stone.

Lambeth council compulsorily bought the cemetery in 1965 and carried out an unsympathetic clean-up. Recently, however, the council has worked with the Friends of West Norwood Cemetery to improve the site.

BURIED AT NORWOOD

- **Thomas Cubitt**, the building contractor who created so many developments in Islington and Belgravia, left the longest will ever written.
- **Isabella Beeton** (d. 1865) wrote the famous *Mrs Beeton's Book of Household Management* in 1861 and died four years later in childbirth.
- **Charles Bravo** (d 1876) was a victim of the Balham poisoning case (☞p. 254). His face had 'acquired the dark hue of a mummy, the teeth almost entirely black', according to the inquest verdict.
- **William Burges** (d. 1881), high Gothic designer and architect extraordinaire, was buried in the tomb he designed for his mother. Mordaunt Crook, the architectural historian, wrote his epitaph: 'ugly Burges who designed such lovely things – what a duck'.
- **Sir Henry Tate** (d. 1899) was a sugar merchant. It is to his philanthropy that we owe the Tate Gallery.
- **Hiram Maxim** (d. 1916), an American-born engineer, invented the Maxim gun, an early type of machine gun.

SE27

CHAPTER 10

South-West London

BELGRAVIA, SW1
Cadogan Lane
Chapel Street
Eaton Place
Grosvenor Gardens/Buckingham
Palace Road/Victoria Street
Lower Belgrave Street
Victoria Station Approach
Wilton Crescent

BRIXTON, SW2, SW9
Brixton Road

CHELSEA, SW3
Cheyne Row
Cheyne Walk
Old Church Street
Royal Hospital Road
Tedworth Square
Tite Street

CLAPHAM, SW4
Clapham Common North Side
The Avenue

FULHAM, SW6
Gowan Avenue

KNIGHTSBRIDGE, SW7
Gloucester Road
Kensington Gore
Montpelier Square
Onslow Square
Prince's Gate

WEST BROMPTON, SW10
Fulham Road

BARNES, SW13
Queen's Ride

MORTLAKE, SW14
North Worple Way

PUTNEY, SW15
Kingston Road

STREATHAM, SW16
Bedford Hill

WANDSWORTH, SW18
Heathfield Square
Magdalen Road

Further south-west
RICHMOND
Maid of Honour Row

BELGRAVIA, sw1

A land of embassies and luxurious stucco terraces, Belgravia was built in the 19th century over open land known as the Five Fields, a swamp through which the River Westbourne flowed and 'a place where robbers lie in wait', as Addison wrote in the *Tatler*.

Cadogan Lane

Judy Garland death place, *No. 4*

The actress Judy Garland died of an accidental overdose of sleeping tablets in the bathroom at 4 Cadogan Lane on 22 June 1969, aged 47. She had married for the fifth time only a few months before. At her funeral in New York Ray Bolger, her co-star in *The Wizard of Oz*, commented: 'She was just plain wore out.'

Chapel Street

Beatles manager Brian Epstein died of a drug overdose at No. 24 on 27 August 1967. The Beatles were meeting the Maharishi Mahesh Yogi in north Wales at the time.

Eaton Place

A long stark street of stucco houses, built in 1826–45, which has been home to the wealthy ever since. Recent residents including the musical impresario Andrew Lloyd Webber.

No. 36

One of the first killings carried out in London by Irish nationalists was that of Sir Henry Wilson, the former chief of the Imperial Staff, shot dead as he stepped out of a car outside No. 36, his home, on 22 June 1922. The butler, who was in the pantry at the time, heard four shots and rushed upstairs where he picked up Sir Henry's sword 'as it was out of its scabbard'. He ran outside and, as he later explained, saw Sir Henry 'lying half on the pavement, half on the street'.

Grosvenor Gardens / Buckingham Palace Road / Victoria Street

For hundreds of years this junction was regularly used for burying suicides. A crossroads was used as popular belief had it that if someone's spirit wished to haunt its former home, the choice of four roads would confuse it. Crossroads burial was abolished by an Act of Parliament in 1823 after George IV's carriage was held up by a crowd of spectators that had gathered here to watch the burial of the suicide Abel Griffiths.

Lower Belgrave Street

Lord Lucan's address (1970s), *No. 46*

Richard John Bingham, better known as Lord Lucan, disappeared, never to be seen again, following the murder of the family nanny, Sandra Rivett, and an attack on his wife, Veronica, here on 7 November 1974, both of which were possibly carried out by the peer.

The drama unfolded when Lady Lucan went down to the darkened basement to find out why the nanny was so long making a cup of tea. She was grabbed around the throat by a gloved hand and hit on the

head by an assailant, who she later claimed was her husband. He told
her he had killed the nanny mistakenly, thinking it was her.

Lady Lucan saved her own life, she later explained, by reasoning
with the peer while she nursed her wounds. Once Lucan had left the
house she fled in her nightclothes, running into the nearby Plumbers
Arms pub, her head wet with rain and blood, shouting: 'Murder, there's
been a murder. He's in the house... my children... he murdered the
nanny.' Despite a number of alleged sightings in places as far apart as
Goa and Gibraltar, Lord Lucan has never been found.

Victoria Station Approach

Victoria station

After Queen Victoria died at Osborne House on the Isle of Wight on
22 January 1901 the coffin was taken by train to, appropriately, Victoria
station where the huge crowd awaiting it included the King of Portugal,
the Crown Prince of Siam and the King of the Hellenes.

Just before the cortège left for Buckingham Palace a mounted soldier galloped out of the station to the point where he could be seen by
the next look-out. The funeral procession then made its way up
Buckingham Palace Road towards Buckingham Palace.

Going the other way one day in spring 1936 was the funeral cortège
of Leopold von Hoesch, the German ambassador to Britain, who supposedly died of heart failure after collapsing in the bathroom of the
German embassy on The Mall (☛p. 105), but was more likely a victim
of political assassination by the Nazis.

Wilton Crescent

The northern approach to Belgrave Square was designed by Seth Smith
around a grassed area decorated with classical embellishments.

No. 40

In 1912 Lady Drogheda held her séances here in a room designed in
contemporary pagan by the modernist artist Wyndham Lewis. He provided silver-foil ceilings, matt black velvet walls bordered by a Vorticist
frieze, and blue glass witch-balls standing on columns in the centre of
the room – all bathed in the unnatural glow of yellow alabaster lamps.
Guests at Lady Drogheda's occultist gatherings included Jacob Epstein,

the sculptor; Sir Ernest Cassel, who had been Edward VII's personal financier and tended to the king on his death-bed; and the painter Augustus John.

BRIXTON, sw2, sw9

A cosmopolitan suburb developed as a retreat for City merchants following the opening of Brixton station in 1862. After the Second World War it became one of the most popular destinations for Caribbean immigrants.

Brixton Road

Brixton police station, No. 367

The death of Wayne Douglas, a young black man, in custody at the police station on Wednesday 13 December 1995 provoked the third Brixton riots. Douglas was arrested in a children's playground in the early hours of Tuesday 5 December and severely beaten up by officers who sat on him so heavily that witnesses said they could hear the sound of his bones crunching. After Douglas's death a peaceful protest outside the station turned nasty when one public speaker described the police as 'killers'. An hour later, during a march along Brixton Road, scuffles broke out and bottles were thrown by youths wearing masks. Soon there were running battles between the police and rioters, shops were attacked and cars were set on fire.

CHELSEA, sw3

Chelsea's name derived from either Ceoles-ige ('place of ships'), Chesil ('a gravel bank'), or Celchyth ('a chalk wharf') in medieval times and it grew as a fishing village. Since the Victorian era Chelsea has been one of the most picturesque of London's inner suburbs.

Cheyne Row

St Thomas More, No. 7

The funeral of the hell-raising actor Richard Harris took place at St Thomas More on 29 October 2002 before his ashes were scattered in the Bahamas. In attendance was the equally uproarious fellow actor Russell Crowe who flew 5,500 miles to be there and told reporters: 'I love him – and I miss him.' The admiration was mutual for Harris. Just before he died of lymphatic cancer at 72, Harris wrote of Crowe: 'Top bloke, loves his rugby, doesn't give a stuff, brilliant actor, a much loved new friend. He will carry the baton on' – but which baton he didn't specify. After the service six pall bearers carried Harris's coffin, draped in an Irish flag, out of the church. The throng then left for a wake at the Goring Hotel near Victoria station, where Crowe leapt on to the bar and raised a pint of Guinness before reciting an Irish poem.

Cheyne Walk

A riverside street lined with the finest Jacobean and Queen Anne properties, it was named after the Cheyne family, lords of the Chelsea manor in the late 17th century. Its sweeping vistas and excellent light have attracted several painters including J. M. W. Turner, who died here in 1852.

George Eliot's address and death place (1880), *No. 4*

The great Victorian novelist George Eliot died on Cheyne Walk shortly after marrying John Cross, 20 years her junior. They had just spent a largely unhappy honeymoon in Venice, where he had tried to commit suicide. Despite his best efforts to drown, he was rescued from a canal by gondoliers. When they moved into their house, Eliot optimistically announced: 'I find myself in a new climate here, the London air and this particular house being so warm.' Nevertheless she died a few weeks later from kidney disease.

James Neild deathsite, *No. 5*

Neild, who lived in the property for 60 years from the end of the 18th century, inherited his father's wealth but became a miser. Dressed in rags, he walked everywhere, particularly to collect the rents from his many properties, ate little, and had no friends, other than his cat. In his will he left half a million pounds to Queen Victoria.

No. 27

Bram Stoker, author of *Dracula* (1897), lived here in the 1870s, and one day fished a drowning man out of the adjacent river. Stoker laid him on the table after failing to revive him, and went off to get assistance. In the meantime his wife entered the room oblivious to the drama to find a dead man on the dining-room table. The couple moved a few months later.

J. M. W. Turner's death place, *No. 119*

The watercolourist J. M. W. Turner died in this property, then 6 Davis Place, after spending the last six years of his life living incognito as 'Mr Booth', a retired admiral as far as locals were concerned. Turner built a gallery on the roof of the cottage so that he could watch the sunsets. On his deathbed on 19 December 1851 his last words were: 'The sun is God,' predictable given his body of work. Some, however, have interpreted it as the more devout 'The Son is God.'

Chelsea Old Church

Rebuilt after Second World War damage, the church nonetheless contains a fine set of monuments. Among those honoured are Sir Hans Sloane (d. 1753), whose collections formed the basis of the British Museum and the Chelsea Physic Garden. When the tablet was unveiled the vicar announced: 'We have given this great man the best spot we could find. The new plaque is beside the tomb of the family of the squire who picked up the crown at the battle of Bosworth and presented it to the knight who then handed it to the new Tudor King.'

There is also a memorial to Henry James, the revered *fin de siècle* author who lived nearby, which reads: 'In memory of Henry James, Novelist Born in New York, 1843. Died in Chelsea, 1916. Lover and interpreter of the fine amenities of brave decisions and generous loyalties: resident of this parish, who renounced a cherished citizenship to give his allegiance to England in the first year of the Great War.' When James died in March 1916 a notice appeared in *The Times* which simply read 'James – On the 28th Feb Henry James OM in his 73rd year. Funeral service at Chelsea Old Church, Cheyne-walk. Friday March 3 at 2.opm. Will friends kindly accept this as the only intimation. No flowers, by request.'

Old Church Street

No. 44

Steve Clark, guitarist for 1980s metal band Def Leppard, died in his sleep in this cottagey, three-storey house on 8 January 1991 at the age of 30 after years of drug and alcohol abuse. According to the band's biographer, Dave Dickson, Clark had an alcohol level in his blood of 0.59 when admitted to hospital. 'When you consider that 0.30 would reduce any ordinary mortal to a coma, and that 0.41 was allegedly the amount that killed Led Zeppelin's drummer in 1980...'

Royal Hospital Road

Royal Hospital

The grandest funeral in London history – dwarfing even those of Winston Churchill and Ronnie Kray – was that of the Duke of Wellington, victor over Napoleon at Waterloo, following his death on 14 September 1852. The cortège left the Royal Hospital, en route to St Paul's, led by a funeral coach made out of metal from the guns used during the battle. It took the 12 horses pulling it four and a half hours to complete the journey.

Tedworth Square

No. 23

It was while the 61-year-old Mark Twain, author of the timeless American classics *Tom Sawyer* and *Huckleberry Finn*, was lodging in Chelsea during a worldwide lecture tour in 1896–1897 that he was visited by a reporter from the *New York Journal* carrying two cablegrams from the paper. One read: 'If Mark Twain dying in poverty, in London, send 500 words,' the other: 'If Mark Twain has died in poverty send 1000 words.' Writing in the *New York Journal*, Twain noted: 'The rumors of my death have been greatly exaggerated' – usually misquoted as 'News of my death has been greatly exaggerated.'

Tite Street

Peter Warlock's death place (1930), *No. 30*

A minor composer but a major eccentric, Warlock, real name Philip Heseltine, who was born in the Savoy Hotel, was a manic-depressive, 'unable to work unless surrounded by cats and mistresses', according to his biographer Cecil Gray. After dabbling in black magic Warlock gassed himself shortly before Christmas 1930.

CLAPHAM, SW4

To the west of Clapham Junction station, the largest in the country, the streets are charmless. Further east, near the common, one of the largest open spaces in the vicinity, they soon give way to spacious villas. Clapham took on its present-day appearance in the late 19th century after tube stations were opened on the high street.

Clapham Common North Side

Samuel Pepys's address (1700–1703), *No. 29*

Towards the end of the 17th century, after he quit the Navy, the great diarist Samuel Pepys retired to a huge black-brick villa, described by his fellow diarist John Evelyn as 'very noble & wonderfully well furnished', which belonged to William Hewer, his former secretary. After

Pepys died here on 26 May 1703 seven large stones were found in his kidneys.

It was remarkable that Pepys had lasted so long. He had been afflicted for years with kidney stones, as he revealed in the opening section of his diary, and in his youth had undergone a painful operation, without anaesthetic, to remove them.

The house was later demolished and replaced with a property designed by Charles Barry, architect of the Houses of Parliament, who died here in 1860.

The Avenue

Clapham Common

The discovery of the battered body of Leon Beron, an immigrant Russian Jew and a slum landlord, on Clapham Common on New Year's Day 1911, led to a web of intrigue involving the two most dramatic East End events of the period – the Houndsditch Murders (☛p. 18) and the Siege of Sidney Street (☛p. 131).

Beron was found with his head bashed in, probably by a blunt instrument, his legs crossed, his wallet empty and an 'S' carved on to his cheek 'like the holes on a violin', according to the police surgeon. The 'S' was probably a punishment mark, perhaps standing for the Polish word *spiccan* or spy, and a rumour soon swept through the Jewish Ghetto in the East End that Beron had divulged to the police the identities of those implicated in the Houndsditch escapade.

Earlier on the day Beron was found, some of those involved in robbing the Houndsditch jeweller's store and killing the police who came to arrest them had holed themselves up at 100 Sidney Street in Whitechapel. They died in the fire that engulfed the property some hours later. Beron's murder was probably connected with both events, witnesses told the authorities.

Detectives established that the murderer was a 'tall, strong, left-handed man', and they soon arrested such a man. He was Steinie Morrison, a petty felon and fellow Russian Jew, real name Alexander Petropavloff, with whom Beron had often been seen dining at the Warsaw Kosher Restaurant, 32 Osborn Street, Whitechapel. Circumstantial evidence against Morrison was strong. He had been working near the common, and on the morning of the murder had deposited a revolver and bullets at the left-luggage office of St Mary's tube station. A jury found Morrison guilty of murder, and he was sentenced to death, but he failed to become only the third Jew to be hanged in Britain for murder due to the clemency of the home secretary, Winston Churchill, who commuted his sentence. Morrison, far from celebrating his escape, protested his innocence with a series of hunger strikes that so weakened him that he died in prison ten years later.

FULHAM, sw6

A mostly pleasant riverside middle-class neighbourhood with little eventful history but a rich sporting tradition thanks to the Hurlingham Club, where the first polo match was played in 1874, and Fulham and Chelsea football clubs.

Gowan Avenue

Jill Dando deathsite, *No. 29*

Television presenter Jill Dando was shot dead on the doorstep of her Fulham house on 26 April 1999 by an unknown gunman, believed by some to be local eccentric Barry George, who was jailed for her murder following one of the highest-profile court cases in London history.

As Dando arrived at the house at about 11.30 a.m. after visiting her fiancé, she was shot once in the head with a 9mm semi-automatic pistol. The murder enquiry soon began to focus on a smartly dressed man carrying a mobile telephone who was spotted leaving the scene. A few days later it emerged that Dando had received a letter from a 'Serbian source' attacking a charity appeal she had made for Kosovan refugees two weeks previously.

Nevertheless a month later police arrested George, following surveillance of his home. The evidence against him was slim, but he could not satisfactorily account for his movements at the time of Dando's death. It soon became clear that George would not have been competent enough to stage such a calculated killing, and the investigation was clouded by further inconsistencies which were concealed in the authorities' relentless pursuit of so easy a target.

KNIGHTSBRIDGE, sw7

An enclave of South-West London exuding wealth and importance thanks to the charming mews and alleys of Knightsbridge village, and the museums by Exhibition Road.

Gloucester Road

Originally Hogmore Lane but renamed after Maria, Duchess of Gloucester, in 1826.

Gloucester Road station

The Polish countess Teresa Lubienska was killed – possibly assassinated – in the tube station after getting off a train on 24 May 1957. As the lift opened at ground level the countess staggered out with blood pouring from her chest, crying 'bandits, bandits'. She collapsed into the arms of the ticket collector and though an ambulance was called, she died a few hours later at St Mary Abbots hospital. She had been stabbed five times in the heart.

The 73-year-old countess had spent the Second World War as a member of the Polish resistance, and had been arrested by the Nazis, who incarcerated her in Ravensbruck concentration camp, where she had the number '44747' tattooed on her arm. In London, in the 1950s, she campaigned for compensation for Poles imprisoned for political reasons during the war.

The murder investigation was led by John Du Rose, head of Scotland Yard's Murder Squad, who went by the nickname 'Four Day Johnny', on account of the speed with which he usually solved cases. Du Rose showed how the murderer could have stabbed the countess on the platform and raced up the emergency stairs quickly enough to beat the lift by 13 seconds. He sent scores of officers to Lubienska's funeral at Brompton Oratory looking for clues, but no one was ever apprehended for the murder. Historians believe she was murdered by a Nazi revenge organisation.

Acid Bath Murder site, No. 79

John George Haigh, a suave businessman, carried out a gruesome series of homicides in the 1940s, some at his basement workshop at 79 Gloucester Road, until he was unveiled as the 'Acid Bath Murderer'.

Haigh rented the property as a workshop for making plastic fingernails, and in September 1944 invited an acquaintance, William McSwan, to the premises. There Haigh battered McSwan to death with the leg of a pin table. He then made an incision in McSwan's neck, collected the blood in a tea cup, and drank it. Once sated, Haigh put the body in a water butt and covered it with concentrated sulphuric acid. The corpse failed to dissolve completely and Haigh had to finish off the process with a cleaver and a mincer he had bought from the department store Gamages.

Haigh kept in contact with McSwan's parents, writing them letters which suggested their son was still alive but had disappeared to avoid joining the army. A year later he invited Mr and Mrs McSwan to Gloucester Road to show them some contraptions he had been working on. When they arrived he shot them and immersed the bodies in a vat of acid, taking care to wear a full-length leather apron and gas mask. He then posed as their son to claim a share of their £5,600 estate.

Events finally caught up with Haigh after the disappearance of a guest at the Kensington hotel where he lived, whom he murdered. Haigh admitted his crimes but explained that he had committed them simply to satisfy a fascination for blood which dated back to his child-hood, rather than for profit. His plea of insanity was not accepted, and he was hanged in August 1949.

Kensington Gore

Royal Albert Hall

A week after the death of Arthur Conan Doyle in 1930 some 10,000 people turned up at the hall to witness his resurrection. On the stage was an empty chair bearing a reservation card in the Sherlock Holmes author's name. During the meeting, which Conan Doyle, a keen spiritualist, had arranged, relatives gave speeches, fellow writers read tributes and the crowd sang hymns. Conan Doyle failed to attend – in corporeal terms at least.

Montpelier Square

Arthur Koestler deathsite (1983), *No. 8*

The writer Arthur Koestler and his third wife, Cynthia Jeffries, killed themselves in a suicide pact here on 3 March 1983. They were both members of the voluntary euthanasia society Exit, and left all their worldly goods to fund a chair in parapsychology at Edinburgh University.

Onslow Square

No. 105

Gunter Podola, a German exile, shot dead Detective Sergeant Purdy outside this block of flats on 12 July 1959 after escaping the police's clutches. Podola, a one-time member of the Hitler Youth, had emigrated to Canada, where he was imprisoned for burglary. He returned to Germany on his release and decided to move to London in May 1959. Unemployed, he stayed in various hotels in Kensington, and that July burgled a Mrs Verne Schieffman at a local flat. Podola then went to a telephone box by South Kensington tube station, phoned Mrs Schieffman and tried to blackmail her, claiming he had embarrassing photos and tape recordings of her. As Mrs Schieffman knew she had nothing to hide she went to the police, who tapped her phone. When Podola rang again on 13 July they were able to trace the call to the telephone box.

Two detectives raced there and arrested Podola. But as they were walking to the police car Podola escaped and ran into Onslow Square. He was recaptured and, while one of the detectives, Sergeant Sandford, went to get the police car, Detective Sergeant Purdy was left guarding

Podola in the hall of a block of flats. Podola distracted Purdy, pulled out an automatic pistol, and shot him in the heart. He died soon after. Officers later caught up with Podola in a nearby hotel. He was hanged at Wandsworth, the last person to be executed in Britain for the murder of a policeman.

Prince's Gate

A peeling stucco terrace set back from Knightsbridge that was built as an entrance to Hyde Park, it was opened by Edward, Prince of Wales, in 1848, and attained notoriety for the Iranian Embassy siege that took place here in 1980.

Iranian Embassy (1980s), *No. 27, south side*
Five gunmen were killed when the SAS stormed the building to end the Iranian Embassy siege on 5 May 1980. The siege began on 30 April when gunmen demanding autonomy for the Khuzestan province of Iran and the release of 99 political prisoners took over the building. The events were captured live on television and unfolded amid enormous media attention as the prime minister, Margaret Thatcher, stipulated that there would be no surrender to terrorism.

On the sixth day the terrorists threatened to kill the hostages one by one unless their demands were met. At 6.40 p.m. shots were heard and the body of an Iranian diplomat was pushed out of the front door. Half an hour later the SAS launched their successful rescue operation, freed the hostages and killed five gunmen. Twenty-four of the 26 hostages were released unharmed.

WEST BROMPTON, SW10

Though less visually enticing than Chelsea, with which it effortlessly blends, West Brompton contains some of London's most expensive and luxurious properties, particularly those on The Boltons.

Fulham Road

Brompton Cemetery

Readers all as you pass by,
As you are now so once was I,
As I am now so you will be.
Prepare for death and follow me!
          Brompton epitaph

One of the seven great Victorian London cemeteries – Gardens of the Dead – Brompton was created in the 1830s to ease the overcrowding of the City graveyards. It was built on a flat, featureless sliver of land owned by Lord Kensington, nearly 40 acres in size, nestling on the banks of the Kensington Canal (since replaced by the District Line).

The original architect was Stephen Geary, founder of Highgate Cemetery, who was also responsible for the monument to George IV known as King's Cross. He was soon replaced by Benjamin Baud whose ambitious design included two grand entrances, a water gate to the canal, a circular colonnade and three chapels. This was all part of Baud's master plan to create a symmetrical, open-air 'cathedral' where the ceremonial drive which runs south from the main entrance is the sacristy, a high altar is created by the Anglican chapel, and the 100-yard diameter Great Circle symbolises the Piazza at St Peter's, Rome.

Financial problems and disagreements over who owned the land delayed the start of burials. The lack of access on to Fulham Road until 1846 also hampered the cemetery in its early days. By the time Brompton was in regular use fashion had moved away somewhat from Baud's rigid classicism towards romantic Gothic. Baud's work was scaled down and, when structural defects were found, he was sacked, just like his predecessor, Geary, had been.

The cemetery was initially divided into 60,000 plots. On the west side common graves took several coffins in a deep cut with no marker. Many of these were of soldiers as Brompton's was London's main military cemetery. On the east side were the private graves, sold in perpetuity, 20 feet deep and containing brick-lined vaults.

Brompton is now managed by the Royal Parks and closed for burials except where old graves can be reopened.

‖ Beatrix Potter, who lived nearby in *The Boltons*, took the names of many of her animals from tombstones in the cemetery after spotting a Mr Nutkins, a Tod, Jeremiah Fisher, Tommy Brock and even a Peter Rabbett. She also based Mr McGregor's walled garden on the colonnades.

BURIED AT BROMPTON

‖ **John Snow** (d. 1858) single-handedly prevented the spread of cholera in the West End thanks to his tireless campaigning for clean water (☞ p. 79).

‖ The magazine *The Builder* was not impressed with the monument for **Coombes**, the champion sculler (d. 1866), describing the upturned skiff as 'bad and vulgar, so ugly as a whole, so execrable in the details'.

‖ **John Wisden** (d. 1884) was the late-Victorian cricketer after whom the games' annual handbook is named.

‖ **Frederick Leyland** (d. 1892), patron of the Pre-Raphaelites, has Brompton's grandest tomb, designed by Edward Burne-Jones.

‖ **Long Wolf** (d. 1892), the American Indian Sioux chief, was buried here, having died at the age of 59 of bronchial pneumonia while touring Europe with Buffalo Bill's Wild West Show. In 1997 his remains were moved to the Wolf Creek Community Cemetery in South Dakota.

‖ **Emmeline Pankhurst** (d. 1928), the suffragette leader, died only a few weeks after women were granted the vote. Her grave is marked by a Celtic cross with figures carved in relief in the style of Eric Gill.

11 **Luisa Casati** (d. 1957) was a socialite at whose parties guests were served by nude servants gilded in gold leaf and wearing live snakes as jewellery. She was buried with a stuffed Pekingese dog at her feet, and her tomb was inscribed with the well-known line from Shakespeare's *Antony and Cleopatra*: 'Age cannot wither her, nor custom stale her infinite variety'.

SW10

BARNES, SW13

One of the most picturesque 'villages' in London, equalling Highgate and Hampstead in visual appeal on account of its riverside setting, Barnes was built on land owned by the canons of St Paul's in the Middle Ages. It developed when the railway arrived from Waterloo in 1848, and was soon covered with streets of elegant houses and a high street of cosy shops.

Queen's Ride

Marc Bolan death place, *at railway bridge*

Marc Bolan, the best-selling rock star in Britain in the early 1970s, was killed on the night of 16 September 1977 when his purple Mini, driven by his girlfriend, Gloria Jones, crashed into a sycamore as it came over the bridge from the east. The impact at 45 mph flattened the engine compartment, snapped off the gear lever, and forced the steering wheel into the roof. Neither passenger was wearing a seat belt, and though Jones suffered only a broken jaw and facial injuries, Bolan took the full force of the impact and died instantly. The tree has since become a site of pilgrimage, particularly on 16 September every year, and is festooned with flowers and ribbons, and covered in graffiti.

MORTLAKE, SW14

The name has nothing to do with 'mort' – death – but simply means Morta's Lake, Morta being a Saxon chief. Nine years before Mortlake resident and Somerset MP Edward Colston died in 1719 he left detailed funerary instructions which must have caused his executors many nightmares.

As to what to relate to my funeral, I would not have the least pomp used at it; nor any gold rings given; only that my corpse shall be carried to Bristol in a hearse and met at Lawford's Gate, and accompanied from thence to All Saints Church by all the boys at my Hospital on St Augustine's back, and by the six boys maintained by me in Queen Elizabeth's Hospital in the College green.

And also by the twenty-four poor men and women or so many of them are able in my almshouse on St Michael's hill, and only to the church door of All Saints. Likewise by the six poor old sailors that are kept at my charge in the Merchants' almshouse in the Marsh.

And likewise by the forty boys in Temple parish, that are clothed and otherwise provided by me. To be drawn directly thither, so it may be there in the close of the evening, or the first part of the night; and my further desire is, that at my interment the whole burial service of the church, as it is now appointed, may be decently read and performed.

North Worple Way

St Mary Magdalene

On the first Sunday in May every year a procession of Ghanaian pilgrims dressed in purple, brown and green sashes – members of the Noble Order of the Knights and Ladies of Sir James Marshall – come to St Mary Magdalene, a Roman Catholic church, to lay a wreath on the tomb of their founder, who revived the Catholic Church in their country in the mid-20th century.

The churchyard is home to Richard Burton's remarkable mausoleum which is in the shape of a large stone tent. There is a ladder which allows visitors to get a view of the inside. Burton was a 19th-century explorer who was the first European to enter Mecca (he was disguised as an Arab). After he died in Trieste in 1890 his wife, Isobel, burned all his diaries and unpublished manuscripts and produced a sanitised version of his life. His wish, to be buried in a tent in the desert, was evidently only partly carried out. Alongside him is Isobel. The vault was partly sealed in the 1950s after a number of thefts.

Nearby is the less visited crumbling Gothic vault for Guillaume Henry, Comte de Vezlo, a French noble who died in 1901 aged seven.

PUTNEY, SW15

Putney's name derives from Putta's landing place. Now quintessential London suburbia, until Putney Bridge was built in 1729 it was a farming and fishing community where a third of males were employed as watermen. Growth around Putney High Street followed the arrival of the railway in 1846, and much of the modern-day housing stock was erected towards the end of the 19th century.

Two Cabinet ministers, George Canning, the foreign secretary, and Viscount Castlereagh, secretary for war, were lucky not to die when they fought a duel on Putney Heath on 21 September 1809. Canning challenged Castlereagh to a duel when he discovered that troops he had sent to Portugal had been diverted to Holland by the viscount. Canning was shot in the thigh; Castlereagh was slightly injured by a bullet that ricocheted off a button.

Kingston Road

Putney Vale Cemetery

Wandsworth Council bought farmland in 1887 for a new cemetery as land on Putney Common was by then full, and four years later the first burial took place. In typical late-Victorian style the cemetery is dominated by massed monuments, Egyptian-styled mausoleums, and much granite and limestone. A crematorium was added in 1935, and a Garden of Remembrance two years later.

BURIED AT PUTNEY VALE

- **Bruce Ismay** (d. 1937), owner of the *Titanic*, survived the disaster and saved many lives during its capsizing but was berated, particularly in American newspapers, for not going down with the vessel. Ismay's tomb features three masted schooners sailing in a stormy sea.
- **Howard Carter** (d. 1939), the discoverer of the tomb of Tutankhamun, surprisingly did *not* fall victim to the so-called curse responsible for the deaths of many connected with the findings (p. 74). On Carter's gravestone is written: 'May your spirit live, May you spend millions of years, You who love Thebes, Sitting with your face to the north wind, Your eyes beholding happiness.'
- The sculptor **Jacob Epstein** (d. 1959) created the monument on Oscar Wilde's grave in Paris's Père-Lachaise Cemetery.
- **Alexander Kerensky** (d. 1970), the last prime minister of Russia before the Bolsheviks seized control in 1917, lasted considerably longer than his contemporaries, dying at home in New York City in 1970. Local Russian Orthodox churches refused to bury him, blaming him for allowing their country to fall into revolutionary hands. Eventually the body was flown to London so that it could be buried at non-denominational Putney Vale.

ıı **Sandy Denny**, the honey-voiced singer of folk rock exponents Fairport Convention, died aged only 31 in 1978, after falling down the stairs at her parents' home.

ıı **Jim Laker** (d. 1986) still holds the probably unbeatable record of taking 19 wickets out of a maximum 20 in a single match for England (against Australia in 1956).

ıı **Bobby Moore**, England's World Cup-winning captain, was cremated here in May 1993 after his premature death from cancer. The ashes were then interred at the City of London Crematorium.

ıı **James Hunt**, the 1976 motor-racing champion, was terrified of dying in a Grand Prix crash but instead died of a heart attack at 45 in 1993.

STREATHAM, sw16

The main suburb south of Brixton, its name, which is of Saxon origin, means 'the dwellings by the street'. After Streatham Hill station opened in 1856 the population mushroomed from 6,000 to 20,000 in forty years.

Bedford Hill

Charles Bravo murder place (1876), *The Priory, No. 225*

Lawyer Charles Bravo died a slow, agonising death, poisoned with potassium antimony, at the Priory, a whitewashed Gothic folly, on 21 April 1876, a few months after getting married. Although the case was never solved, his wife, Florence, whom he abused, remains the main suspect. But Bravo had no shortage of enemies and the culprit may have been Jane Cox, Florence's long-time companion; or George Griffiths, a stableman who nursed a grudge against Bravo; or a Dr James Gully, who had been Florence's lover. On his deathbed Bravo failed to say who he believed might have poisoned him – someone had slipped the poison into the water on his bedside table – and he remained so calm during his last days that some think he committed suicide. The inquest concluded that Bravo had been 'wilfully murdered by the administration of tartar emetic. But there is not sufficient evidence to fix the guilt upon any person or persons.'

WANDSWORTH, SW18

A dull traffic-choked suburb occupying a U-shaped bank of the Thames opposite Fulham, its name, Wandsworth, means 'Place of Wendel'. It grew around the River Wandle, and is best known for Wandsworth Prison, site of one of Britain's main 20th-century gallows.

Heathfield Square

Wandsworth Prison
Built in 1851 as the Surrey House of Correction, the prison initially used the 'silent system', whereby inmates were banned from talking and obliged to wear felt masks with slits for eyes 'to hide their shame'.

When 𝔥orsemonger 𝔏ane 𝔊aol in Southwark closed in 1878, its executions were transferred to Wandsworth and an execution area – the 'Cold Meat Shed' – was constructed in the yard. Over the next 80 years the prison held the second-highest number of executions in Britain, its 117 beaten only by Pentonville, with 120.

When Monty Saphir was released from Wandsworth jail after serving time for receiving stolen goods in 1943, the army was at hand to arrest

him for desertion. However, a team of villains led by London gangster Frankie Fraser arrived on the scene to spirit Saphir away. Shots were fired at the getaway lorry carrying Saphir, which was driven by his brother. Then soldiers clambered on the back to overcome the escapers, whereupon the vehicle careered from side to side, the driver lost control and a couple of army men were killed in the ensuing crach.

Wandsworth's gallows wasn't dismantled until 1994, and was still being tested every six months, because the death penalty remained in force for the crimes of treason, piracy with violence and mutiny in the armed forces. The former execution chamber is now a staff recreation room.

HANGED AT WANDSWORTH

‖ **Robert Rosenthal** (d. 1915) was the only man hanged at Wandsworth for spying during the First World War. He was caught soon after arriving in Britain from Copenhagen with an American passport, and was convicted under the Treachery Act of 1914.

‖ **John Amery** (d. 1945) was a British traitor who sought help from Hitler to form a British volunteer force. During the war Amery broadcast propaganda for the Nazis, which was particularly embarrassing for his father, Leo, Secretary of State for India and Burma.

‖ **William Joyce**, the Nazi sympathiser known as Lord Haw-Haw following his mannered broadcasts on German radio during the Second World War, went to the gallows in January 1946 after being convicted of high treason.

Joyce was captured at the end of the war near the Germany–Denmark border and brought back to Britain. As the plane neared the coast he exclaimed, 'The white cliffs of Dover! God bless old England!', which fooled no one. He was sent for trial, which was delayed by wrangling over his nationality (he had been born overseas), but was nevertheless charged with committing treason between 3 September 1939 and 2 July 1940, the date his British passport ran out, and was sentenced to death. He showed no emotion when confronted by news and evidence from the concentration camps, blaming the deaths on starvation and disease caused by Allied bombing of communication lines. He scratched a swastika on the wall of his cell while awaiting execution.

‖ **John George Haigh**, the so-called 'Acid Bath Murderer', went to the gallows in 1949 for killing half a dozen people, in most cases for only

Fighting for Life

When German spy Karl Richter went to the gallows on 10 December 1941 he threw himself against the cell wall and fought with the hangmen, Albert Pierrepoint and Harry Allen. Warders managed to strap his hands behind him, but Richter's arms were so strong he freed himself from the leather strap and had to be restrained again. When Pierrepoint finally pushed the lever, Richter jumped up and loosened the noose which caught under his lip. However, his neck was broken by the force of the drop and he died. After the execution Albert Pierrepoint was given the broken strap as a memento.

small financial gain, but mainly to satisfy his desperate urge to drink the victims' blood. The Wandsworth hangman Albert Pierrepoint believed Haigh to be a special case and used a leather wrist strap to hold him down before the drop.

- The execution of **Derek Bentley** in 1953 horrified many. Bentley was robbing a Croydon warehouse with a juvenile, Christopher Craig, when a policeman interrupted them. Bentley shouted: 'Let him have it, Chris,' and Craig shot the policeman dead. Yet Craig, the murderer, escaped the gallows because he was under age, while Bentley, who was deemed to have been urging Craig to shoot, rather than to hand the officer the gun, was hanged. As he went to the drop a large crowd gathered outside the jail singing 'Abide With Me'. The hanging gave considerable ammunition to those campaigning to abolish the death penalty and Bentley was later posthumously pardoned.
- The last person to be executed at Wandsworth was the murderer **Henryk Neimasz** on 8 September 1961.

Magdalen Road

Wandsworth Cemetery

It wasn't just the murder weapon discovered wrapped in a plastic bag with his mother's fingerprint on it in the cemetery in 1994 that helped convict Gary Nelson of two murders in 2006, it was the other bizarre activities that went on inside the Victorian burial site. Nelson's aunt, Rose, led an expedition to the cemetery in the middle of the night to retrieve the guns, which were buried here, but could not find them. However the police could, helped by anonymous phone calls and lipstick crosses on the gravestones.

Further south-west

RICHMOND

A gorgeous riverside suburb which was home to a medieval palace used by Elizabeth I.

Maid of Honour Row

Richmond Palace

Sheen Palace was where Anne of Bohemia, wife of Richard II, died of the plague in 1394. She was commemorated by Chaucer in the prologue to *The Legend of Good Women* – 'whan this book ys maad, yive it the Quene/On my byhalf... at Sheene' – but after her death, the lines were deleted from the text.

In 1499 it burnt down and was later rebuilt as Richmond Palace. Elizabeth I died here on a heap of cushions in the room above the gatehouse on 24 March 1603. Or as her doctor, John Manningham, put it: 'Hir majestie departed this lyfe, mildly like a lambe, easily like a ripe apple from the tree.' At the moment of the queen's death Lady Scrope, a courtier, dropped a ring from the window as a signal.

Elizabeth left instructions that she was not be embalmed, and though no one is sure whether her wishes were followed, the corpse was rubbed with spices as part of the preservation process. The body lay at Richmond for three days during which time it supposedly exploded with such force that it split open the lead coffin, although the story was probably made up by her Catholic opponents. Elizabeth was then taken on a barge to Westminster for burial.

CHAPTER 11

West London

BAYSWATER, W2
Bayswater Road
Pembridge Gardens
Praed Street
St George's Fields
Westbourne Grove
Westbourne Terrace

CHISWICK, W4
Church Street
Corney Road

KENSINGTON, W8
Holland Park
Hornton Street
Kensington Church Street
Kensington Palace Gardens
Lexham Gardens
Palace Avenue
Pembroke Gardens

MAIDA VALE, W9

NORTH KENSINGTON, W10
Harrow Road
Southam Street

NOTTING HILL, W11
Bartle Road (formerly
    Rillington Place)
Ladbroke Square
Lansdowne Crescent
Penzance Street

SHEPHERDS BUSH, W12
Braybrook Street

WEST KENSINGTON, W14
Addison Road
Talgarth Road

Further west
SOUTHALL

BAYSWATER, w2

The name Bayswater is a corruption of Bayards' Water, a former
well in Hyde Park, and this once fashionable district was one of
the first suburbs to be colonised by wealthy Londoners moving
west to escape the squalor of the City.

Bayswater Road

The main road running through Bayswater, originally known as The
Way to Uxbridge, is dominated by Hyde Park on the south side and a
succession of once grand stucco properties on the north, many of which
are now crumbling into dereliction.

Hyde Park

In late-medieval times deserting soldiers were shot by firing squad in
Hyde Park near the Tyburn public gallows. Until 1841 soldiers could be
executed for a long list of crimes that included demolishing a house,
ravishing women, carnally abusing children, burning ships with intent
to murder, piracy with violence and joining a rebel chieftain.

Twice Oliver Cromwell narrowly escaped death in Hyde Park. On one
occasion an assassin stalked him but never had the opportunity to
attack. On another occasion in September 1654, while driving a carriage
through the park, Cromwell was thrown to the ground when his horses
bolted. The pistol in his pocket fired, but he remained unhurt.

The southern section of Hyde Park is dominated by the water of the
Serpentine, created from the damming of the River Westbourne in the
1720s, where Harriet Westbrook, wife of the poet Shelley, drowned in
autumn 1816.

That year a man identified by the markings 'S. T. Coleridge' on his
shirt was found hanged from a tree in the park. The death of the poet
Samuel Taylor Coleridge was duly reported in the papers and discussed
by two men in a coffee house within earshot of the great writer who
asked to read the reports of his death and was told by one of the men:
'It is very extraordinary that Coleridge the poet should have hanged
himself just after the success of his play [Remorse]; but he was always a
strange mad fellow.' Coleridge replied: 'Indeed, sir, it is a most extraordinary thing that he should have hanged himself, be the subject of an

w2

inquest, and yet that he should at this moment be speaking to you.' At least he now knew what had happened to his lost shirt.

On 5 July 1969 a huge crowd attended a Rolling Stones concert in the park which was used by the group as a memorial to Brian Jones, the Stones' multi-instrumentalist who had died three days previously in the swimming pool of his Sussex farm. Mick Jagger, wearing a white dress and dog collar, and carrying a wooden cross, read from Shelley's 'Adonais' ('Peace, peace, he is not dead, he doth not sleep, he hath awakened from a dream of life') at the beginning of the gig and released thousands of – mainly dead – butterflies into the air.

Pembridge Gardens

Pembridge Court Hotel (The Lennox), No. 34

The sadist Neville Heath suffocated 32-year-old Margery Gardner in Room 4 of the Pembridge Court Hotel on 20 June 1946 after a night of violent sex during which he cut diamond-patterned whip marks into her flesh and bit off her nipples.

When the chambermaid found the body the next morning, Gardner's ankles were bound tightly together with a handkerchief and her face had been washed – or possibly licked – clean of blood, although there was no evidence that intercourse had taken place.

Police eventually linked Heath to the crime but in the meantime he struck again, in Bournemouth, posing as Group Captain Rupert Brooke (surely too obvious a pseudonym). He was hanged by Albert Pierrepoint on 26 October, 1946, his last request being for a large whisky.

Praed Street

Paddington station

The coffin of Queen Victoria, which had been brought to London by train from the Isle of Wight, where she had died in January 1901, was taken out of the capital from Paddington station, en route to Windsor, where the funeral service was held.

One hundred and fifty sailors led the gun carriage containing the body of George VI which also travelled from here to Windsor after he died at Sandringham in February 1952.

St George's Fields

Lawrence Sterne, author of the comic classic *Tristram Shandy*, was buried in 1768 in a now disused graveyard which once stood on this site and which was opened for the society church of St George, Hanover Square. A few days after Sterne was interred bodysnatchers dug up the corpse to sell it to an anatomy professor who wanted fresh cadavers for dissection. On the slab Sterne was recognised, and his body was returned to the graveyard.

When the site was redeveloped in 1969 the coffin was opened and two heads were found inside. The authorities had to examine paintings of the time to decide which one was Sterne's. The correct one was then placed back in the coffin and sent for reburial in Yorkshire.

Westbourne Grove

Bayswater's first major shopping street was developed in the mid-19th century and later became known as Bankrupt Avenue, because of the closure of many businesses. In 1958 the street saw much violence during the Notting Hill race riots, but surprisingly no deaths resulted.

Whiteley's (1863–1911), No. 43

William Whiteley, owner of London's leading 19th-century department store, was murdered in his office above the store on 24 January 1907 by his long-lost son, Horace Rayner.

Whiteley had opened the store in 1863, aiming to cater for every need – 'from a pin to an elephant at short notice'. Whiteley's grew quickly, spreading over fifteen neighbouring premises within ten years, but the owner was not popular with everyone. Local butchers burnt effigies of him on Guy Fawkes Night 1876 after he opened a meat counter, and the store suffered a number of arson attacks.

Whiteley's murder was the culmination of unfortunate events that had begun in Brighton nearly thirty years previously. Whiteley and a friend, George Rayner, had spent a weekend there with two girls, one of whom later gave birth to a boy, Horace, whom she brought up with Rayner. When the boy grew up Rayner told him: 'Any time you're in trouble, go and see your real father, William Whiteley.' When Horace did so, a bemused Whiteley, by then 75, suggested he went abroad. Horace then produced a gun and shot Whiteley dead, as well as injuring

W2

himself. He left a note which read: 'To all whom it may concern William Whiteley is my father and has brought upon himself and me a double fatality by reason of his own refusal of a request perfectly reasonable. R. I. P.' He was tried at the Old Bailey but was acquitted following a wave of public sympathy for a son wronged by a rich father.

Westbourne Terrace

Nina Hamnett, one of the great characters of post-war bohemian Fitzrovia, impaled herself on the railings of her Westbourne Terrace balcony in December 1956 after taking offence to a mention of her in a radio play. By this time Hamnett was toothless and drink-sodden, her wit and charm dissipated. The late Aleister Crowley, satanist and terror of middle-class London, with whom she had long tussled, was blamed for putting a curse on her.

CHISWICK, w4

Chiswick, originally Chesewic, from 'chese' (cheese) or 'ceosil' (stoney beach) and 'wic' (village), grew as a fishing community around the riverside church of St Nicholas.

On 8 September 1944 the first V2 rockets fell on Chiswick and also on Epping to the north-east of the capital. The V2, 45 feet long, weighing 14 tons, and travelling at a speed of 3,600 mph, was considerably more powerful than anything that had previously been used in airborne combat. It was fired from Wassenaar, a suburb of The Hague, left the earth's atmosphere during flight, and re-entered at a speed that made defence impossible.

On that September evening a mother and her daughter were in bed in their Chiswick home when the air-raid siren sounded. The mother heard what she thought was a V1 flying bomb overhead and the engine cut out. It was likely that the bomb would land nearby, she mused, so she grabbed the baby and smothered herself and the child with pillows. Sure enough the bomb hit their block of flats, which collapsed on top of them. Mother and baby were injured but alive. The woman's enduring memory was of the bomb landing just as the ARP warden was making his way up the garden path. It exploded near him and though

she saw his head blown clean off, for a second or two the warden continued along the path towards the front door – headless.

Church Street

St Nicholas

This handsome parish church, dedicated to Nicholas, patron saint of
sailors and fishermen, is supposedly haunted by Mary Fauconburg and
Frances Rich, daughters of Oliver Cromwell. After their father was
posthumously beheaded at Tyburn (p. 62) in 1660, Mary seized the
headless corpse and buried it in a vault at St Nicholas's in which she and
her sister were later also buried. During the rebuilding of the church in
1882 the vicar decided to look closer into the story and opened the vault,
where he found three coffins. Fearing a stream of visitors gawping at
what might be Cromwell's remains, he bricked it up.

The tomb of the painter William Hogarth (d. 1764) contains the
epitaph:

> Farewell, great painter of mankind
> Who reached the noblest point of art
> Whose pictured morals charm the mind
> And through the eye correct the heart.

W4

Corney Road

Chiswick Old Cemetery

One of London's least attractive burial sites, flat and largely free of trees, the old cemetery is near to the burial ground of St Nicholas's church. James Hitch's granite tomb has a draped Union Jack topped with a pith helmet. The monument for the painter James McNeill Whistler has lost its corner statuettes.

KENSINGTON, w8

One of London's most luxurious and prestigious inner suburbs, dominated by Kensington Palace, became a royal retreat after William III moved here in the late 17th century. Sherlock Holmes expert Richard Lancelyn Green, a prolific author and avid collector of Holmesian memorabilia, was found dead in his Kensington flat in 2004, garrotted with a shoelace, after complaining that a rival American bookseller was following him. At the time the coroner returned an open verdict, but friends and relatives of Green later claimed that it was suicide made to look like murder, and that he had set up a trail of false clues similar to those used in the last Sherlock Holmes story, 'The Problem of Thor Bridge' (1922).

Holland Park

Holland House

The ghost of Sir Walter Cope, property dealer, money-lender and favourite of James I, carrying his severed head, allegedly haunts Holland House, the only surviving E-plan Jacobean manor house in inner London.

As the house's late 18th-century owner, Henry Fox, lay on his deathbed in June 1774, a servant announced that George Selwyn, an associate known for his predilection for viewing corpses, had come to visit him. Fox told the servant: 'If Mr Selwyn calls again show him up. If I am alive, I should be delighted to see him. If I am dead, presumably he would like to see me.'

Hornton Street

The body of Scottish prostitute Frances Brown was found on waste ground behind a car park in Hornton Street on 25 November 1964 during a killing spree now believed to be part of the so-called 'Jack the Stripper' murders. Brown's body was covered with rubble and her head with a large dustbin lid. Death, according to the autopsy, had been caused by 'asphyxia due to pressure on the neck by persons unknown'.

Ironically Brown and a friend, Kim Taylor, having a drink in a Notting Hill pub, had joked about meeting the murderer. One evening, back on the streets, each one was approached by a motorist, and were driven off in separate cars. Taylor never saw Brown alive again.

Brown, like an earlier similar victim, Hannah Tailford, had minor connections with the Profumo affair. At a court hearing she revealed that she had once been hired by Dr Stephen Ward, the society osteopath who pimped Christine Keeler and Mandy Rice-Davies, the two girls at the centre of the scandal. No one was ever charged with the murders of Brown or Tailford, which some blame on the former boxing champion Freddie Mills (☛ p. 81).

Kensington Church Street

The main link between Notting Hill and Kensington, famous for its antique shops, was originally Silver Street at its northern end and Church Lane further south. When the funeral cortège of Queen Caroline, wife of George IV, passed along Kensington Church Street in summer 1821 the crowd rioted, strewing obstacles across the road and overturning vehicles to show their distaste for the way the king had treated her. George had humiliated Caroline by banning her from his coronation at Westminster Abbey, and when he heard of her death (from 'obstruction of the bowels') his only comment was: 'Is she? By God!' The cortège turned back and made for Hyde Park, where troops fired on the crowd and killed two people, provoking further rioting.

Kensington Palace Gardens

Russian Embassy, No. 5

Hugh Gaitskell, the Labour Party leader, was fatally poisoned here, according to intelligence sources, as 'punishment' for hounding communists out of the Labour Party. Gaitskell had come to the Soviet consulate to obtain a visa for a visit to the USSR in December 1962. A week later he complained of feeling unwell, and was taken to Middlesex Hospital, where he was questioned about his recent diet. Gaitskell could think of nothing unusual until he remembered that while at the visa office he had been given some tea and biscuits. On 18 January 1963 he died from heart and kidney failure.

Peter Wright, the British secret agent who wrote *Spycatcher*, later explained that the biscuits could have contained hydralazine, a drug that produces the symptoms of *lupus disseminata erythematosis*, a tropical disease rare in Britain – and even rarer in someone who had not visited the tropics. The disease, which is not usually seen in men over 40 (Gaitskell was 56), induces heart and kidney failure, and had been described as a method of assassination in a Soviet journal.

Lexham Gardens

Shellbourne Hotel, No. 1

Christine Granville, one of Britain's most successful Second World War secret agents, was murdered on the stairs of the Shellbourne Hotel in

June 1952 by a would-be suitor, Dennis Muldowney, who had followed her to London.

Granville was a Polish countess, born Krystyna Skarbek, and spent the war working for Britain's Special Operations Executive, a crack unit of agents hand-picked to cary out covert sabotage missions. After the war she took a number of mundane jobs, including that of second-class stewardess on a liner travelling to Australia. There she met Muldowney, who unsuccessfully tried to inveigle his way into her affections.

On the night of 15 June 1952 Granville returned to the hotel. As she climbed the stairs she heard a voice behind her. It was Muldowney, clutching a knife. The night porter heard a desperate cry of 'Get him off me' and rushed to the scene, but she was dead. 'I killed her,' cried Muldowney who made no attempt to escape but sat still until the police arrived. He then told the officers: 'I built all my dreams around her, but she was playing me for a fool.'

Following the murder the press dubbed Granville 'the modern pimpernel no man could resist... [the woman] who ordered the Gestapo and set agents free.' Muldowney's Old Bailey trial was one of the shortest ever – three minutes almost to the second – after which he was sentenced to death. He was hanged on 30 September 1952 at Pentonville.

Palace Avenue

Kensington Palace

Nottingham House was redeveloped into the grander Kensington Palace at the end of the 17th century by William III, who wanted a London residence away from 'the smoak of London' to ease his chronic asthma. When Mary Stuart, who ruled jointly with her husband, discovered she was dying of smallpox at the age of 32 in 1694 she ordered those not contaminated with the disease to leave the palace. Then she locked herself away, and calmly awaited death.

Riding through Hampton Court Park two years later, William fell from his horse and broke his collar bone. He returned to Kensington Palace to recuperate but lay down by an open window and caught a chill that turned to pneumonia, which killed him.

William, Duke of Gloucester, son of (Queen) Anne, who embodied hopes of a Protestant, English male succession, was too delicate to survive and died in the palace soon after his 11th birthday in 1700. His head was too big for his body and he may have suffered from hydro-cephalus.

George II was the last monarch to live in Kensington Palace. His consort, Caroline, died here in 1737 after failing to cure a hernia with snake-root. George banished his son, Frederick, from the palace. Later, given the news that Frederick had died (➦p. 95), he simply replied: 'Dead is he! Why, they told me was better,' and returned to his game of cards. George died in the palace in 1760, after falling off the toilet and smashing his head on a cabinet. As the writer Horace Walpole put it in his memoirs of the king's life: 'The German valet de chambre heard a noise louder than royal wind, listened, heard something like a groan, ran in, and found the [King] on the floor... expired.'

After the death of George VI in 1952 the medium Lilian Baylis was invited to meet the royal family to try and communicate with the late monarch. Blindfolded, Baylis was taken to a mystery address, probably Kensington Palace, where the mask was removed and she found herself looking at the Queen, Prince Philip, the Queen Mother and other royals grouped around the table for a séance.

Following the death of Princess Diana in 1997 the largest collection of flowers ever seen in London was placed outside the palace, her occasional home.

Pembroke Gardens

No. 31

Ernest Oldham, a Foreign Office clerk, was murdered in his Pembroke Gardens flat by the KGB, a few years after he had begun to sell government secrets to the Russians. Oldham started working for Moscow after visiting Paris, where he presented himself at the Soviet Embassy as a 'Mr Scott', demanding payment for documents in his possession. When he was refused, he simply left the package on his chair. Embassy staff later examined the goods and found to their surprise that they were valuable, but they had no idea how to contact 'Scott'.

They sent a Soviet agent, Hans Galleni, to London, where they thought it likely the English 'Mr Scott' lived. Galleni wandered into a police station and spun a highly unlikely story about how he and his sister had been involved in a car crash in Paris, witnessed by an Englishman whose name and address they had unfortunately lost but who they knew worked at the Foreign Office.

The duty sergeant was eager to help and phoned the Foreign Office, obtaining the names and addresses of the four FO personnel who had been in Paris that weekend. Galleni visited each one in turn, until he caught a glimpse of Oldham walking along Pembroke Gardens. Realising this was indeed his man he approached him and thrust an envelope containing £2,000 into his hand. Oldham soon became a full-time agent for the Soviets, but the relationship soured when, racked with guilt, he resigned his Foreign Office post. No longer of any use, Oldham was assassinated by KGB agents in September 1933.

MAIDA VALE, w9

Frederick Knott's play *Dial 'M' for Murder*, famously filmed by Alfred Hitchcock in 1954, is set at 61a Charrington Gardens in Maida Vale. To phone Maida Vale in those days you started by dialling the letter 'M'.

NORTH KENSINGTON, W10

The shabby northern part of Notting Hill, between the Westway motorway and the unlovely Harrow Road, is home to one of London's greatest cemeteries – Kensal Green.

Harrow Road

Kensal Green Cemetery

The first of the great mid-Victorian 'Gardens of the Dead', officially the General Cemetery of All Souls at Kensal Green, is rich with memorials, mausoleums, catacombs and chapels. It is also the burial place of some of the greatest writers of the 19th century including Wilkie Collins, Anthony Trollope and William Thackeray.

Kensal Green was conceived by George Frederick Carden, a barrister who announced plans in 1825 to build a cemetery similar to Paris's Père-Lachaise in Primrose Hill. Five years went by before a committee was formed, after which an exhibition held in Parliament Street displayed plans by Francis Goodwin for an elaborately designed cemetery with temples, cloisters and other romantic effects. It took some time to complete the planning stages but in 1831 a Strand banker, Sir John Dean Paul, bought 54 acres of land here for the new cemetery's proprietors.

It was an appropriate time, for in October 1831 England was in the grip of a cholera epidemic, which some blamed on decaying bodies in the capital's overcrowded graveyards. In July 1832 a bill for 'establishing a General Cemetery for the Interment of the Dead in the Neighbourhood of the Metropolis' received royal assent.

The 54 acres of land at Kensal Green were well situated. Though the area was then almost entirely rural, there was good access to the centre of London along the Harrow Road and an alternative route along the Grand Union Canal. Here everything was neat and sedate; the wild romance of Highgate was absent. Kensal Green Cemetery was consecrated in 1833, and incorporated an Anglican chapel, dissenters' chapel and gardens of remembrance.

The cemetery should have been designed in the Gothic style but the board of directors were worried about the connections between Gothic and Catholicism, and particularly about Catholicism's links with superstition. They replaced the chosen architect, H. E. Kendall, with John

Griffith. But not everyone was enamoured of Griffith's classical layout and design. 'What a rendezvous of dreary inanities it is!' protested *The Builder*, which was particularly irked by Ducrow's Egyptian mausoleum, slighted in the magazine as an example of 'ponderous coxcombry'.

During its first twenty years Kensal Green saw nearly 20,000 burials. After the 1843 funeral of the Duke of Sussex the cemetery became fashionable and now has graves of around 500 members of the aristocracy. The most spectacular tombs are those of Princess Sophia (d. 1848), daughter of George III, who scandalised society by having an illegitimate child and is commemorated with a *quattrocento* sarcophagus in Carrara marble on a podium, and the octagonal 1866 monument for the Molyneux family by John Gibson, with its rich polished granite.

Vandalism and neglect have taken their toll on the cemetery in recent decades but Kensal Green continues to enchant.

BURIED AT KENSAL GREEN

‖ **Mary Hogarth (d. 1837)** The death of Charles Dickens's sister-in-law when she was only 17 caused the author immense grief, and was the only event that ever stopped him writing. Rumours even circulated that the writer had committed suicide, but Dickens and his wife, Catherine, Mary's sister, had simply gone to Hampstead to mourn. The author paid for Mary's grave at Kensal Green Cemetery and composed the epitaph for her tombstone that reads: 'Young, beautiful and good. God in His mercy numbered her among His angels at the early age of seventeen.'

Dickens continued to show what many termed an overly morbid obsession with Mary, indicating his wish to be buried in the same grave, which he had to relinquish on the death of her brother, George, in 1841. 'It is a great trial for me to give up Mary's grave,' he wrote to his biographer, John Forster. 'The desire to be buried next to her is as strong upon me now, as it was five years ago. And I *know*... that it will never diminish... I cannot bear the thought of being excluded from her dust...'

‖ **Thomas Hood (d. 1845)** The tomb of the 'Song of the Shirt' poet was originally accompanied by a bronze bust designed by Matthew Noble, who sculpted Prince Albert for the original Albert Memorial in Manchester. The bust was later stolen.

‖ **Leigh Hunt (d. 1859)** was the publisher of Shelley and proprietor of

The Examiner, a controversial Sunday paper in which he once slammed the Prince Regent as 'a corpulent man of fifty, a violator of his word, a despiser of domestic ties, who has just closed half a century without one single claim on the gratitude of his country...'

‖ **William Thackeray (d. 1863)**, the author of *Vanity Fair*, has a plain stone slab surrounded by a low railing. Dickens was among the 2,000 mourners at Thackeray's funeral.

‖ **Anthony Trollope (d. 1882)** A restrained red granite memorial reading 'He was a loving husband, a loving father and a true friend' commemorates the prolific Victorian novelist.

‖ **Wilkie Collins (d. 1889)** The *Woman in White* author and friend of Dickens wrote in his will: 'I desire to be buried in the Cemetery at Kensal Green and that over my grave there may be placed a plain stone cross and no other monument.'

‖ The French acrobat **Charles Blondin (d. 1897)**, real name Jean Francois Gravelet, crossed Niagara Falls dozens of times in the 1850s and 60s, on one occasion blindfolded, on another pushing a wheelbarrow, but also on a bike, on stilts and while cooking an omelette – but nearly messed up while carrying a man on his shoulders.

W10

Southam Street

With the 1958 Notting Hill race riots fresh in the memory, Kelso Cochrane, an Antiguan carpenter, was surrounded by six white men outside the Earl of Warwick pub at the corner with Golborne Road on 16 May 1959. They taunted Cochrane with cries of 'Hey! Jim Crow!' (a reference to the 'Jim Crow' laws of the southern US states which barred blacks from jobs and public places), attacked him with a knife, and left him to bleed to death.

Three days later *The Times* reported an interview with a local youth 'with sideburns two inches long and a pencil slim tie' who, when asked what he felt about the murder, replied: 'One less of the blacks, that's the way I look at it. We've got too many of them around here.' No one was ever caught for the murder but a local youth later revealed that he had been approached by a fascist organisation to kill a black man – any black man – for £200.

NOTTING HILL, w11

Fashionable London par excellence, a magnet for writers, actors, rock stars, journalists, designers and film-makers, Notting Hill was also the location of 10 Rillington Place, setting of some of the most notorious of London murders.

Bartle Road
(former Rillington Place)

No. 10

10 Rillington Place, a shabby three-storey terraced house (now demolished) overlooking the Hammersmith & City line, became the most infamous address in London in the late 1950s as a result of the killing spree carried out by John Christie who murdered eight women, mostly prostitutes, while living there between 1938 and 1953, burying their bodies on the premises.

Christie, a Yorkshireman who was shelled in the Great War, and his wife, Ethel, moved into No. 10 a year before the Second World War broke out. Once war was declared he was taken on as a special constable,

despite having a criminal record for a murderous assault on a prostitute. With his zealous, officious manner he earned the nickname of the
'Himmler of Rillington Place'. He affected a middle-class demeanour
which, in what was then a heavily proletarian area, gave him a feeling of
superiority and made him a magnet for poorly-educated neighbours
with problems. He first struck on 10 August 1943 while his wife was in
Sheffield visiting her brother.

Victim 1, Ruth Fuerst, August 1943

Christie's first victim was Ruth Fuerst, a student nurse, daughter of
the Austrian artist Ludwig Fuerst and part-time prostitute. Christie
invited her back to No. 10 and strangled her during sexual intercourse. A few minutes later came a knock on the door. It was the
telegraph boy bearing a message stating that Christie's wife would
soon be returning home with her brother.

Christie quickly buried the body under the floorboards. Later that
night, he put his brother-in-law in the same room, retrieving the
corpse after he left. He then cut off Fuerst's head, dumping it in a
broken dustbin, where it still lay unnoticed six years later when
police searched the house over another murder, and reburied the
body in the yard. The Austrian's disappearance was blamed on an air-
raid.

Victim 2, Muriel Eady, October 1944

Muriel Eady was a respectable 32-year-old woman whom Christie met
while working for the Ultra Radio company in Park Royal. Once he
had decided to murder Eady, Christie invited her to Rillington Place
with the excuse that he could cure her catarrh. Eady visited while
Christie's wife was away in Sheffield and agreed to have a cup of tea.
Meanwhile Christie rigged up a glass jar containing Friar's Balsam,
pierced two holes through the lid and inserted some rubber tubing,
which he connected to the gas mains. As Eady breathed the mixture
he turned on the mains and she was soon poisoned by the carbon
monoxide fumes.

Christie carried her to his bed, sexually assaulted and strangled
her. He buried the body in the back yard, first removing her thighbone which he used to hold up his rickety fence. Eady's skull,
however, he threw into a bombed house on nearby St Marks's Road,
where some boys found it a few weeks later. They handed it in to the
police, but an officer explained that it was probably the remains of

the resident who had died in the bombing. Christie's wife, Ethel, knew nothing of either murder.

Victims 3 and 4, Beryl and Jeraldine Evans, 8 November 1949

In May 1948 Welshman Timothy Evans and his pregnant wife, Beryl, moved into the top-floor flat at 10 Rillington Place. That October, Beryl gave birth to a girl, Jeraldine. When she fell pregnant again a few months later Evans, worried about not being able to afford another child, told his wife to get an abortion, which was then illegal.

Christie offered to carry out the abortion himself while Evans was at work. During the operation Beryl panicked, and Christie raped and strangled her, leaving her to die on the bed. This time Mrs Christie was party to the affair, though she believed Beryl Evans had died of complications during the abortion.

When Evans returned home and found out what had happened, he was devastated. He accepted that he couldn't go to the police immediately, as Christie might be prosecuted for manslaughter – poor reward for selflessly performing a home abortion – and he, Evans, might be viewed as an accomplice. So they disposed of the body in the washhouse. Christie promised to take care of baby Jeraldine by placing her with 'a nice couple' in east Acton, but within a few days the child was dead, strangled either by Christie or, as some believe, including the crime expert Colin Wilson, by a distraught Evans.

Christie encouraged Evans to go to Wales, but a few days later he went to the police and announced: 'I want to give myself up. I have disposed of my wife and have put her down the drain.' An officer went to Rillington Place where, watched by an anxious Christie, he realised that it would take three men to lift the manhole cover. When they found nothing down the drain, the police accused Evans of lying, and he admitted that he had done so 'to protect a man called Christie'. Officers returned to No. 10 and searched the garden, but failed to notice Muriel Eady's thighbone propping up the fence. Nor did they find any bodies. However, during another search they at last discovered the corpses of Evans's wife and child in the washhouse, dead by asphyxiation.

But it was Evans not Christie who was prosecuted. He was found guilty and hanged in what has gone down in history as one of London's worst miscarriages of justice, instrumental in bringing about a change of public feeling towards the death penalty.

‖ **Victim 5, Ethel Christie, 14 December 1952**

After Evans's hanging Christie's murderous tendencies stayed dormant for a few years. But by the end of 1952 his wife was annoying him. With Ethel out of the way, Christie reasoned, he could do as he pleased, and so on 14 December that year he strangled her in bed, leaving her to decompose for three days before burying her under the floorboards.

‖ **Victim 6, Kathleen Maloney, January 1953**
‖ **Victim 7, Rita Nelson, January 1953**
‖ **Victim 8, Hectorina Maclennan, 6 March 1953**

There were three more victims. After murdering the last, a 26-year-old Scottish woman called Hectorina Maclennan, Christie moved out and sublet the property, failing to mention to prospective tenants the eight corpses secreted in various places throughout the house: two in the garden, two in the washhouse, one wife under the floorboards and three prostitutes in an alcove. A few weeks later one of the new tenants, engaged in a spot of DIY, shone his torch into the alcove where Christie had buried his three most recent victims and became hysterical. He called the police who searched the property further and uncovered the remaining corpses. Now officers realised that *Christie* was the culprit and launched a nationwide search for him. He was spotted in Putney a week later.

W11

Christie was convicted of the various murders at the Old Bailey, where three years previously Timothy Evans had been sentenced to death for a crime Christie had committed. Like Evans, he was hanged at Pentonville.

Ladbroke Square

No. 22, a grand stucco house in the exclusive Ladbroke estate, was home in the 1940s to Dr Archibald Henderson and his wife Rose, victims of John George Haigh, the 'Acid Bath Murderer'. They fell prey to the serial killer in 1948 simply by having their property for sale.

He posed as a potential buyer and befriended them, taking Dr Henderson to his Crawley workshop where he shot him with a revolver. He then drove to London and urged Henderson's wife to return with him to Crawley as her husband was 'ill'. At the workshop he shot her too, and then threw both their bodies into vats of sulphuric acid. Haigh

also committed murder in his Gloucester Road workshop (➻p. 243) and
was caught after killing a woman who was staying in his Kensington
hotel.

Lansdowne Crescent

Jimi Hendrix's death place, *No. 22*

The virtuoso rock guitarist died on the morning of Friday 18 September
1970 in the room rented by him and his girlfriend, Monika Danneman,
in what was then the Samarkand Hotel and is now private apartments.
Hendrix had returned to the room at around 3 a.m., eaten a tuna
sandwich and taken a sleeping tablet. He woke about seven, spoke to
Danneman, and fell asleep again. A few hours later she found she
couldn't wake the guitarist, and noticed that he had taken a number
of pills and been sick. She called an ambulance, which took him to St
Mary Abbot's Hospital in Kensington where he was pronounced dead.
A doctor at the hospital explained that Hendrix had drunk so much red
wine that he had drowned trying to regurgitate it. The official cause of
death given at the time was 'inhalation of vomit due to barbiturate
intoxication', but later this was changed to an open verdict.

W11

Penzance Street

Ossie Clark, the well-known fashion designer, was murdered in his
Penzance Street council flat by his lover, Diego Cogolato, in August
1996. But this was no ordinary murder or even crime of passion.
Cogolato stabbed Clark to death 23 times with a kitchen knife in what
the tabloids called a 'drug-induced attack'. Cogolato was convinced
that he was the Messiah and Clark the devil. Two days previously he
had heard voices telling him he was the new anointed one, and he had
travelled to Richmond Park to receive a 'revelation from God'.

The Old Bailey later heard that Cogolato, who had a long history
of drug and alcohol abuse, underwent a 'transient psychotic episode'
because a prescribed drug he had taken reacted unfavourably with
amphetamines he was consuming illegally. After the stabbing Cogolato
had battered Clark over the head with a plank of wood, a stone and a
terracotta flower pot. A day after the murder he contacted police and
confessed.

SHEPHERDS BUSH, w12

Lively but charmless, the area takes its name from the local
shepherds who rested their flocks on what is now Shepherd's
Bush Common on their way in and out of London.

Braybrook Street

Harry Roberts and two accomplices shot three unarmed police officers
on Braybrook Street, close to Wormwood Scrubs Prison, on 16 August
1966. The first officer to be killed was a Sergeant Head. He thought
Roberts's car might be used in a prison escape attempt and approached
the vehicle. Noticing the absence of a tax disc on the windscreen,
Head began speaking to Roberts who, worried that the policeman
would search the car and find the gun he had secreted inside, shot him.
A second officer, DC Wombwell, ran back to his police car to take cover,
but Roberts chased him and shot him in the head. He then ordered an
accomplice, John Duddy, to shoot the third officer, PC Fox, as the latter
tried to flee.

As the villains sped off a passer-by, who assumed there had been a

jailbreak, took down their registration number. This led officers to a third member of the gang, John Witney, who during questioning implicated Duddy and Roberts. The latter two went on the run for 90 days, camping out in the Hertfordshire woods until they were spotted by a schoolboy. Roberts was jailed for 30 years.

WEST KENSINGTON, w14

Seedy hotels created out of once grand terraced houses make up much of West Kensington, particularly around the roaring Talgarth Road and Cromwell Road. Nearer Holland Park, however, stand some of London's most glorious properties, mostly designed for the area's late 19th century artistic community.

Addison Road

The Lodge
Early 20th-century home of Violet van der Elst, a leading campaigner for the abolition of capital punishment, who used to organise demonstrations and hire marching bands to play hymns before executions. Mostly her efforts were treated with wry amusement, but when she drove up in her white Rolls-Royce to oppose the execution of Dr Hakim Bakhtyar Rustomji Ratanji missiles were thrown at the car windows. The doctor had been convicted for strangling his wife and the nursemaid who watched him do it, before throwing their remains into a Scottish ravine known as the Devil's Beef Tub. When van der Elst's husband died in 1934, she kept his lead-lined coffin in the basement for a year and held regular séances in the house.

Talgarth Road

No. 53
While living here in May 1940 Marcus Garvey, the leading mid-20th-century black civil rights campaigner, suffered a stroke. It was wrongly reported in the press that he had died, which gave him the chance to read his own obituaries.

Further west

SOUTHALL

A suburb named after the southern wood, located alongside
the Grand Union Canal, is now home to one of Britain's most
vibrant Asian communities, mainly Punjabis, whose antecedents
began arriving at nearby Heathrow airport in the 1950s.

At an anti-National Front demonstration in Southall in April 1979
officers from the Metropolitan Police Special Patrol Group attacked a
New Zealand-born teacher, Blair Peach, at the junction of Beechcroft
Road and Orchard Avenue, clubbing him to death as he sought to
escape from the fighting. It was the worst incident on a day of extreme
violence beset by fighting between skinheads and Asians, and the
ominous sound of policemen beating their batons against their riot
shields to scare the public. Three years previously a racist gang had
stabbed an Asian, Gurdip Singh Chaggar, in Southall. After the killing
Kingsley Read of the National Front was quoted as remarking: 'One
down – a million to go.' Chaggar's killers were never caught. Peach died
in hospital four hours after running into the police. His death became
a cause célèbre for the left throughout the Thatcher years. No one was
ever apprehended.

CHAPTER 12

The London Underground

Aldgate

The station is built on the site of the 'terrible [Plague] pit' that Daniel Defoe described in *A Journal of the Plague Year*. More than 1,000 people were buried in it in two weeks in 1665 as the bubonic plague swept through London.

Seven people died and more than 100 were injured when Shehzad Tanweer detonated a bomb on a Circle Line train as it left Liverpool Street bound for Aldgate, at 8.50 a.m. on 7 July 2005. It was part of a four-pronged attack on the London transport network that day with Tanweer's associates setting off bombs at Edgware Road, and on the Piccadilly Line between King's Cross and Russell Square. A year later Muslim extremists released a video suicide note in which Tanweer explains that 'Non-Muslims of Britain deserve to be attacked because they voted for a government which continues to oppress our mothers, children, brothers and sisters in Palestine, Afghanistan, Iraq and Chechnya.'

In Baroness Orczy's 'The Mysterious Death on the Underground Railway' (1901), a woman is found murdered at Aldgate station. In the Sherlock Holmes short story 'The Bruce-Partington Plans' (1912) the dead body of a plate-layer is discovered on the tracks outside Aldgate station. The first mystery Holmes wants to unravel is why the dead man did not have a ticket.

Balham

Sixty-eight people died on 14 October 1940 when the station was hit by a wartime bomb that destroyed a water main, sending thousands of tons of earth and water into a tunnel where some 600 people were sheltering.

Bank
A bomb that fell in the road directly above the station booking hall on 11 January 1941 caused the road to collapse and killed 58 people.

Barbican
The Dynamiters, an anarchist group, left a bomb at the station (then Aldersgate) in 1897, killing one man. It was a revenge attack for the seven-year sentence given to one of their members the previous April for blowing up a train as it was passing through Paddington.

The demolition of the original booking hall and roof in 1955 inspired John Betjeman's poem 'Monody on the Death of Aldersgate Street Station'. The station became Barbican in 1968.

Bethnal Green
One hundred and seventy-eight people died at the foot of the station's steps on 3 March 1943 as they rushed away from what they believed were bombs but turned out to be a false alarm. The station where the tragedy occurred was not identified nor the number of fatalities disclosed for two years.

Bounds Green

Nineteen people sheltering here on 13 October 1940 during the war died when a bomb hit the station. Sixteen of the victims were Belgian refugees who had been allotted the east end of the platform. The other three were members of local families bombed out of their homes.

British Museum

According to local myth the station, which closed in September 1933, is haunted by the ghost of an Ancient Egyptian dressed in a loincloth and headdress, presumably connected with the nearby museum. When a newspaper offered a reward to anyone who would be prepared to spend the night inside the station, there were no takers. The 1935 film *Bulldog Jack* tapped into the station ghost story. On the night the film was released two women supposedly disappeared from the platform at Holborn, the next station along on the Central Line.

The station was commandeered by the Ministry of Defence during the Second World War and has since been occupied by various military organisations.

Edgware Road

One of four bombs detonated on the London transport network on the morning of 7 July 2005 was that left by Mohammed Sidique Khan which went off 20 seconds after the train left. Passengers later recalled an orange fireball sweeping through carriages. Six people were killed and 163 injured as part of what was Britain's worst terrorist attack.

Farringdon

The eastern terminus of the first ever underground line holds the dubious honour of being the only tube station out of which crowds have poured en route to a public hanging. This bizarre mix of the medieval and the modern happened on 26 May 1868 for the execution of Michael Barrett, the Irish nationalist accused of causing a horrific explosion at the Clerkenwell House of Detention (p. 38), in which six people were killed and hundreds injured.

Finsbury Park

Graham Bond, the innovative British R&B organist, threw himself under the wheels of a Piccadilly Line train at Finsbury Park on 8 May 1974. He had just carried out an exorcism of Long John Baldry's house and was under the delusional belief that he was the son of the notorious Satanist Aleister Crowley.

Gloucester Road

The Polish countess and war heroine Teresa Lubienska was murdered by an unknown assailant at Gloucester Road on 24 May 1957. Seconds after alighting from a train she staggered into the lift with blood pouring from her chest, crying 'bandits, bandits'. No one was ever apprehended for the crime, despite a huge police manhunt, and experts later claimed that she had probably been murdered by Nazi sympathisers.

King's Cross

Thirty-one people died when fire ripped through the King's Cross tube station concourse at half past seven in the evening on 18 November 1987. The blaze, which may have been caused by a discarded match, began in the machine room beneath a wooden escalator and took more than two hours to get under control. Following the King's Cross tragedy smokers were banned from lighting up anywhere in the confines of the station.

Germaine Lindsay was one of four bombers to attack the London transport system on 7 July 2005, detonating a bomb in his rucksack on a packed Piccadilly Line train 250 yards out of King's Cross station that killed 26 people and left more than 340 injured.

Marble Arch

Twenty-one people died during a wartime air raid on the station on 17 September 1940.

Moorgate

The London Underground system's worst train accident occurred at the at the end of Platform 9, the terminus of what was then the Northern Line's Great Northern & City Railway branch (now part of WAGN), on 28 February 1975. A train approaching Moorgate failed to brake and slammed into the buffers at 40mph tunnel, killing 42 passengers including the driver, Leslie Newson. It took four days to clear the rubble and prise Newson's body from the cab. No reason for the crash was ever found, and the discovery that Newson had an unblemished work record made it all the more puzzling.

Russell Square

The 1974 horror film feature *Death Line* was based around the fantastic notion of a gang of navvies, entombed by a landslip during the station's construction, having mutated into a race of man-eating ghouls who pick unwary passengers off the platform at Russell Square.

Sloane Square

Peter Llewellyn Davies, the inspiration for Peter Pan, committed suicide in 1960 by throwing himself under a train at Sloane Square tube station.

South Kentish Town

The disused former Northern Line station was the setting for a bizarre John Betjeman short story about the demise of a civil servant, Basil Green. Engrossed in the newspaper he's reading, he accidentally disembarks from a tube train as it comes to a stand at the platform where the driver has opened the doors to check a fault. To his horror, Green finds the doors closing behind him, the train speeding off and himself stranded. He tries to flag down passing trains to no avail. In the pitch black, interrupted only by the light of passing trains, all of which ignore him, Green finds an opening on the platform and climbs the spiral stairs until his head hits the floor of the shops above. He eventually gives up and goes back to the platform to lie down and die, which is where the story ends.

Stockwell

Jean Charles de Menezes, a 27-year-old Brazilian electrician, was shot dead at Stockwell on 22 July 2005 by police marksmen who mistakenly thought he was a bomber on the run connected with a series of recent failed attacks on the London tube. Initially the police claimed that de Menezes had failed to respond to an order to stop. They also unofficially briefed the press that the man had leapt over the barriers and was dressed like a suicide bomber, both of which turned out not to be true.

A report into the shooting, released two years later, alleged that the Metropolitan Police Commissioner Sir Ian Blair was not told for 24 hours that his officers had eliminated the wrong man. Many believe the killing to have been part of an unofficial Metropolitan Police 'shoot-to-kill' policy, designed to alarm the public and smooth the way for the introduction of more draconian security measures. No one has been indicted for the killing, and Cressida Dick, the officer believed to have given the order to shoot, has been promoted.

Swiss Cottage

Thousands sheltered in the station during the Second World War and even produced their own magazine, *The Swiss Cottager*. After a child died of meningitis in the station the magazine railed against the authorities' 'indifference almost amounting to callousness, neglect soulless contempt for elementary human decencies...red tape, authoritarianism and officialdom'.

West Ham

Tube train driver Stephen Julius was shot dead by Irish terrorist Vincent Kelly at West Ham station on 15 March 1976. Kelly had brought a bomb on board the train and when it started to smoke, panicked and threw it on the floor. It exploded, injuring ten passengers. The bomber fled but was pursued by the driver, Stephen Julius. Kelly shot him dead, and then turned the gun on himself.

Bibliography

Abbott, Geoffrey, *Execution: A Guide to the Ultimate Penalty*, West Sussex, Summersdale, 2005

Bland, Olivia, *The Royal Way of Death*, London, Constable, 1986

Curl, James Stevens, *The Victorian Celebration of Death*, Newton Abbott, David and Charles, 1972

Dodson, Aidan, *The Royal Tombs of Great Britain*, London, Duckworth, 2004

Glinert, Ed, *The London Compendium*, London, Penguin, 2003

Glinert, Ed, *East End Chronicles*, London, Penguin, 2005

Glinert, Ed, *West End Chronicles*, London, Penguin, 2007

Harding, Vanessa, *The Dead and the Living in Paris and London, 1500–1670*, Cambridge, Cambridge University Press, 2002

Kerrigan, Michael, *Who Lies Where? A Guide to Famous Graves*, London, Fourth Estate, 1995

Linnane, Fergus, *The Encyclopaedia of London Crime and Vice*, Gloucestershire, Sutton, 2003

Litten, Julian, *The English Way of Death*, London, Robert Hale, 1991

Meller, Hugh, *London Cemeteries: An Illustrated Guide and Gazetteer*, Aldershot, Ashgate, 1981

Parsons, Brian, *The London Way of Death*, Gloucestershire, Sutton, 2001

Smith, Stephen, *Underground London: Travels Beneath the City Streets*, London, Little, Brown, 2004

Photo Index

Types Of Death

Cemeteries, Churches and Burial Grounds

People Index

Places Index

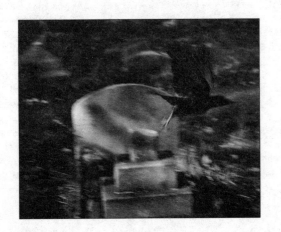